HEALTH AND HEALING
THE NATURAL WAY

YOU AND
YOUR HEART

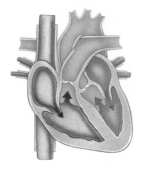

HEALTH AND HEALING
THE NATURAL WAY

YOU AND
YOUR HEART

Reader's
Digest

PUBLISHED BY

THE READER'S DIGEST ASSOCIATION LIMITED

LONDON NEW YORK SYDNEY MONTREAL CAPE TOWN

YOU AND YOUR HEART
was created and produced by
Carroll & Brown Limited
5 Lonsdale Road, London NW6 6RA
for The Reader's Digest Association Limited, London

Managing Editor Denis Kennedy
Art Director Chrissie Lloyd

Series Editor Arlene Sobel
Series Art Editor Johnny Pau

Editor Sharon Freed

Assistant Editor Laura Price

Art Editor Louisa Cameron
Designer Helen George

Photographers Ian Boddy, David Murray

Production Lorraine Baird, Wendy Rogers,
Amanda Mackie

Computer Management John Clifford, Caroline Turner

First English Edition Copyright © 1996
The Reader's Digest Association Limited,
11 Westferry Circus, Canary Wharf,
London E14 4HE

Copyright © 1996
The Reader's Digest Association Far East Limited
Philippines Copyright © 1996
The Reader's Digest Association Far East Limited

Reprinted with amendments 1997

ISBN 0 276 42196 5

Reproduced by Colourscan, Singapore
Printing and binding: Printer Industria Gráfica S.A., Barcelona

CONSULTANTS

Professor A.J. Camm QHP, MD, FRCP,
FESC, FACC, CStJ
Department of Cardiological Sciences
St George's Hospital, London

Lucille Daniels BSc (Nutrition)
State Registered Dietician

Susanna Dowie LicAc, MTAcS, RWTA
Licentiate in Acupuncture and Chinese Medicine
Member of the Traditional Acupuncture Society

Dr Lesley Hickin
MB, BS, BSc, DRCOG, MRCGP
General Practitioner

Roger Newman Turner BAc, ND, DO
Member of the Register of Naturopaths
Member of the Register of Osteopaths

Bob Smith

MEDICAL ILLUSTRATIONS CONSULTANT

Dr Frances Williams MB, BChir,
MRCP, DTM&H

CONTRIBUTORS

May Winnifred Annexton
Anita Bean BSc
Ellen Dupont
Richard Emerson
Elaine Harbige
Nigel Howard
Sharon Talbot
Stephen Ulph

The information in this book is for reference only;
it is not intended as a substitute for a doctor's diagnosis and care.
The editors urge anyone with continuing medical problems
or symptoms to consult a doctor.

YOU AND YOUR HEART

More and more people today are choosing to take greater responsibility for their own health rather than relying on the doctor to step in with a cure when something goes wrong. We now recognise that we can influence our health by making an improvement in lifestyle – a better diet, more exercise and reduced stress. People are also becoming increasingly aware that there are other healing methods – some new, others very ancient – that can help to prevent illness or be used as a complement to orthodox medicine.

The series *Health and Healing the Natural Way* will help you to make your own health choices by giving you clear, comprehensive, straightforward and encouraging information and advice about methods of improving your health. The series explains the many different natural therapies now available – aromatherapy, herbalism, acupressure and many others – and the many circumstances in which they may be of benefit when used in conjunction with conventional medicine.

The approach of YOU AND YOUR HEART reflects the idea that a healthy person is one whose mind and body work in concert to achieve that goal. Throughout the following pages, the message you will see time and again is that the responsibility for a healthy heart is in your hands.

The well-being of your heart should be *a* major health issue for everyone. For without a healthy heart, the quality of human life is significantly reduced. It is vital to understand the underlying causes of heart disease so that you can keep your heart functioning at its maximum capacity.

Keeping your heart healthy, and helping it recover after heart disease, may mean changing your behaviour, your habits, your lifestyle, and even aspects of your personality. Throughout the book natural therapies are suggested for maintaining and helping to restore the health of your heart, and the book shows you how these therapies can be used with orthodox medicine for the greatest benefit.

CONTENTS

5 DIAGNOSIS AND TREATMENT OPTIONS

6 HEART AND CIRCULATORY DISORDERS

7 THE ROAD TO RECOVERY

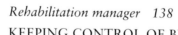
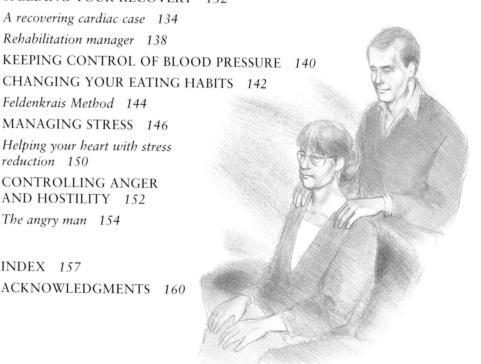

A HEALTHY HEART

Modern life is providing your heart with its toughest trial. How you treat this vital organ will determine your health now and for the future.

THE MYTHICAL HEART
The heart has held a privileged position for centuries as the seat of our emotions. In this 16th-century painting, the heart is connected with the feeling of love.

THE HEALTHY HEART DIET
Eating at least five servings of fruit and vegetables every day provides antioxidants which help fight disease. Complex carbohydrates, such as wholemeal bread and pasta, contain vitamins and nutrients as well as fibre which helps reduce cholesterol levels.

Few people need to be reminded of the crucial role played in the body by the heart. Unlike most other organs, the heart makes its presence palpably felt in one way or another every day. Its dramatic leap into pulsating life in response to feelings of attraction, excitement, alarm and the whole spectrum of human emotion has always aroused interest and wonder, and the mystery of its action has secured for it a privileged place in the folklore, mythology and even the language of men and women the world over.

Although anatomical study has long since ousted the heart from its position as the conscience and centre of a person's being, modern medical research is now bringing to light the sensitivity of the heart to factors such as exercise, diet, habits and personality, so we are now able to take a fuller responsibility for our health. Although the heart is an involuntary muscle working without our conscious effort, most people tend to take the functioning of the heart for granted until something goes amiss, without realising how much influence they can actually have on its health.

Statistics show that heart problems are now occurring with an alarming frequency. This century has seen a massive increase in the number of people suffering from degenerative heart disease, which is now the biggest cause of death and disability in the Western world. In America and Great Britain it kills as many people as all other diseases put together, including cancer. Coronary heart disease alone accounts for one-third of all registered deaths and as many as one in five of the population suffer from high blood pressure – a poor prognosis for the future. In America, over 300 in 100 000 people die from coronary heart disease every year, and in Scotland it is over 500, the highest rate of deaths in the world. In Great Britain, some 350 000 men and women die from coronary heart disease annually.

Many people associate problems with the functioning of the heart with the onset of middle age. But there is nothing inevitable about heart disease. It is not necessarily a natural product of old age or decline. It can also result from a lifetime of bad habits and diet, when it is largely self-inflicted and avoidable. The tragic fact is that it is striking people down in the prime of their lives.

THE CAUSES OF HEART DISEASE

The heart is the 'pump' at the centre of the body's plumbing system, the transportation network of tubes which supplies blood to the various parts of the body. Along with input from the brain and nervous system, the heart regulates the rate at which blood is pumped to the various organs, as well as how much blood is needed in various situations, such as exercise or stress. Even a minor defect in the heart or its arteries can cause major symptoms and problems.

In a very few cases the heart may be defective at birth or sustain damage to the valves from the effects of rheumatic fever or other infectious illnesses. The damage to heart muscle as a result of illnesses or factors such as alcoholism may cause heart failure. But in the vast majority of cases, 'heart disease' is actually the end result of the gradual deterioration of the coronary arteries.

In the Western world we eat too much (often of the wrong things), drink too much alcohol, smoke too much tobacco, exercise too little and live in an unhealthy environment. All these things contribute to damage to the blood vessels. When they start to fur up and become constricted, the heart has to work much harder to ensure the all-important free flow of blood, and is consequently put under strain. A heart attack is simply a pump giving up when the odds are stacked against it.

MODERN MEDICINE

Today, there are ingenious and sophisticated methods for diagnosing heart and circulatory ailments. These range from a simple physical examination (taking pulse and blood pressure, listening to the heart with a stethoscope), to an electrocardiogram (ECG) and exercise stress test, to the more complicated scans, and invasive procedures such as cardiac catheterisation and coronary

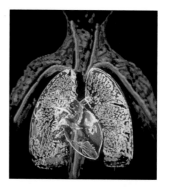

POSITION OF THE HEART
This coloured x-ray shows a healthy heart just behind the lungs and a little to the left.

PETER SELLERS
The comedian and film star, Peter Sellers (1925–1980), suffered seven heart attacks within two hours in 1964 but recovered and went on to star in several more films before he finally died of heart failure 16 years later.

LIFE AFTER A TRANSPLANT
These men have had a heart transplant, and are regular competitors in the British, European and World Transplant Games. They are keen athletes and participate in transplant support groups, which encourage returning to an active life after surgery.

HEART RELAXATION
Overcoming stress is essential for the health of your heart. Relaxation exercises, reading books and listening to music can all help to combat stress.

angiography. In terms of countering the effects of damage to the heart, bypass operations, valve replacements, pacemakers, heart transplants and the techniques of intensive care, have enabled many heart patients to live reasonably healthy lives. However, treating heart disorders with such methods is expensive, and includes the risks of further medical complications. Since most heart disease is caused by damaged arteries as a result of an unhealthy lifestyle, doctors are realising more and more that changes in lifestyle can both prevent and reverse many heart-disease cases, and patients who acknowledge this are increasingly taking a greater level of responsibility for their own health.

Now, before advising surgery, many specialists prefer to recommend simpler measures such as changing the patient's diet or devising an exercise programme, aimed in either case at improving the efficiency of the heart and reducing the deposits that are clogging up the arteries. And now that it is increasingly accepted that the condition of the mind is vital for heart health too, doctors propose treatments that reduce stress – and consequently high blood pressure – and increase cardiovascular efficiency.

MIND OVER MATTER

Statistics are showing that in addition to lifestyle there is another, and perhaps far greater, determinant of heart disease. There is evidence that in addition to being physically unhealthy, many heart patients are leading unhappy lives. People are more vulnerable to premature death from heart disease if they suffer stresses in their social and professional environments, if they feel isolated from others, or if they have low or negative self-esteem through feelings of emotional deprivation and psychological inadequacy. Our environments, our habits, our behaviour, and our attitudes are all major contributors to the development of heart disease.

As the miss of a beat and a quickening pulse graphically indicate, a disturbance in a person's mind very quickly reverberates in the heart and the entire cardiovascular system. Emotional stress or anxiety triggers physical stress. How much the cardiovascular system holds up against the extra pressures exerted this way will depend on several factors: the level and intensity of the pressures, genetic tendency, individual personality and emotional resources, the amount of exercise taken and the quality of the person's diet.

THE HOLISTIC APPROACH

The sensitivity of the heart to personality factors, rather than just issues of strictly medical interest, means that cardiovascular problems are particularly responsive to a broader treatment approach that embraces the psychological, along with the physical, aspects of health. The conventional medical idea of the body as a system made up of purely mechanical parts is now falling out of favour. The traditional approach to heart treatment, in which blood pressure, cholesterol level and the structure of the blood vessels are viewed in isolation from personality, is regarded as far too limiting. At least equally as important are questions about the patient's relationships with family members and work colleagues, the way he or she deals with problems and stressful situations, the way the body is treated and the success with which the patient can maintain the balance of the physical body, the intellectual mind and the emotional spirit.

This is precisely the emphasis of the various natural therapies that holistic medicine is introducing, or, in many cases re-introducing, into modern medical practice. These include naturopathy, homeopathy, hydrotherapy, aromatherapy, massage, acupuncture, biofeedback, herbalism, Chinese medicine and nutrition. Holistic medicine aims to cater to the whole person, beyond the contours of the body and on into the patient's psychological and emotional environment. To do this it dispenses with the conventionally passive role of the patient and encourages a full 'partnership for health' with the doctor or therapist.

The holistic way with heart disease naturally emphasises prevention first and foremost and seeks to offer treatment that does not require the use of symptom-relieving drugs or interventionist surgery. More importantly, holism makes many more demands upon the patient to develop skills to adapt to the changing circumstances of age, social environment and pressures of work. To stay physically healthy we must elaborate methods of coping with the demands made on us, of maintaining our self-esteem and spiritual well-being.

HEALING HERBS
There are a number of herbs that can play a part in restoring your heart to health. Some can be taken as teas or infusions, while others, such as garlic, onions and ginger, can be used in cooking. Still other herbs, such as lavender, are used in aromatherapy and aid relaxation.

BEING SOCIABLE
Many studies have shown that living in social isolation increases the risk of heart disease and slows recovery from heart surgery. Relaxing with the family can help your heart to heal.

EXERCISE TO HEALTH
Walking briskly for at least 20 minutes three times a week can help lower blood pressure and strengthen your heart. Walking is an essential component of any cardiac rehabilitation programme.

FOOT MASSAGE
The first weeks after heart surgery are stressful and uncomfortable. A foot massage is a gentle and effective way to help you to relax and recover.

Holism should not be seen in opposition to orthodox healing, rather as complementary to it, and to be employed in full cooperation with the advanced methods of technological medicine.

Many heart attacks and strokes need not occur. But lack of information on what can be done, passive belief in the capabilities of technological medicine and a fatalistic resignation to the apparent all-conquering power of heart disease, has prevented the general public from appreciating just how much they are responsible for their own health.

The purpose of *You and Your Heart* is to provide you with the knowledge you need in order to make your own decisions on your health, and to introduce you to a wider spectrum of care for the heart, where the roles appropriate to conventional and complementary medicine are given their due place.

After an explanatory chapter on the functioning of the heart and cardiovascular system, *You and Your Heart* is divided into two parts: the first is on prevention and the second is on treatment of heart disease. Chapter 2 describes the many factors that increase the risk of heart disease, such as gender, family history, age and personality. It also covers lifestyle risks such as smoking tobacco, a high intake of alcoholic beverages, high levels of stress and a sedentary life, and gives techniques for stopping smoking and relieving stress. Chapter 3 is about how you should eat to protect your heart and gives up-to-date information on the importance of unsaturated fats, antioxidants, fibre and other foods that you should incorporate into your diet if you want to keep your heart healthy. Chapter 4 explains the necessity for regular and programmed exercise, and tells you how to get moving, with illustrated toning and stretching programmes that you can follow.

Chapter 5 deals with the diagnosis of heart and circulatory disorders and takes a look at the natural treatment options that are available. Chapter 6 explains these disorders in detail and lists conventional treatments together with natural therapies that can assist in relieving symptoms. The final chapter discusses recovering after you have had a heart attack or heart surgery, and it covers such topics as returning to work, resumption of sex, stress management techniques and ways to control anger – an emotion that contributes to the development of heart disease.

How much do you really know about heart disease?

Heart disease has received a great deal of media attention over the last three decades, with the result that people feel that they are much more knowledgeable about it. But is this really true? This quiz tests what you know about heart disease. You may be in for one or two surprises.

Q IS IT TRUE THAT DEATHS FROM HEART DISEASE HAVE BEEN RISING STEADILY SINCE THE BEGINNING OF THE CENTURY?

Yes and no. In most Western countries there has been a noticeable rise due to a number of factors, including a high-fat diet, an increase in smoking, a more sedentary lifestyle and the effects of stress. In the UK and US, however, since the 1960s, there has been a decline, which is due to a combination of lifestyle changes and advances in medical technology, which treat conditions which were once invariably fatal far sooner, thus reducing the mortality rate.

Q WHEN I HAD MY BLOOD PRESSURE TAKEN IT WAS 135/85. IS THIS TOO HIGH FOR AN ADULT WITH REASONABLE HEALTH?

No, your blood pressure is completely normal. It is now generally agreed by doctors that a reading that is consistently higher than 140/90 indicates high blood pressure or hypertension and warrants therapy, as there is an increased risk of heart attack, heart failure and stroke. Note, however, that blood pressure in children and the very fit is markedly lower. Blood pressure can rise normally as people get older but should always be monitored during routine health checks.

Q CAN I LOWER MY CHOLESTEROL BY EATING LOW CHOLESTEROL FOODS?

No. The only way you can reduce your cholesterol level is to eat foods that do not contain saturated fat. Monounsaturated and polyunsaturated fats are preferable as they conserve the good, high-density lipoprotein (HDL) cholesterol and lower the bad, low-density lipoprotein (LDL) cholesterol. Nevertheless, you should aim to reduce all fat in your diet. (See Chapter 3 for further information.)

Q IT'S OBVIOUS WHY SMOKING CONTRIBUTES TO LUNG CANCER, BUT WHY SHOULD IT AFFECT THE HEART?

Smoking has a number of negative effects on the heart and the other organs, which is why smokers have two to three times the risk of developing heart disease of non-smokers. The nicotine in cigarettes makes the adrenal glands produce more adrenaline, and this causes an increase in the heart rate and also in blood pressure. The walls of the arteries become constricted and there is more risk of blood clots and cholesterol build-up. The constriction of the blood vessels in the brain can lead to a stroke.

Q DO MEN AND WOMEN HAVE THE SAME RISK OF HEART DISEASE?

No. Until the menopause, women have a lower risk than men because the female hormones, especially oestrogen, have a protective role in maintaining levels of high-density lipoprotein-cholesterol (HDL), and lowering levels of low-density lipoprotein-cholesterol (LDL). After the menopause, when oestrogen declines, the levels reverse and women and men become more equal in risk.

Q DO YOU ALWAYS KNOW WHEN YOU ARE HAVING A HEART ATTACK?

No. In a few cases, mainly the elderly and diabetics, a heart attack will occur without pain. More typically, though, the pain of a heart attack starts as a mild ache that builds up over half an hour to an hour, becoming more distinct and quite severe. There may be a squeezing feeling in the chest, as well as pain that radiates to the arms and shoulders, sweating, dizziness, nausea, breathlessness and a feeling of dread. Because 60 per cent of heart-attack victims die within the first hour, it is critical that anyone with these symptoms gets emergency medical treatment.

Q WHY ARE HIGH-INTENSITY EXERCISES LESS BENEFICIAL FOR THE HEART THAN AEROBIC ONES?

Aerobic exercises, which consist of at least 20 minutes of a prolonged activity, including walking, swimming, rowing, and jogging, are best for using oxygen as fuel, for burning fat and and for making the heart pump more efficiently. Anaerobic or high-intensity exercises, such as sprinting, squash and skiing, which consist of short bouts of activity, burn carbohydrates, not fat, as fuel and do not improve cardiovascular health. In fact, anaerobic exercises may actually put excess strain on unfit hearts.

CHAPTER 1

HOW THE HEART WORKS

A healthy heart is essential for pumping blood around the body. From life in the womb until old age, the heart is constantly working. An understanding of how the heart and circulatory system works and what affects their well-being is essential for maintaining a healthy life.

THE HEART AND CIRCULATION

At the centre of the circulatory system lies the heart, which forces blood around the body via the arteries, sending nutrients to every tissue and receiving blood back through the veins.

Figure-of-eight

The blood travels around the body in a roughly circular path, going from the heart to the lungs and then on to nourish the body. But this circular flow is actually a figure-of-eight because the blood must return from the lungs back to the heart so that it can be pumped out to the rest of the body.

Arteries to the lungs | Veins from the lungs

Veins from the body | Arteries to the body

THE TWO CIRCLES
The top circle of this figure-of-eight is the circulation through the lungs where blood picks up oxygen, while the bottom circle is the circulation through the body where oxygen and nutrients are delivered to the tissues.

Blood is necessary for the nourishment of every cell in the body. It moves ceaselessly, carrying life-giving oxygen and nutrients to the cells and taking away waste products such as carbon dioxide. The blood travels around the body in a

THE CIRCULATORY SYSTEM
The heart pumps the blood through the main arteries throughout the body, and it is then returned to the heart via the veins.

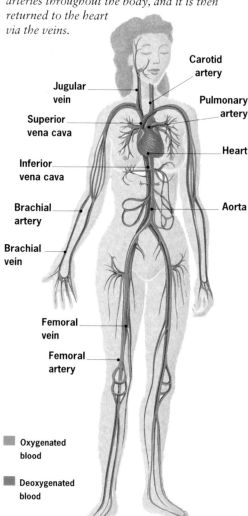

Jugular vein
Superior vena cava
Inferior vena cava
Brachial artery
Brachial vein
Femoral vein
Femoral artery
Carotid artery
Pulmonary artery
Heart
Aorta

■ Oxygenated blood

■ Deoxygenated blood

roughly circular path, actually creating a figure-of-eight (or almost two circles) as it delivers nutrients and oxygen throughout the body. The heart is the pump that keeps this circular system going.

THE CIRCULATORY SYSTEM
The heart is divided by a wall called the septum. The right side of the heart deals with deoxygenated blood, while the left side deals with oxygenated blood.

The cycle begins on the right side of the heart (the 'right heart'). The deoxygenated blood (bluish in colour) from the trunk and legs enters the right atrium through one vein (the inferior vena cava) while that from the head and arms enters the right atrium through another vein (the superior vena cava). When the heart walls contract, the blood is pumped down into the right ventricle. When the right ventricle contracts, the blood is forced up into the pulmonary artery which takes it into the lungs to deposit carbon dioxide and pick up oxygen. (When it leaves the heart, the pulmonary artery divides into two branches – one leads to the right lung, the other to the left.)

The oxygenated blood leaves the lungs and enters the 'left heart' through the pulmonary veins which then take the blood into the left atrium, which contracts, pushing the blood down into the left ventricle. When the thick muscular wall of this ventricle contracts, the blood is forced out through the aorta to begin its journey to the rest of the body via the main arteries, such as the femoral arteries in the legs, brachial arteries in the arms and carotid arteries in the neck.

Once the blood has completed its circuit of the body, it returns to the heart through the superior and inferior venae cavae into

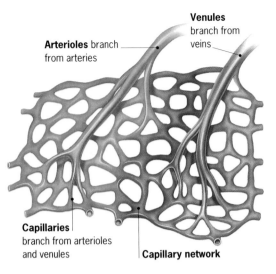

Venules branch from veins

Arterioles branch from arteries

Capillaries branch from arterioles and venules

Capillary network

CAPILLARY NETWORK
Oxygen, nutrients and waste products pass between the bloodstream and the body tissues via the very thin capillary walls, and blood flows from arteries to veins through the network.

the left side of the heart. The whole process then begins again. The heart pumps the blood around the body about 70 times a minute every minute of your life. The entire journey of a single blood cell around the body takes just about a minute.

THE BLOOD VESSELS

The circulatory system is made up of an extensive network of blood vessels, which include arteries, arterioles, veins, venules and capillaries. In total, the length of these vessels is 96 000 km (60 000 miles).

Arteries

The arteries are thick-walled, muscular tubes through which the blood flows to all parts of the body. As the heart pumps blood through them, they widen, then recoil automatically to push the blood onwards, assisting the heart in pushing the blood around the body.

Arteries branch into smaller tubes (arterioles), which branch into tiny blood vessels called capillaries. These link up with venules which link up with the veins.

Veins

The veins eventually carry blood back to the heart. But by the time the blood reaches the venules and veins it has run out of pressure. Because they are not elastic like arteries or able to expand and recoil to force the blood through, most veins have valves that prevent

the backflow of blood. It is the movement of muscles surrounding the veins that helps the blood to get back to the heart.

Capillaries

Although they keep the tissues supplied with oxygen and nutrients, capillaries are so small they can only hold a single file of blood cells and their walls are very thin to allow molecules to pass through them. The pulmonary capillaries allow oxygen from the lung's air sacs (alveoli) to be absorbed into the blood. Blood carries the oxygen to the body's cells, where it is exchanged via the capillaries for carbon dioxide. The capillaries link up with the venules, returning the carbon dioxide-rich blood through the venous system to the heart to be circulated to the lungs again for exhalation of the carbon dioxide it contains. The blood also picks up nutrients from the small intestine via the capillaries, exchanging them for waste products which are then taken to the liver or kidneys for excretion. The nutrients are circulated around the body.

THE LYMPHATIC SYSTEM

The capillaries exchange fluid with all tissue cells in the process of delivering oxygen and nutrients and taking away carbon dioxide

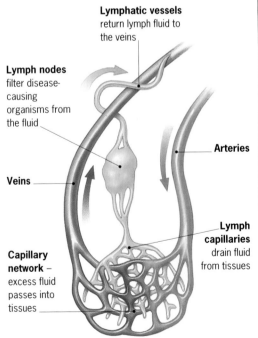

Lymphatic vessels return lymph fluid to the veins

Lymph nodes filter disease-causing organisms from the fluid

Arteries

Veins

Capillary network – excess fluid passes into tissues

Lymph capillaries drain fluid from tissues

LYMPHATIC SYSTEM
The drainage system of the body draws off excess fluid from tissue, filters out bacteria and other foreign organisms, and then returns the fluid to the veins.

How the blood carries oxygen

Red blood cells carry haemoglobin, an iron-rich pigment which chemically links up with oxygen. When deoxygenated blood passes through the lungs, its haemoglobin picks up the oxygen in the air sacs of the lungs until it has taken up the full complement and has become saturated once more. This oxygen-rich blood is then returned to the heart and pumped out to the tissues. The haemoglobin then gives up its oxygen to cells which are low in oxygen.

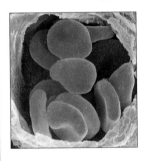

RED BLOOD CELLS
This electron micrograph shows red blood cells travelling through an arteriole. A red blood cell lives for about four months and travels about 15 km (9.3 miles) every day. There are about 5000 billion red blood cells per litre (1¾ pints) of blood.

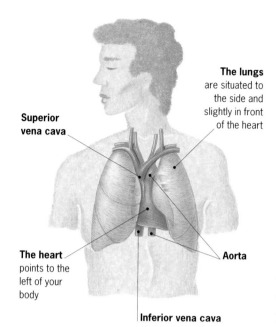

THE POSITION OF THE HEART
A hollow muscular organ about the size of two fists, the heart sits in the chest (thoracic) cavity just to the left of the centre of the chest. It is protected by the breastbone (sternum) at the front and the spinal column at the rear as it nestles between the lungs.

Superior vena cava

The lungs are situated to the side and slightly in front of the heart

The heart points to the left of your body

Aorta

Inferior vena cava

and other waste products. But more fluid passes from the capillaries into the tissue cells than returns to them so in this exchange the lymphatic drainage system removes this excess fluid from the tissues and returns it to the veins via lymph nodes, where the fluid is filtered for disease-causing organisms.

THE STRUCTURE OF THE HEART
The heart is a hollow muscular organ, made up of four chambers: two atria and two ventricles, with a septum dividing the left side from the right. Blood enters and exits from these chambers via valves.

The heart is made up of three layers: the myocardium which is thick and muscular, and the epicardium and the endocardium which are thin membranes. The epicardium covers the outer surface of the myocardium, and the endocardium lines the inside of the heart's four chambers, the heart valves and the muscles that attach to the valves.

How the myocardium works
It is the myocardium, made up of individual muscle cells called myocytes, which actually pumps out the blood. The myocytes act in concert to contract and relax the chambers of the heart in the correct sequence in response to electrical messages which pass between them directing the entire operation. Fine threads called filaments contract to shorten the myocytes, and thus contract the heart muscle. As the pumping chambers get smaller, the blood is squeezed out. When

FINDING OUT ABOUT THE HEART

Galen of Pergamon, a Roman who lived in the 2nd century AD, developed theories about the heart that were accepted for centuries. His theory – that the blood flowed from one side of the heart to the other – remained unchallenged until Andreas Vesalius (1514–64) proved that the heart's septum was solid, preventing blood from passing from one side to the other. Vesalius also proposed that blood flowed in a circular, not a lateral, route around the body.

William Harvey (1578–1657), an English physician and anatomist, discovered that blood flows from the arteries to the veins and back to the heart, proving that blood is in constant motion and moves in one direction only.

Harvey based his theories on a mathematical calculation of the heart's output, that is, with each contraction the heart ejects about 59 ml (2 fl oz). Since it beats about 70 times a minute, it would pump about 248 litres (436 pints) every hour. Harvey concluded that this was possible only if the blood flowed back to the heart to be pumped out again. Thus he was able to deduce that the heart is a pump and that it keeps the blood moving in a circular direction around the body.

DISCOVERING THE CIRCULATION
William Harvey uses a heart to demonstrate to Charles I his theory of the circulation of the blood in 1628.

THE ANATOMY OF THE HEART

The heart is the hardest working muscle in the body. The walls of the ventricles are much thicker than the walls of the atria because they have to work harder to pump the blood out. The aorta is the largest blood vessel in the body and pumps oxygenated blood. The pulmonary veins are the only veins carrying oxygenated blood, and the pulmonary artery is the only artery that carries deoxygenated blood.

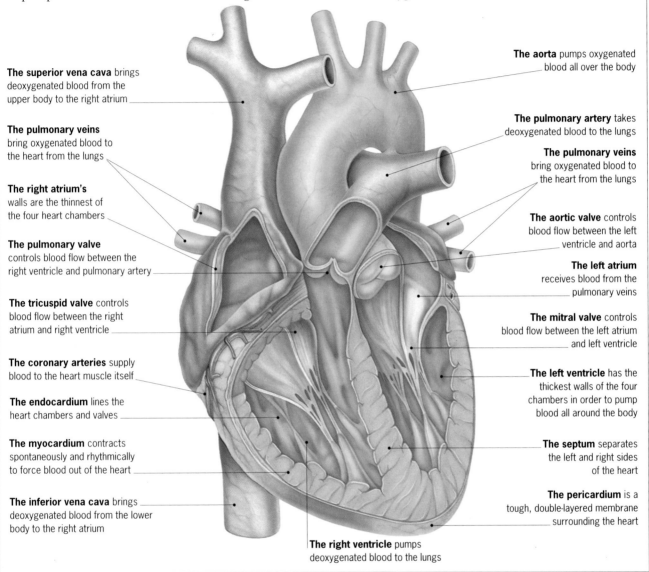

The superior vena cava brings deoxygenated blood from the upper body to the right atrium

The pulmonary veins bring oxygenated blood to the heart from the lungs

The right atrium's walls are the thinnest of the four heart chambers

The pulmonary valve controls blood flow between the right ventricle and pulmonary artery

The tricuspid valve controls blood flow between the right atrium and right ventricle

The coronary arteries supply blood to the heart muscle itself

The endocardium lines the heart chambers and valves

The myocardium contracts spontaneously and rhythmically to force blood out of the heart

The inferior vena cava brings deoxygenated blood from the lower body to the right atrium

The aorta pumps oxygenated blood all over the body

The pulmonary artery takes deoxygenated blood to the lungs

The pulmonary veins bring oxygenated blood to the heart from the lungs

The aortic valve controls blood flow between the left ventricle and aorta

The left atrium receives blood from the pulmonary veins

The mitral valve controls blood flow between the left atrium and left ventricle

The left ventricle has the thickest walls of the four chambers in order to pump blood all around the body

The septum separates the left and right sides of the heart

The pericardium is a tough, double-layered membrane surrounding the heart

The right ventricle pumps deoxygenated blood to the lungs

the filaments relax, the chambers get larger and fill with blood again. It is this in-out process that you feel when you take your pulse or put your hand on your chest.

The pericardium

Covering the whole heart is a bag made of tough fibrous tissue called the pericardium. It is attached to the large blood vessels emerging from the heart, but not to the heart itself. Unlike the muscles of the heart, the pericardium does not stretch. It is loose-fitting and is lined with a moist membrane.

The space between the pericardium and the heart contains a tiny amount of lubricating fluid which allows the heart to expand and contract easily without any danger of irritation from contact with the inner surface of the pericardium.

THE VALVES

The amount of blood that enters and leaves the heart's left chambers is exactly the same as that which passes through the chambers on the right side of the heart. The movement of the blood in and out of the chambers is

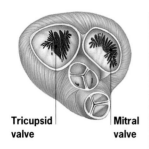

Tricuspid valve | **Mitral valve**

BLOOD ENTERS HEART
This view of the heart from above shows the mitral and tricuspid valves open, as blood enters the ventricles from the atria.

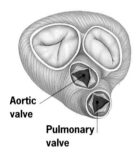

Aortic valve

Pulmonary valve

EXIT OF BLOOD
The aortic valve and pulmonary valve are open here, as blood passes from the left ventricle into the aorta and from the right ventricle into the pulmonary artery.

controlled by the precise movements of the valves. In order to keep the blood in the heart flowing in only one direction and at the right rate, the heart has four one-way valves. Each valve has flaps or cusps which open to let the blood in and then close to prevent it flowing back the way it came.

The atrioventricular valves 'guard' the openings from the atria into the ventricles. On the right side, the tricuspid valve keeps blood from flowing back into the right atrium after it has entered the right ventricle. The mitral valve performs the same function on the left side of the heart. The other two valves are shaped like half moons: the pulmonary valve between the right ventricle and pulmonary artery, and the aortic valve between the left ventricle and aorta. They open and close on cue to keep the blood flowing out of the ventricles to the body and at the proper rate.

Heart sounds

In addition to the regular sound of its beating, the heart makes a number of other sounds that are audible with amplification. The stethoscope is the most commonly used amplifying device. Abnormal heart sounds (such as clicks, snaps, murmurs, whooshes) can indicate disorders of the heart and your doctor may carry out further investigation.

By listening at four different places on the chest, your doctor can hear sounds made by the four heart valves opening and closing in rhythm. In a normal heart, there are two

sounds, known as 'lubb' and 'dupp'. One of the sounds is caused by the slamming shut of the tricuspid and mitral valves. The other occurs when the aortic and pulmonary valves shut. In young adults and children, the second sound may be split because the two valves do not close at exactly the same time, but this is normal and not dangerous.

Another abnormal sound is a rushing sound that indicates a heart murmur caused by turbulent blood flow. This noise may suggest that there are problems with one of the heart valves. Heart murmurs are more common in children, but are also found in adults. They are also common in newborn babies and usually disappear within a few days, although they can indicate a congenital heart defect (see page 106).

HOW THE HEART BEATS

The heart beats an average of 70 times per minute. The timing of the heartbeat is controlled by the sinoatrial (sinus) node, the heart's natural pacemaker. In a healthy heart the sinoatrial node directs the heart's conduction system (see opposite) and maintains a regular rhythm. The node is a group of cells located in the upper part of the right atrium. These cells send out electrical impulses which make the heart muscle contract. Their rate of discharge is modulated by nerve impulses from the brain.

The electric current is initiated and controlled from the sinoatrial node. It travels to the atria and then to the atrioventricular node (a cluster of cells between the atrium and the ventricle) and on to the ventricles.

The group of nerves that make up the electrical network of the ventricles is called the His-Purkinje system which directs the current through the cells in both ventricles.

The atrioventricular node slows down the current to make sure the atria contract before the ventricles. The time required for the electrical impulse occurring in the sinoatrial node to reach the myocardial cells averages about one-quarter of a second in a heart beating 70 times a minute.

The rate set by the sinoatrial node changes according to the demands of the body. The sinoatrial node can increase the heartbeat from an average of about 70 beats per minute when resting, to about 180 beats per minute during strenuous exercise, and it slows down the heart as you rest or sleep. Other impulses and hormonal activity can

LISTENING TO THE HEART

The doctor will place the stethoscope at four different positions on your chest, which correspond to the four valves.

Depending on which noises are heard, a diagnosis can be made. Further tests may be needed to confirm the diagnosis.

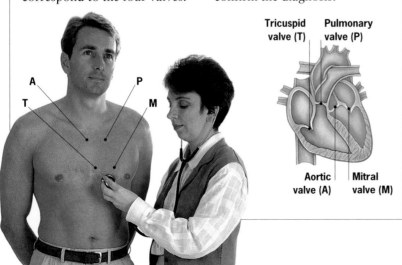

Tricuspid valve (T) | **Pulmonary valve (P)**

Aortic valve (A) | **Mitral valve (M)**

also affect the pace that the sinoatrial node sets. Factors such as smoking, alcohol and caffeine intake as well as some prescription drugs, speed the heartbeat by affecting the sympathetic nervous system (see below), and hormones such as adrenaline.

THE PULSE

Your heart beats at a rate of about 100 000 times a day throughout your life. Each beat can be felt as a pulse around the body where arteries lie close to the surface of the skin.

The flow of blood in the arteries increases and decreases as a new volume of blood is pumped into them with each heartbeat. The arterial walls expand as blood enters them and recoil as it empties into the capillaries, creating a pulse. The pulse can be felt most easily over a bone or other firm spots where an artery lies, such as the wrist and the neck. The pulse can also be felt at points just in front of the ear, on the outer side of the eye, and on the upper surface of the foot.

CARDIAC OUTPUT

Even though it beats constantly, the heart does not pump all the blood from the ventricles at any one time. The proportion which leaves the heart when it contracts is called the ejection fraction, and consists of about half the blood in the ventricle. The ejection fraction in a healthy body increases by about five to ten per cent when there are increased demands for oxygen made on the heart, such as during exercise or times of stress.

The stroke volume is the amount of blood which is pumped into the aorta by the left ventricle in one contraction. The cardiac output is the total volume of blood pumped by the heart in 1 minute. It is determined by the heart rate (the number of heartbeats per minute) and the stroke volume.

When you exercise, not only does the heart pump more but it also contracts more forcefully and the muscle stretches so that more blood is pumped with each beat and the overall cardiac output increases.

The coronary arteries

The fuel lines of the heart stem from the aorta and provide blood to the heart muscle itself. These arteries form a crown encircling the top of the heart and running along its surface. They then branch off into increasingly smaller branches that penetrate the heart muscle. Finally the branches become capillaries in which the blood's oxygen and nutrients are exchanged for waste products. Blood flow through the coronary arteries averages 200 ml (7 fl oz) per minute. The heart uses four to five per cent of the blood it pumps.

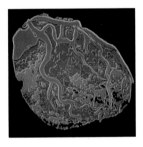

HEART IMAGE
This scan shows mostly healthy coronary arteries but one artery, in the top right hand corner, shows an abnormal narrowing, (stenosis). When fatty deposits build up in these arteries due to unhealthy eating habits, they become blocked.

THE CONDUCTION SYSTEM

The sinoatrial node sends nerve impulses to the atria, atrioventricular node and on to the ventricles. The brain, in response to the nervous system, regulates the sinoatrial node. The sympathetic nervous system, which prepares the body for action, speeds up the heart in response to stress or exercise, while the parasympathetic nervous system, which regulates processes such as digestion, slows it down.

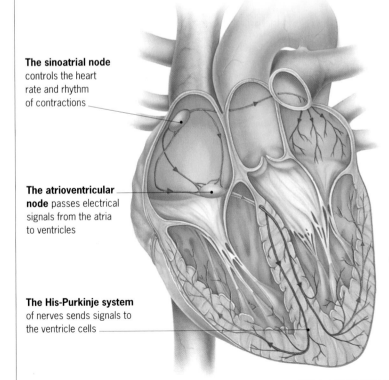

The sinoatrial node controls the heart rate and rhythm of contractions

The atrioventricular node passes electrical signals from the atria to ventricles

The His-Purkinje system of nerves sends signals to the ventricle cells

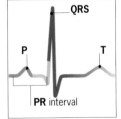

QRS

P   T

PR interval

ECG READING
This represents the electrical pathways in the heart. The P wave shows the impulse travelling through the atrium; the PR interval as it passes through the atrioventricular node; the QRS complex as it travels through the ventricles; and the T wave as the heart relaxes before the next beat (see page 91).

BLOOD PRESSURE

The heart pushes the blood through the circulatory system with great force. Without this pressure, the blood would be unable to reach every part of the body.

Blood pressure measurements
Blood pressure is recorded in millimetres of mercury (mm Hg) as the earliest blood pressure measuring devices used a column of mercury calibrated against a millimetre scale.

The action of pumping the blood through the heart is called a systole. With each heartbeat, the blood surges through the arteries and arterioles and pressure is at its highest – this is systolic pressure. It is then followed by a very short pause, called a diastole, which occurs between heartbeats when the pressure is at its lowest. This period of low pressure is called diastolic pressure.

The heart rests during diastole so that the muscles can relax and fill with blood before the heart contracts again, forcing the blood into the arteries. At a rate of 70 beats per minute, the diastole or rest period is about three-fifths of a second.

The arteries, which carry the blood away from the heart, are resilient and elastic and are able to withstand the varying flow of blood as the heart pumps. Healthy vessels also have no obstructions or narrowings. The two pressures audible in the heartbeat, the diastolic (resting phase) and systolic (pumping phase), remain within normal limits when the blood flow from the heart neither meets nor creates too much resistance in the arteries. However, if the artery walls become inflexible, any additional fluid will cause a rise in pressure as more blood is forced through a confined space. This can result in serious health problems.

High blood pressure
When arteries are narrowed or become rigid due to disease or ageing, the walls cannot expand to relieve pressure so blood pressure levels rise. If they remain elevated, high blood pressure, clinically known as hypertension, can result. High blood pressure itself further damages the cells of the artery walls, making them even less elastic, which drives the blood pressure up even more.

Blood pressure is naturally elevated during exercise or exertion, as the heart has to pump more blood to supply the muscles.

High blood pressure is symptomless in the majority of cases, but may sometimes cause headaches, giddiness, visual disturbances and shortness of breath.

Low blood pressure
Blood pressure that is lower than the average of 140/90 (see opposite) usually causes no problems, apart from occasional light-headedness. Very fit people often have low blood pressure, as do young women.

Blood pressure that is dangerously low (a systolic pressure less than 60 mm Hg) is known as hypotension, and is usually associated with shock or serious bleeding.

WHAT INFLUENCES BLOOD PRESSURE

Blood pressure rises if the heart pumps blood into the arteries at an increased rate (as during exercise), or if the arteries are constricted and therefore resist blood flow from the heart.

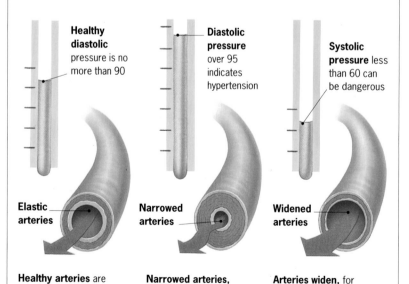

Healthy diastolic pressure is no more than 90

Diastolic pressure over 95 indicates hypertension

Systolic pressure less than 60 can be dangerous

Elastic arteries

Narrowed arteries

Widened arteries

Healthy arteries are elastic and expand and recoil easily, keeping blood pressure normal

Narrowed arteries, which result from disease or ageing, cause blood pressure to rise

Arteries widen, for instance during shock or heavy bleeding and cause blood pressure to drop

MAINTAINING BLOOD PRESSURE

Keeping your blood pressure at a healthy level is of paramount importance to avoid damaging the artery walls, including those of the heart, brain and kidneys, and raising the risk of heart disease.

Medical professionals and other scientists agree that eating a healthier diet, exercising more and avoiding stress can all help to keep blood pressure low or help to lower it if it has become too high.

People who are at risk of high blood pressure should have check-ups regularly. Risk factors include: obesity, contraceptive pills, smoking, excessive alcohol intake, family history, pregnancy and stress. To monitor the impact of lifestyle changes, some people have blood pressures machines at home (see page 96), but this is not usually necessary.

If your blood pressure level is high, your doctor may prescribe medication but changes in diet may also be vital (see page 51). Foods that are good for your heart are fresh fruit and vegetables, and fish. Fats are to be avoided, particularly the saturated fats found in dairy products and red meat. Moderation in all things, particularly in salt and alcohol consumption, is also important. Smoking is definitely to be avoided.

MEASURING BLOOD PRESSURE

Attempts have been made to measure blood pressure since the 19th century. In 1863, Etienne-Jules Marey of Paris introduced the first practical instrument to measure the way the blood pulsed and the amount of pressure in the arteries. The instrument, which was called a sphygmograph, contained an arrangement of screws and levers for altering tensions on the arm. Other scientists improved on Marey's design.

Blood pressure is now measured with an instrument called a sphygmanometer, which is a refinement on Marey's early efforts. It measures the pressure in the brachial artery (the main artery in the upper arm) by means of a cuff which is wrapped around the arm.

The cuff is attached by a rubber tube to a squeezeable bulb and to another tube attached to a column of mercury marked off in millimetres. The cuff is inflated to a pressure above the systolic so that no blood can get through the brachial artery. Pressure in the cuff is then slowly released, and the doctor listens with a stethoscope placed over the artery in the elbow below the cuff. As the blood starts to flow, it creates a thumping noise and the pressure in the cuff at this time is equal to the systolic pressure.

As the pressure in the cuff falls further, the sound suddenly becomes muffled and then disappears as the blood flow is no longer obstructed. This is the time when a measurement of the diastolic pressure is taken.

Normal adult pressure readings register somewhere below 140 mm Hg systolic pressure and 90 mm Hg diastolic pressure and is written down as: 140/90 mm Hg. Healthy, young people will have lower readings, in particular, young women. Anything higher than 160/95 mm Hg is defined as hypertension and may need medical treatment. Low blood pressure is not normally a cause for concern unless it has fallen to dangerous levels due to shock or blood loss.

MEASURING BLOOD PRESSURE
The doctor will place a cuff on your arm and listen to the blood pressure changes. It is important to be calm and relaxed while your blood pressure is being measured.

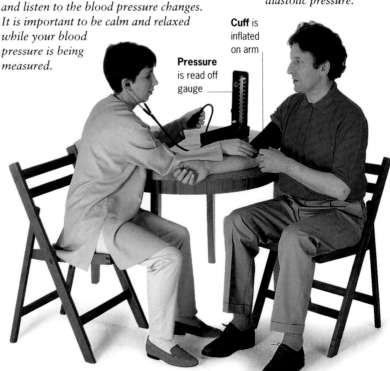

Cuff is inflated on arm

Pressure is read off gauge

Blood pressure
When blood pressure is measured, figures are taken for systolic and diastolic pressure.

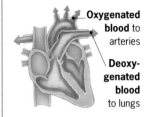

Oxygenated blood to arteries

Deoxygenated blood to lungs

SYSTOLE
When ventricles contract to force blood into the arteries, arterial blood pressure is at its highest; this is called systolic pressure.

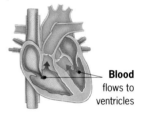

Blood flows to ventricles

DIASTOLE
Blood flows into the ventricles from the atria as the heart relaxes between beats. Arterial blood pressure is then at its lowest; this is called diastolic pressure.

A HEART FOR ALL SEASONS

Throughout your lifetime, your heart will adjust to biological, psychological and environmental changes. It starts out beating rapidly in childhood, then slows down into adulthood.

THE HEART IN ADOLESCENCE
Prior to adolescence boys and girls have a similar heart rate. During adolescence, however, girls have a higher resting heart rate.

BLOOD PRESSURE AND ADOLESCENCE
Systolic blood pressure in girls rises rapidly until menstruation begins and then levels off. Systolic pressure also rises steadily in boys before puberty, but the change is not as dramatic as for girls. Diastolic pressure does not fluctuate much for either boys or girls.

The heart of a foetus starts to beat approximately 20 days after conception. It can first be heard at about eight weeks, and the heart rate at this stage is between 140 to 150 beats per minute (bpm) – approximately twice that of the mother's resting heart rate.

HEART DEVELOPMENT
The foetal circulatory system, which begins to develop in the second week, is well established at eight weeks, and the heart has already developed into a four-chamber pump, strong enough to pump the embryo's blood around its network of blood vessels.

It is during the first eight weeks of life that the foetal heart is most vulnerable to outside influences, such as illness in the mother, or x-rays. However, fewer than one per cent of babies have heart defects at birth (see congenital heart disease on page 106). These may be detected during routine ultrasound, or may only be noticed when the newborn baby is being examined by the doctor.

By the end of the 12th week of gestation the foetus has started to produce its own blood cells, in preparation for taking over an independent system of nourishment. By the 28th week, the baby has taken over full responsibility for the production of red blood cells.

At birth the baby's heart and circulatory system are fully functional, and continue to grow through childhood with the rest of the body until adolescence.

Adolescence
At adolescence there are various noticeable changes in blood pressure, heart rate and other physiological functions. For both boys and girls, systolic blood pressure rises steadily until puberty, but then levels off. Diastolic pressure does not change much. The rise in systolic pressure occurs earlier in girls than in boys and the changes are more dramatic, but systolic pressure is ultimately higher in men. As blood pressure increases throughout the growing years, there is a corresponding decrease in the heart rate. During adolescence girls have a heart rate that is ten per cent higher than boys at the same age. In adulthood women continue to have a higher resting heart rate than men.

Adulthood
Women tend to have smaller hearts and narrower coronary arteries than men. Some doctors believe that this size difference

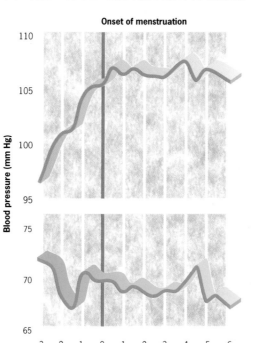

Onset of menstruation

Blood pressure (mm Hg)

110
105
100
95
75
70
65

3 2 1 0 1 2 3 4 5 6
Years before **Years after**

Diastolic   Systolic

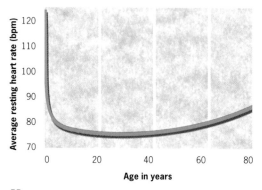

HEART RATE AND AGE
A newborn baby has a heart rate of about 120. This decreases sharply until the thirties when it begins to rise again more gradually.

makes women more susceptible to the effects of atherosclerosis (hardening of the arteries). There is also some evidence which suggests that women's coronary arteries contract more strongly than men's as a response to stress.

But if size puts women at a disadvantage, the female hormone oestrogen puts them at a distinct advantage. It seems to protect women against cardiac disease until it stops being produced after the menopause. That is why women do not have as many heart attacks as men until they are over 65. After 65 the differences between the sexes are no longer a factor in heart disease (see page 29).

THE DEMANDS OF PREGNANCY

The body has a remarkable ability to adjust to change. Nowhere is this more apparent than during pregnancy. The heart and circulatory system make the nourishment of the foetus possible throughout the nine months of pregnancy.

During pregnancy, the blood volume increases to about 30 to 40 per cent above nonpregnant levels and can rise to 50 per cent above normal by the 32nd week of gestation. The pregnant woman is carrying 1.2 to 1.7 litres (2 to 3 pints) of body fluid more than she usually does. At about 34 weeks of gestation, the blood volume reaches its maximum limit and stays at that level throughout the rest of the pregnancy.

The extra volume of blood creates more work for the heart, which must pump it to the woman's body and to the developing foetus. The heart beats faster, pumping out more blood with each contraction (cardiac output) in order to handle this extra load.

The pulse rate when measured at rest is about 10 to 15 beats higher than in a woman who is not pregnant.

Blood pressure in the arteries is affected by the woman's position. It is highest if she is seated or standing and lowest when she is lying on her back. The blood pressure is usually lowest during the second or middle trimester of pregnancy and rises from then on. The pressure in the veins, however, is not affected by pregnancy and remains unchanged. Despite this, a pregnant woman is prone to varicose veins because her uterus may impair the return blood flow from the legs causing the veins to swell.

As high blood pressure can cause complications during pregnancy, blood pressure should be checked regularly (see page 41).

AGEING AND THE HEART

There are two main effects of ageing on the heart: increased heart rate and reduced amount of blood pumped with each beat (cardiac output and stroke volume, see page 21).

PREGNANCY AND CIRCULATION
The mother's blood supplies oxygen and nutrients to the baby via the placenta. The baby and placenta require 25 per cent of the mother's cardiac output.

Heart rate and output increase during pregnancy

Kidneys have to filter more waste

Placenta allows exchange of nutrients from mother to baby

Baby depends on mother for oxygen

Blood volume increases by 30 to 40 per cent during pregnancy

Is treatment necessary?

Although blood pressure naturally rises with age in many people, studies show that it is worth treating even mild hypertension as keeping blood pressure levels down markedly reduces the risk of stroke and heart disease in people over 65. Treatment does not necessarily mean medication. There are several other measures that can be taken first, including losing weight, giving up smoking, cutting down on fat, salt and alcohol, learning to relax and exercising regularly.

Atherosclerosis

As arteries get older and more rigid, fats are more likely to deposit and form plaques.

Fats in blood

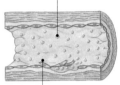

DAMAGED WALLS
When cells lining artery walls are damaged, fats (including cholesterol) build up.

Cells lining artery

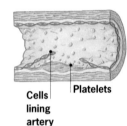

Cells lining artery | **Platelets**

PLAQUES FORM
White blood cells and platelets get 'stuck' on the fatty deposits and the artery narrows.

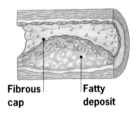

Fibrous cap | **Fatty deposit**

FURTHER BLOCKAGE
A fibrous cap forms over the fatty deposit. Blood clots may form in the narrowed artery.

The heart muscle becomes progressively weaker and therefore less efficient. The aorta (main artery of the body) becomes less elastic. These ageing processes of the heart start at age 20, after which the heart loses nearly one per cent of heart muscle strength every year. Other changes occurring with age include the thickening of the heart valves, increased blood pressure and atherosclerosis (fatty deposits in the arteries), although these are not inevitable but are related to your lifestyle. These changes may sound depressing, but the decreasing efficiency of the heart is offset by a drop in the metabolic rate and less intense demands by the body to respond to activity. However, the heart's ability to cope with stress is impeded, as arteries are less elastic and do not respond as well to fluctuating blood pressure (see page 22).

Ageing arteries

The high-fat diets as well as several other unhealthy habits that are common in the Western world mean that even children and teenagers may have fatty streaks in their arteries. After the age of 20 fibrous plaque is more likely to develop and between 30 and 45 the plaques may become calcified, especially if the person is inactive and has a poor diet. After this time heart problems may develop, depending on other risk factors, such as smoking, amount of exercise and family history.

Blood pressure and age

Healthy blood pressure levels are relative to age. In Western countries, blood pressure tends to rise until people are in their seventies, and then levels off. A blood pressure reading of 160/100 would be considered hypertension in a young person but would be more usual in a person over 80, due to the natural ageing of the arteries. It should, however, be reduced if possible.

Although fewer than three per cent of children suffer from high blood pressure, if the condition begins in childhood it may go undetected for many years. This could then lead to serious problems in later life. All cases of elevated blood pressure under ten years should be investigated. Often there will be a specific, and treatable, cause. A child under six years of age should have a blood pressure of 110/75 mm Hg, and between six to ten years, 120/80 mm Hg.

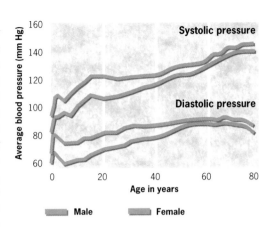

CHANGING BLOOD PRESSURE
Blood pressure tends to rise with age in Western populations, in large part due to high-fat diets, low exercise, too much stress and unhealthy habits such as smoking.

In some population groups such as Fijians and Amazon Indians, Bushmen in the Kalahari and highlanders in New Guinea, there has been no association between age and rising blood pressure.

Lifestyle factors (such as diet, smoking, alcohol, exercise, stress) play a large part in determining the effect of ageing on your blood pressure levels. You can keep your blood pressure relatively healthy by following the lifestyle recommendations in the next chapter.

HEART DISEASE AND AGE

Heart disease is most common among the middle-aged and elderly. The changes that occur in the heart with age may contribute to coronary heart disease, the most common heart disease in older patients. This is where the arteries become blocked or high blood pressure damages arteries.

There are, however, some forms of heart disease that occur in babies (congenital heart disease, see page 106) and sometimes teenagers and young adults may be affected, most commonly by rheumatic heart disease caused by a throat infection (see page 117). Heart diseases are covered in more detail in Chapter 6.

Although the heart and circulatory system show signs of wear and tear as they age, they can be kept in good health by controlling your weight, getting regular exercise, controlling blood pressure and cholesterol levels, giving up smoking, and cutting down on alcohol. Managing stress is also essential for preventing damage to your heart.

CHAPTER 2

LIFESTYLE AND A HEALTHY HEART

Keeping your heart well is one of the many good reasons for maintaining a healthy lifestyle. Your diet, exercise, habits and personality can all play a part in the health of your heart. Factors such as gender and family history cannot be changed, but a healthy lifestyle can also go a long way towards controlling these non-acquired risks.

WHO IS AT RISK FROM HEART DISEASE?

Many deaths from heart disease can be prevented if people modify the way they live. But there are some factors for heart disease that are impossible to change.

The contraceptive pill
Early oral contraceptive pills increased the risk of heart disease by raising blood pressure and blood cholesterol levels and making the blood more likely to clot. Although modern versions have lower doses of hormones, women on the Pill should always have their blood pressure taken when getting a new supply. And, if they smoke, they should quit, as this can also lead to high blood pressure.

There are several risk factors that increase the likelihood of suffering a heart attack. Two ground-breaking research projects – the Ancel Keys' Seven Countries Study (Finland, Greece, Italy, Japan, Netherlands, US and the former Yugoslavia) and the Framingham Study (US) – provided much of the scientific information on reducing risk factors. The Seven Countries Study of 12 000 men aged 40 to 59 years from 1957–62 showed the importance of blood cholesterol as a risk factor for heart disease. The main findings of the Framingham Study (1948 until now) of 5000 men and women over 40 years old confirmed the contribution of smoking, cholesterol and high blood pressure. All of these major risk factors can be changed and are therefore known as lifestyle or acquired risk factors. Physical inactivity is another important acquired risk factor.

Those who stop smoking, restrict their intakes of dietary fat, exercise regularly and follow advice on reducing high blood pressure will reduce their coronary risks. The benefits of following these guidelines will be greatest for people who are at a particularly high risk and for younger people.

Unfortunately, there are also major risk factors for coronary heart disease that cannot be changed. These are being male, heredity (family history), having diabetes, being a member of certain ethnic groups, personality and increasing age.

HEART DISEASE LEAGUE

Amongst the industrial nations Japan has the lowest risk of death from heart disease, followed closely by China. This chart shows some other countries in comparison with Japan between 1985 and 1987, resulting from a major international World Health Organisation study which looked at coronary heart disease death rates per 100,000 population.

Among both men and women, the death rates from heart disease were the highest in Scotland and Northern Ireland, while the lowest rates were seen in France and Italy. Differences between the countries are attributed mainly to dietary factors, with an emphasis on the Mediterranean diet (see page 56).

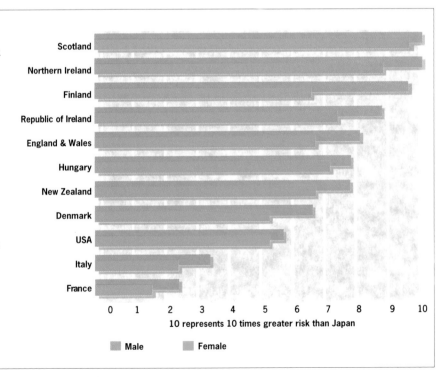

10 represents 10 times greater risk than Japan

Male   Female

GENDER

Coronary heart disease is often thought of as a man's disease. It is true that between the ages of 35 and 44, a man is five or six times more likely to die from coronary heart disease than a woman.

But in countries where coronary heart disease is a major problem, it kills more women than any other disease. Every year in the UK, coronary heart disease kills 76 000 women (compared with 16 000 from breast cancer).

Women and coronary heart disease

Women with coronary heart disease are more likely to die from the disease than men. This is partly because they are older when they develop heart disease and partly because coronary heart disease is perceived as a man's disease. The result of this is that symptoms of heart disease are generally taken less seriously in women by doctors who sometimes assume that a complaint of chest pain is psychosomatic. Studies have shown that women who have symptoms of coronary heart disease are less likely to be referred to a hospital for diagnosis and treatment, and are less likely to receive surgery than men with the same condition.

Menopause

A woman's risk of dying from coronary heart disease increases dramatically after she stops menstruating. This is because female hormones, particularly oestrogen, which offer some protection against coronary heart disease, are no longer produced after the menopause. After the age of 65, the risk of dying from heart disease is almost the same for women as it is for men.

Although the mechanism is not understood, oestrogen in premenopausal women helps to maintain high levels of high-density lipoprotein-cholesterol (HDL), the 'good'

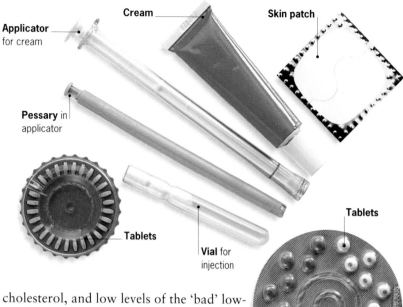

Applicator for cream · **Cream** · **Skin patch**

Pessary in applicator

Tablets · **Vial** for injection · **Tablets**

HRT
HRT can be given as tablets, skin cream, skin patch, implant or vaginal creams and pessaries.

cholesterol, and low levels of the 'bad' low-density lipoprotein-cholesterol (LDL), thus reducing the risk of heart disease (see page 38). After menopause this reverses – HDL levels decrease and LDL levels increase, increasing the risk of heart disease.

However, studies in the US have shown that postmenopausal women who have hormone replacement therapy (HRT) in the oestrogen-only form can reduce their coronary risk by up to 50 per cent. Oestrogen replacement therapy reduces the total blood cholesterol and increases HDL-cholesterol. Unfortunately, oestrogen replacement therapy also increases triglycerides (see page 53) which are bad for the heart and may be related to increased risk of uterine cancer.

Another form of HRT which is a combination of oestrogen plus progestogen (the synthetic form of progesterone) may offer protection from the triglyceride and cancer effects, but have other side effects. Newer forms of HRT are still being researched to maximise benefits and minimise side effects.

FAMILY HISTORY

Coronary heart disease sometimes runs in families. Studies have suggested that if your father or brother has a heart attack before the age of 50, or if your mother or sister has a coronary before 55, then your risk of a heart attack may be doubled or even quadrupled.

Scientists do not believe that there is a specific genetic factor that is responsible for familial clusterings of coronary heart disease. Rather, it is probable that there are *continued on page 32*

DID YOU KNOW?

Race plays an important part in determining the risk of coronary heart disease. For reasons that are unclear, the percentage of African-Americans with hypertension is 50 per cent greater than that of whites or Asians, and they are more likely to suffer congestive heart failure.

Why take HRT?

About 20 per cent of women experience unpleasant symptoms after menopause due to the sudden reduction in oestrogen levels. They include hot flushes, night sweats, loss of vaginal lubrication, decreased libido, fatigue, depression and irritability. The drop in oestrogen levels can also contribute to the onset of osteoporosis (bone-thinning disease) and atherosclerosis. Individual symptoms may be treated or your doctor may advise that you take HRT. However, women who have had cancer of the breast or uterus will not usually be given HRT as it may lead to a recurrence.

The Postmenopausal Woman

After the menopause, when oestrogen levels fall, women's risk of heart disease increases as their protective mechanism is lost. It is therefore vital that their blood pressure and blood cholesterol levels are monitored regularly. Women who have several risk factors for heart disease should consider hormone replacement therapy as an effective way of reducing the risk.

At 58, with husband Ronald, a married daughter Jenny, and three grandchildren, Lesley feels she leads a fairly normal life. She has smoked throughout her married life, but never more than 15 cigarettes a day, and would be the first to admit she is overweight, though not excessively so – anyway Ronald says he likes her like that. She often tries out the latest diet but soon lapses, snacking on biscuits, crisps and cakes, especially when busy.

Her job as a consultant for a computer company involves entertaining so she often drinks slightly more than is wise, but aside from high blood pressure, for which she receives medication, her health is reasonably good.

Lesley went through the menopause in her early fifties but, unlike her friends, she was fortunate not to suffer serious symptoms such as depression, mood swings, night sweats or hot flushes.

Though she has never been very interested in sport or fitness, Lesley feels she is still very active; she enjoys gardening – when she has time – and is often called on to look after her energetic grandchildren.

Her daughter and son-in-law both have very busy careers and enjoy a full social life so she also helps out with some of their domestic chores, but she is beginning to find this too much of a strain.

She is thinking of retiring but because of recent redundancies at her husband's firm she is starting to worry about the future and how they will manage financially. Recently she has been suffering from chest pains as well as panic attacks.

Both her parents died of heart disease in their sixties and Lesley is frightened that she might too.

FAMILY
Even after they are grown up, children often remain dependent on parents and forget they are only human and may also need support.

DIET
When you are busy with household chores it's easy to neglect your diet in favour of high-fat snacks. This increases the risk of heart disease.

EMOTIONAL HEALTH
The link between mental stress and heart disease is well known. Yet people invariably wait until serious symptoms appear before acting.

MEDICATION
Women often do not realise that the risk of heart disease increases after the menopause but that HRT can help to reduce this risk.

EXERCISE
Many people associate exercise only with strenuous activities such as aerobics, or jogging. As they age, people often feel such pursuits are beyond them and so become increasingly inactive.

WHAT SHOULD LESLEY DO?

Lesley should visit her doctor immediately to discuss her health and lifestyle and to talk over any family problems that are worrying her.

The doctor will want to carry out a thorough physical examination, including exercise tests to check her heart and lungs. She will measure her blood pressure and take blood samples to test cholesterol levels and also to discover whether Lesley has already suffered heart damage (painless heart attacks are more common in women than men).

In view of Lesley's family history of heart disease, she should discuss with the doctor whether hormone replacement therapy is appropriate. Oestrogen therapy has been shown to reduce the risk of coronary heart disease in postmenopausal women by up to 50 per cent, but it may also have other risks.

However, Lesley must also make major lifestyle changes. A somewhat unhealthy diet, overweight, relatively high blood pressure, a smoking habit and high alcohol consumption over recommended levels all combine to increase the likelihood of heart attack. The stress in her life, which has been causing panic attacks, is an added risk factor. High stress levels increase the risk of heart disease and may cause angina, although in Lesley's case the chest pain was actually caused by panic attacks.

Action Plan

FAMILY
Encourage family to take responsibility for their own chores and make their own arrangements. Help only when it does not interfere with exercise programme and own commitments.

EMOTIONAL HEALTH
Identify sources of stress and find ways to manage them, especially dealing with panic attacks. Spend more time on own activities.

DIET
Improve diet by eating low-fat snacks like fruit and raw vegetables. Do not buy any more sweet and fatty foods and ask friends to help by not offering anything tempting.

EXERCISE
Walk at least three times a week, and go to a local swimming club with Ronald every weekend. Walk instead of catching a bus when there is time. Use stairs not lifts.

MEDICATION
Visit doctor after the first cycle of HRT treatment and again at three months for a check-up to make sure HRT is the right combination. Tell the doctor about any severe side effects.

HOW THINGS TURNED OUT FOR LESLEY

Lesley was started on a course of hormone replacement therapy, with skin patches. The doctor prescribed a combination of oestrogen and progestogen, as this minimised the remote danger of cancer of the uterus that might arise with oestrogen therapy alone.

Lesley attended a woman's health clinic for a diet and exercise programme designed to reduce her weight and cholesterol levels and strengthen her heart. The diet involved reduced levels of fat and increased fruit, vegetables and complex carbohydrates.

She began regular sessions of walking and swimming, building up to 20 minute sessions three times a week, to give her heart a boost and lower her stress levels.

Lesley reduced her alcohol intake, and with hypnotherapy she gave up smoking.

Lesley's daughter and son-in-law stopped calling on her to help out as often as before, at Lesley's request. Lesley and Ronald also looked at their finances and realised that their pension scheme and savings would enable them to live reasonably comfortably if she retired. Ronald also started to exercise and cut down on smoking.

Lesley's panic attacks stopped after two months and her chest pain disappeared, and she was able to spend more time doing things she enjoyed, together with Ronald.

FAMILY TREE
Inherited medical conditions such as familial hyperlipidaemia can increase the risk of a heart attack. It is important to be aware of your family history in order to inform your doctor of any possible risk factors. You may wish to construct your own family tree and find out which conditions run in your family.

combinations of certain genes that affect the risk factors, such as blood cholesterol or blood pressure, for coronary heart disease. Environmental influences also play a role, for instance, bad eating habits that are passed on from parent to child.

Familial hyperlipidaemia

In Britain 1 in 500 people suffers from the inherited condition, familial hyperlipidaemia – too much fat in the blood. Fats, or lipids, including cholesterol and triglycerides, are normal constituents of the watery part of the blood, known as plasma.

Familial hypercholesterolaemia (FH) is the most serious form of hyperlipidaemia, and the gene is inherited in a dominant manner. So, if one parent has the FH gene the chances are that half of the children will inherit it.

The family of a diagnosed individual should be tested for the disease as it requires special care. The disease can be detected at birth if a sample of umbilical cord blood is taken and cholesterol levels are measured. Individuals with FH are at an increased risk of early death from coronary heart disease: it is possible for FH sufferers as young as 20 to have heart problems.

The disease is usually treated by a combination of diet and drug therapy. In most cases, cholesterol-lowering drugs are essential, but many FH sufferers can decrease their risk of coronary heart disease significantly by following a low-cholesterol, low-fat diet from early childhood. Also, they should never smoke or take the contraceptive pill without medical advice.

DIABETES

Diabetes mellitus is a condition in which the body cannot properly use sugar from the diet because the pancreas is not producing enough insulin. There are two kinds of diabetes mellitus. Insulin-dependent diabetes mellitus occurs in children and young adults. It is controlled with daily injections of insulin. Noninsulin-dependent diabetes mellitus can develop in people who are over 40 and usually obese. It is largely controlled by diet and exercise, though medication is sometimes necessary. People with insulin-dependent diabetes are at an increased risk of kidney disease, blindness, and nerve and blood vessel damage, as well as being at a greatly increased risk of coronary disease.

More than 50 per cent of insulin-dependent diabetics die of either heart or blood vessel disease. Part of the reason for this is that diabetes affects cholesterol and triglyceride levels; another is that insulin-dependent diabetics have raised levels of a clotting agent in their blood. Diabetics used to be advised to follow a high-fat, low-carbohydrate diet until the 1980s when it was shown that a high-fat diet is bad for the heart. Diabetics are now urged to eat a diet that is high in fibre and low in fat and sugar.

Diabetes and ethnicity

In the UK and in other Western countries, people of Indian, Sri Lankan, Pakistani and Bangladeshi descent have an average of 40 per cent higher mortality from coronary heart disease than Europeans. One of the reasons may be that the incidence of diabetes is five times higher in south Asians than in whites. With a low-fat diet, this risk factor can be reduced.

PERSONALITY

In the 1950s, two San Francisco doctors, Meyer Friedman and Ray Rosenman, developed a theory that a certain personality type was more susceptible to coronary heart disease than others. They claimed that Type A individuals, who are aggressive, competitive and impatient, are more likely to get coronary heart disease than Type B individuals, who are patient and easy-going.

Although the Type A and B classification is no longer used – it was based on men with white-collar jobs and did not represent the general population – certain psychological characteristics, such as coping badly with stress, are associated with coronary heart disease and considered to be important.

AGE

In both men and women, deaths from coronary heart disease increase with age. About three out of five people who die of a heart attack are aged 65 and older.

Ageing in its own right has little effect on the risk of coronary heart disease. The age factor is primarily due to the cumulative effects of lifestyle risk factors. Over a lifetime, the effects of smoking, raised blood cholesterol and raised blood pressure take their toll. Modifying these in the earlier years, however, may protect against developing coronary heart disease later on in life.

IS YOUR HEART AT RISK?

This quiz is designed to tell you if you are at risk of coronary heart disease. Read each question carefully and be sure to answer honestly. Place a tick in all the boxes that apply to you, then add them up and check your score below.

ARE YOU MALE AND UNDER 65? ☐

If you are male, you are five to six times more likely to die in your 40s from coronary heart disease than a woman of the same age. But by the time women reach age 65, coronary heart disease is the leading killer of women.

ARE YOU OVER 65? ☐

Most heart disease occurs in people over 65, so the older you are, the more likely it is that you could be affected.

DO YOU HAVE A FAMILY HISTORY OF HEART DISEASE? ☐

Doctors define a family history of heart disease as having a mother or sister who developed heart disease before age 65 and a father or brother who developed it before age 55. Having such a family history is the single greatest risk factor for developing coronary heart disease.

DO YOU SMOKE? ☐

Smoking cigarettes is the single greatest risk factor for coronary heart disease, after family history. Smokers at least double their risk of coronary heart disease.

DO YOU HAVE HIGH BLOOD PRESSURE? ☐

High blood pressure, or hypertension, puts extra strain on the walls of your arteries, which can damage them, causing heart attacks. Blood pressure over 140/90 mm Hg is too high (see page 41).

ARE YOU OVERWEIGHT? ☐

If you are more than 30 per cent over the ideal weight for your height (see page 97), you are more likely to have raised cholesterol levels, high blood pressure and develop diabetes, and be at greater risk of heart disease.

DO YOU DRINK HEAVILY? ☐

Heavy drinkers run a far greater risk of developing heart disease. Moderate drinking (up to three glasses of wine a day for a man or two for a woman, for example) seems to lower the risk of heart attack compared to abstaining.

IS YOUR DIET HIGH IN SATURATED FATS? ☐

Saturated fats are turned into cholesterol by the liver. Too much cholesterol can clog your arteries (see page 38).

DO YOU HAVE A RAISED CHOLESTEROL LEVEL? ☐

A total cholesterol level of over 5.2 mmol (200 mg/dl) greatly increases your chances of developing coronary disease. Doctors recommend that you keep your LDL level below 3.4 mmol (130 mg/dl) and your HDL above 1.6 mmol (35 mg/dl). Very high levels of HDL actually protect against heart disease (see page 38).

IS YOUR DIET LOW IN FRUITS AND VEGETABLES? ☐

Eat at least five servings of fruit and vegetables every day. They help your heart by providing antioxidant vitamins (A, C and E) which stop the LDL-cholesterol from oxidising and clogging arteries more rapidly, and they are also a good source of water-soluble fibre which can help to remove cholesterol from your body (see page 59).

DO YOU HAVE A STRESSFUL JOB? ☐

If your job is making you tense and irritable, it could raise your blood pressure. People who have little control over their working conditions may actually be more stressed than high-powered executives.

DO YOU TAKE LITTLE OR NO EXERCISE? ☐

People who are active have a 45 per cent lower risk of developing coronary heart disease. To help your heart, you need to do 20 minutes of aerobic exercise at least three times a week (see page 71).

HOW DID YOU SCORE?

If you answered 'yes' to fewer than six of these questions, you run a low risk of coronary heart disease, but it is worth examining those questions to which you answered 'yes' to see if you can lower your risk level further. If you answered 'yes' to six or more questions, you should consult your doctor for advice on decreasing your risk.

Avoiding heart disease

Coronary heart disease can often be avoided by decreasing risk factors. Stopping smoking, lowering blood pressure and reducing cholesterol are essential measures against heart disease.

The primary avoidable risk factors in coronary heart disease are smoking, high blood pressure and high cholesterol. Each one is associated with heart disease, so a combination of any two or all three should give serious cause for concern. The more risk factors that individuals have, the more likely that they will develop coronary heart disease. A person who smokes, has raised blood cholesterol and high blood pressure is eight times more likely to have a heart attack than someone without any of these risk factors.

Obesity, physical inactivity and stress also contribute to a person's increased risk. They, too, should be avoided.

THE EFFECTS OF SMOKING

Smoking is responsible for 3 million deaths a year worldwide. If the current smoking patterns continue, this toll will rise to about 10 million deaths by 2025. This gloomy forecast refers to deaths not only from lung cancer but from all tobacco-related diseases, including coronary heart disease.

Major investigations have shown that smokers are at two to three times higher risk of developing coronary heart disease than non-smokers. The more cigarettes that people smoke and the more years they smoke, the greater the risk of a heart attack.

Much of the evidence concerning the health risks posed by cigarette smoking was gathered in a landmark study by doctors Richard Doll and Richard Peto from Oxford University, from 1951 to 1971. This study of the hazards of tobacco use in 34 000 British male doctors showed that about half of all regular cigarette smokers will eventually die as a result of their habit. It also showed that half of these will die prematurely in middle age, losing 20 to 25 years life expectancy.

Many studies that have looked at the effect on coronary risk of giving up smoking have shown that the risk falls quite rapidly as soon as a person stops smoking. But some studies have shown that it takes between five to ten years after quitting for

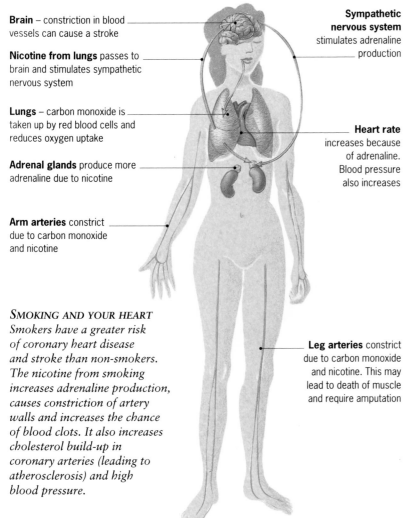

Brain – constriction in blood vessels can cause a stroke

Nicotine from lungs passes to brain and stimulates sympathetic nervous system

Lungs – carbon monoxide is taken up by red blood cells and reduces oxygen uptake

Adrenal glands produce more adrenaline due to nicotine

Arm arteries constrict due to carbon monoxide and nicotine

Sympathetic nervous system stimulates adrenaline production

Heart rate increases because of adrenaline. Blood pressure also increases

Leg arteries constrict due to carbon monoxide and nicotine. This may lead to death of muscle and require amputation

SMOKING AND YOUR HEART
Smokers have a greater risk of coronary heart disease and stroke than non-smokers. The nicotine from smoking increases adrenaline production, causes constriction of artery walls and increases the chance of blood clots. It also increases cholesterol build-up in coronary arteries (leading to atherosclerosis) and high blood pressure.

an ex-smoker to have reduced their risk of coronary disease to the level of someone who has never smoked.

All the studies agree that there is every good reason to stop smoking since it will undoubtedly decrease the risk of a heart attack, as well as improving general cardiovascular health and circulation.

Cigarette smoking and heart disease

Carbon monoxide and nicotine are the most important substances in tobacco smoke that have an effect on the heart.

Nicotine, which is a highly addictive drug, stimulates the sympathetic nervous system (see page 21) and adrenal glands. This increases adrenaline production, makes the heart beat faster and raises blood pressure. The rise in blood pressure, although temporary, may cause damage to the arteries and increase the risk of atherosclerosis.

Carbon monoxide bonds with the blood's red pigment, which is called haemoglobin. Once bonded, the capacity of the blood to carry oxygen to the heart is reduced. Both carbon monoxide and nicotine also encourage blood clotting, which can increase the risk of heart disease.

Passive smoking

Non-smokers who live or work with smokers are at risk from lung cancer, but there is still some debate over whether passive smoking can cause heart disease too. A Chinese study of 200 people, published in the *British Medical Journal* in 1994, claimed to show for the first time that passive smoking is linked to heart disease. Researchers from Xi'an University found that non-smoking women whose husbands smoked were more than twice as likely to develop heart disease than those with non-smoking husbands.

How to quit

Because smoking is so habit forming, giving it up can be difficult. The most common reason smokers give for not quitting is that they are afraid they will get fat. Putting on weight, however, is not an inevitable consequence of stopping smoking. Your appetite will increase once you quit, but it is still possible to avoid weight gain by exercising more. Those who put on weight usually lose it within six months to a year of quitting.

There is no easy way to quit. The simplest method is just to stop – millions of people have done that without any special help. But some people find that 'going cold turkey' is too difficult. They cannot cope with the withdrawal symptoms, which include lack of concentration and nicotine cravings. The physical craving for nicotine can last from a week to several months. To guard against starting smoking again, it is important to recognise and consider how to deal with the times when the craving for a cigarette is likely to be greatest, such as when drinking alcohol or at times of stress (see page 36 for help on quitting).

Other quitting methods include joining a 'stop smoking' group. These groups can provide support and advice for those people who find it difficult to quit on their own. Also available are nicotine chewing gums and nicotine patches that may help, but the addiction to nicotine will still need to be confronted if you use these. Many therapies such as acupuncture and hypnotherapy can be valuable aids in giving up cigarettes.

Reduce or quit?

Some people try to avoid quitting and change their smoking habits instead, hoping to reduce their risk of heart disease. Cutting down does not reduce your risk significantly.

Some smokers switch either to cigars or pipes, filter or low-tar cigarettes, but this will not reduce their risk as cigarette smokers tend to inhale deeply and will do the same with other tobacco products.

The simple fact is that to give up completely would dramatically reduce the individual's chances of getting heart disease. Stopping smoking altogether is the biggest single improvement to health a person can take.

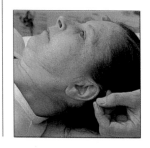

EAR ACUPUNCTURE FOR SMOKING
Needles are inserted into, or tiny metal balls are taped onto, pressure points in the ear for combating addiction.

Pathway to health

Natural therapies can be helpful for stopping smoking and coping with the psychological and physical effects of withdrawal.

Hypnotherapy is recommended for smokers who want to quit. While you are in a very relaxed state of consciousness, the therapist plants suggestions in your mind about quitting smoking.

A very effective way to relieve mental and physical addiction to smoking is with ear acupuncture. The acupuncturist will use standard needles on pressure points in your ear, or may tape tiny needles or metal balls over the pressure points and leave them for a while.

Once you have stopped, you can eliminate some of the chemical pollution of smoking from your body by taking an infusion.

Place 1 teaspoon each of dried red clover and valerian in a cup of boiling water, steep for 10 minutes and drink several times a day. A herbalist can give you more specific advice to help your symptoms.

Quit Smoking

Smoking is an addiction in which there is a psychological as well as a physical dependency. The stress of modern living makes breaking this addiction difficult. It requires great determination, and several techniques are discussed below.

SET THE DATE
A good way to quit is to decide on a day weeks or months ahead, prepare yourself for quitting and then stop on that day.

Letting go of any addiction has to involve an emotional commitment to giving up your habit. Sometimes it can take a long while to get in the right frame of mind to give up, but for most of the methods to work effectively, getting the background mental attitude right is essential. Meditation can help you make your mental commitment to the process, after which you can use one or more ways to help maintain your quitting drive and stop you from slipping back into the habit.

HUMMING MEDITATION

For some people, getting in the right frame of mind is simply a matter of spending time thinking about the benefits of stopping. To reinforce this, you should consider various forms of relaxation exercises, especially those which involve deep concentration on the result you desire. For instance, try meditating daily on your desire for a clean, healthy, smoke-free body. You can use self-hypnosis to the same end, or you can try some relaxation exercises which will enable you to feel calm.

To prepare for giving up you need to feel relaxed, thereby reducing the levels of stress that compel you to reach for a cigarette. One effective form of relaxation is the Humming Meditation. To get the maximum benefit, practise it at the same time every day as part of your routine.

You should pick a place which is quiet and where you will not be overheard or disturbed. Wear loose clothing and sit in a comfortable position: either cross-legged on the floor or in a supportive chair.

Before you begin the meditation, you should formulate an affirmation that you feel is appropriate for you, for instance: 'I am no longer going to pollute my body with nicotine' or 'I want my body to be clean, healthy and vital.' Repeat this meditation once or twice a day or when you feel the need to have a cigarette.

The Humming Meditation gives positive results because the different tones and rhythms of humming induce a hypnotic state, and are very soothing to the mind.

1 *Close your eyes and 'watch' your breath going down, down, down into your abdomen, and then back out again. Concentrate on the breath itself and gently push aside any intrusive or unwanted thoughts.*

2 *After six deep, slow breaths, allow yourself to hum on each out-breath. Choose the pitch of your humming to suit yourself, and try to make the tone as long and drawn out as possible.*

3 *After a few minutes of humming you should be feeling very relaxed and calm. On the in-breath you can now repeat your affirmation in your mind. Continue it for 10 to 15 minutes.*

Focus on your breath

Close your eyes

Wear comfortable clothing

Rest arms on legs

Keep hands relaxed

Wear socks but no shoes

THE QUITTING PLAN

Pick a day a few weeks from now (Q-Day) when no more cigarettes will be smoked and begin to prepare for this day. On Q-Day, the break from cigarettes must be complete. 'Trying just one' will take you straight back to smoking.

PREPARE YOURSELF

In preparation for Q-Day try these methods for making it easier to follow through with your plan:

Make a list of all the situations where you usually smoke, including daily occasions and less common ones. Write down what you will do in each situation to avoid that particular cigarette. For example, instead of having a cigarette after a meal, leave the table and do the dishes.

Tell your friends, family and work colleagues that you are quitting and ask for their support and patience.

Cut out the best cigarette of the day – such as the one on rising in the morning or with after-dinner coffee.

Make yourself conscious of every cigarette you smoke. Try putting a rubber band around the pack.

Smoke your first cigarette one hour later each day. Make a graph of cigarette consumption day-by-day to see the numbers falling.

Avoid very smoky places if at all possible. Try not to socialise with smokers in the first few weeks after you quit, and ask your close friends and family not to smoke around you. Go to places where smoking is not allowed, such as the cinema.

Cut down on your caffeine and alcohol intake. These substances have often been found to be mentally associated with smoking. Also, some research suggests that they increase the craving for nicotine.

Read everything you can about the effects of smoking on your health.

THE DAY ITSELF

On the day you have assigned as your Q-Day there are a number of things you can do to make it easier:

Get your teeth cleaned at the dentist. Wash all your clothes and bed linen, clean the carpets and your car, spray your house with air freshener, open all the windows and wash the curtains. Throw away all ashtrays, matches and cigarettes.

Remind yourself of all the reasons for giving up smoking, including that you will have a healthier heart and circulation, general improved health, improved fitness and better sexual performance. You will save money, enjoy the taste of food, and have better personal odour. Also, you will stop polluting the environment and affecting others with your smoke (especially children).

TROUBLESHOOTING

You are bound to run into a few problems in the days and weeks after you quit. Here are some ways to overcome them.

▶ *Coughing: this is common after quitting. Keep cough drops handy and drink herbal teas.*

▶ *Dry mouth: drink water all day.*

▶ *Irritability: meditate every day. Avoid caffeine. Have a warm bath. Have a massage. Exercise more.*

▶ *Constipation: eat fresh fruit and vegetables for soluble fibre.*

▶ *Hunger: snack on low-fat, low-calorie foods.*

LASTING THE DISTANCE

So you've made it to Q-Day, you've taken the plunge, now what? The weeks ahead will be difficult while you weather the cravings and withdrawal symptoms. You must take further steps to avoid being enticed back to your habit. If you do slip, don't feel that you are a failure. Simply excuse it as a mistake and then continue with the quitting plan. Make sure you meditate or listen to relaxation tapes daily to relieve the stress of withdrawal. Do visualisation exercises: imagine the nicotine flowing out of your body; visualise your lungs filling with healthy air. Sit in non-smoking sections of restaurants and keep your home smoke-free.

KEEP BUSY
Sitting around doing nothing will make it even harder to avoid lighting up. Every time you feel a craving, go for a brisk walk.

REWARD YOUSELF
For every day of success, use the money saved from cigarettes to buy yourself a treat.

STAY RELAXED
Have a long, warm bath every evening. Ask a friend or your partner to give you a massage.

THE HEALTHY HEART DIET

Your daily diet should include five servings of fruit or vegetables, two servings of potatoes, rice or pasta, and four slices of bread. You should also:

► *Avoid fried foods (such as chips) or limit them to one serving per week.*

► *Limit full-fat cheese to two servings per week.*

► *Eat no more than three-quarters of a small chocolate bar a week.*

► *Use semi-skimmed milk instead of whole milk.*

► *Have a maximum of one can of sugary drink a day, though preferably drink fruit juice instead.*

DIET

The second most important lifestyle risk factor after smoking is being extremely overweight. People who are obese, that is, have more than 30 per cent body fat (see page 51) are more likely to develop heart disease than people of normal weight.

Excess weight increases the strain on the heart and is linked to coronary heart disease mainly because being overweight influences blood pressure and cholesterol levels.

Growing evidence also suggests that the distribution of fat over the body is important in predicting the risk of coronary heart disease. 'Apple shaped' people whose weight is mainly around their bellies are at more risk than 'pear shaped' individuals whose weight is around the hips and thighs.

What is a healthy diet?

Eating a healthy diet is really quite simple. For a healthier heart, it is important to reduce the amount of total fat in the diet, and the intake of saturated fats (see page 52) in particular. Saturated fat increases total blood cholesterol levels, particularly the 'bad' low-density lipoprotein-cholesterol (LDL-cholesterol). Mono and polyun-

saturated fats can be broken down in the body and do not cause cholesterol build-up (see page 53). Trans-fatty acids should also be avoided. These are fats that are saturated by processing and are found in some margarines, cakes, biscuits and other packaged foods. They are usually listed as hydrogenated fats on packaging.

CHOLESTEROL

The body needs cholesterol to function normally. It is present in both blood and tissues and is an essential part of body cell walls, hormones and bile salts. Cholesterol is a fat-like substance made by the liver and carried in the bloodstream. Without it, the nervous system would not work properly.

In order to move around the body, it must be attached to one of two lipoproteins (particles that are a combination of lipids, fat and protein) – high-density lipoprotein (HDL) and low-density lipoprotein (LDL).

Good and bad cholesterol

HDL picks up cholesterol from the blood and takes it to the liver for processing or excretion. It actually removes all the excess cholesterol from fat-saturated cells including those of artery walls. HDL-cholesterol is called the 'good cholesterol' and actively protects you from atherosclerosis.

LDL carries 60 to 80 per cent of the body's cholesterol. If there is too much LDL or 'bad' cholesterol in the blood, it may be deposited in artery walls, causing plaques and atherosclerosis.

It is important to know how much 'good' HDL-cholesterol and 'bad' LDL-cholesterol you have, rather than just the total blood cholesterol, as this will indicate how healthy your heart and arteries are. Your doctor will explain these levels after you receive the results of your cholesterol test.

Cholesterol levels

The level of cholesterol in the body is partly determined by genetic factors. Some people naturally have higher cholesterol levels. People who suffer from familial hyperlipidaemia (see page 32) have an abnormality in their genes which affects the way the liver handles cholesterol. As a result, their levels of blood cholesterol are extremely high.

Foods containing saturated fats also raise blood cholesterol levels – particularly 'bad' LDL-cholesterol.

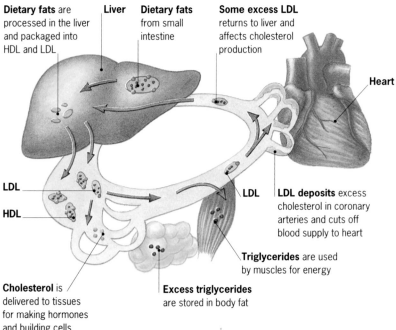

Dietary fats are processed in the liver and packaged into HDL and LDL

Liver

Dietary fats from small intestine

Some excess LDL returns to liver and affects cholesterol production

Heart

LDL

HDL

LDL

LDL deposits excess cholesterol in coronary arteries and cuts off blood supply to heart

Triglycerides are used by muscles for energy

Cholesterol is delivered to tissues for making hormones and building cells

Excess triglycerides are stored in body fat

LDL

HDL

CHOLESTEROL TRANSPORT AND THE HEART
Dietary cholesterol is broken down in the small intestine and then processed by the liver from where it travels in the blood to various tissues for use. Excess LDL-cholesterol may cause atherosclerosis in coronary arteries.

Risks of high cholesterol levels

Elevated blood cholesterol is the most widely known risk factor for coronary heart disease. But when other risk factors such as being overweight, smoking and suffering from high blood pressure are present, this risk increases even more.

If the body has more cholesterol than it needs, this soft, waxy substance builds up in artery walls making them narrower, slowing down blood flow or even cutting off its supply to the heart.

Virtually everyone, therefore, should try and stick to a diet that keeps their cholesterol intake to a minimum, that is, a diet low in saturated fats.

Lowering cholesterol

To reduce cholesterol levels, monounsaturated and polyunsaturated fats should be substituted for saturated fats, and fat intake should be reduced overall.

If a person is overweight, losing weight will lower blood cholesterol. The only way to lose weight is to consume less energy, or calories, than the body needs so that the body begins using up fat stores for energy. To cut down on calories, you should eat fewer fatty foods and sugary foods such as cakes and biscuits.

ALCOHOL

Over-indulgence in alcohol can lead to raised blood pressure, strokes and cirrhosis of the liver. Heavy drinking increases the risk of dying prematurely. Moderate consumption, however, is not harmful. Indeed, there is some evidence that it may have a protective effect (see page 64).

It is thought that red wine may protect against coronary heart disease because it contains a substance which stops LDL from being oxidised by free radicals and forming deposits in the arteries (see page 58). Other types of alcohol are thought to be beneficial, as they may interfere with blood clotting.

It is recommended that men drink no more than 28 units of alcohol (one unit equals half a pint of beer, a glass of wine or a measure of spirits) per week, and women no more than 21 units per week.

EXERCISE

Regular exercise is an important weapon in the fight against heart disease. More than 40 studies have confirmed the link between physical inactivity and heart disease. Overall, these show that inactive people have almost twice the risk of coronary heart disease compared to active people.

How much exercise?

There is some debate as to exactly how vigorous and frequent exercise has to be before it starts to reduce the risk of coronary heart disease, but it is widely accepted that to attain maximum fitness, aerobic exercise (see page 71) should be taken three times a week for 20 minutes.

This could be simply walking briskly, or doing more intense exercise if you are fit. It is better to do moderate exercise several times a week (for at least 20 minutes per session) rather than strenuous exercise only once a week.

Benefits

Exercise reduces blood cholesterol and high blood pressure, and seems to help people give up smoking, all of which reduce the risk of heart disease. It also helps weight loss because the amount of calories used by the body is increased during exercise, and regular exercise increases your metabolic rate even when you are resting.

Type

Exercise can mean anything from sessions in the gym to square dancing to simply leading an active life. Vigorous housework or gardening, walking up stairs rather than using a lift and walking briskly to the train station or the shops rather than driving will all contribute to reducing coronary risk.

See Chapter 4 for more details on exercising to strengthen your heart and improve your circulation.

LOW CHOLESTEROL CHECKLIST

Use these tips to cut down on saturated fats:

▶ *Replace butter with either a low-fat spread or a margarine high in polyunsaturates (check label for 'hydrogenated fats' which indicates trans-fatty acids). Use less fat spreads in general.*

▶ *Change from full cream milk to skimmed or semi-skimmed milk.*

▶ *Avoid hard cheeses and full cream soft cheeses.*

▶ *Choose lean cuts of meat.*

▶ *Trim off excess fat on meat, and remove the skin from poultry.*

▶ *Eat fish and chicken rather than red meat.*

▶ *Grill or steam rather than fry food.*

AEROBIC EXERCISE
An aerobics class is a convenient and fun way to get your weekly exercise. It is important for your heart to exercise at least three times a week for 20 minutes.

The stress tip-off

It is natural to feel stress as part of everyday life, but too much stress is bad for your health. It is important to identify sources of stress and find ways to cope with them or, indeed, to make them less stressful. For instance, try to see the positive side of a situation; and laugh instead of feeling angry. Some psychologists recommend a practice of 'acting as if you are happy' which tends to dissipate negative feelings.

A SOURCE OF STRESS
Waiting for a bus, in a bank queue or for the doctor can be stressful. But if you decide to view waiting as a pleasant opportunity for a rest, to collect your thoughts, to read a book or to perform a visualisation exercise (see page 83), it will no longer be as stressful.

STRESS

All people feel stress, though they may react in different ways. Excessive or long-standing stress may create health problems in some people. For instance, people who feel life is one big struggle with no escape will have trouble managing stress, as will those who often feel angry and out of control. People who approach life's ups and downs with a sense of challenge and purpose are likely to handle stress well.

Some scientists have noted a relationship between coronary heart disease risk and the amount of stress in a person's life. Coronary heart disease rates, for example, have been found to be higher among the recently bereaved and for people in high areas of unemployment.

A theory that was developed in the 1950s by Friedman and Rosenman (see page 32) pointed to the connection between personality and coronary heart disease, where the main component was an individual's susceptibility to stress. This has been modified and now centres around anger (see page 152). A 1994 study of 1000 men who had had a coronary thrombosis found that they were easily annoyed and irritable.

Good and bad stress

Stress is natural and often useful, acting as a stimulant in challenging situations. 'Good' stress can be quite exhilarating. But stress becomes 'bad' when you feel out of control, when everything is too much for you, when you feel life and people are against you, and you are exhausted. This is the time to act (see page 146).

When you feel stressed, take into account that life circumstances may be contributing to it. These may include: change of house, job or partner; death of a loved one; financial problems; illness or injury. Write down exactly what is happening in your life and how you can solve actual problems, or improve your way of coping with them.

Reducing stress

It is important to deal with feelings of stress and anxiety as soon as possible. There are a number of methods that you can try.

Schedule your time reasonably. Write down a weekly timetable showing hours spent at work, relaxing, exercising and socialising. Try to develop interests outside of work. All work and no play is a bad idea.

Exercise regularly. Set yourself an exercise programme (see page 74). Try not to get too serious and competitive about it, especially if you choose to take exercise through a team sport. Exercise should be fun and enjoyable, not an additional source of stress.

Practise relaxation techniques. Join a meditation class or buy some tapes. Try some visualisation methods (see page 83) or simply listen to relaxing music in a peaceful environment. You can even treat yourself to a flotation tank (see page 83) or a massage.

Seek assistance with problems you cannot deal with yourself from a relevant person: accountant, doctor and so on. Or simply talk to a friend about personal worries.

BLOOD PRESSURE

In order for blood to reach the different parts of the body, it must be propelled under pressure. The pressure caused by the heartbeat is the systolic pressure, and when the heart relaxes, it is the diastolic pressure (see page 23).

Blood pressure variations

The upper limit of normal blood pressure in an otherwise healthy person is 140 systolic and 90 diastolic. However, a person less than 30 years old would be more likely to have a reading of 120/80.

CHECKLIST

Tick those symptoms you experience when you feel stressed.

✔ *Diarrhoea or vomiting*
✔ *Headaches, stomach or backache*
✔ *Dizziness, fainting, palpitations*
✔ *Loss of appetite and libido*
✔ *Overeating*
✔ *Depression, low self-esteem*
✔ *Worry and anxiety*
✔ *Anger, hostility, arguing a lot*
✔ *Trouble sleeping, insomnia*
✔ *Fatigue*
✔ *Forgetfulness*
✔ *Skin rashes*

Look at your ticks. When you next have these symptoms, use stress reduction methods.

These values are expressed in millimetres of mercury (mm Hg). Blood pressure readings vary from minute to minute depending on activity and time of day. Blood pressure falls to low levels when sleeping and is raised during times of stress. It also tends to rise with age.

Blood pressure and pregnancy

Pregnancy can cause an increase in blood pressure, as does the oral contraceptive pill in some women.

Normally, blood pressure falls in the first few months of pregnancy then rises again in the later stages of pregnancy. High blood pressure, however, may also develop for the first time in pregnancy, a condition known as pre-eclampsia (pre-eclampsic toxaemia or toxaemia). It occurs in about 15 per cent of pregnant women, but is most common in women who are over 35, those who are having their first babies, or women carrying more than one foetus.

One of the first signs of pre-eclampsia is swelling of the face, feet and hands, and there is protein in the urine. You may also experience headaches, dizziness and nausea, or there may be no symptoms at all.

Pre-eclampsia usually only starts after the twentieth week of pregnancy, but blood pressure may rise progressively before this. It is vital therefore for blood pressure to be checked regularly during pregnancy. If pre-eclampsia develops you will be admitted to hospital for observation. Pre-eclampsia is usually controlled with rest. Occasionally sedatives and blood pressure lowering drugs may be used. Pre-eclampsia rarely causes complications if it is treated as soon as possible. In severe cases, birth may be induced or a Caesarean performed.

Blood pressure and cardiovascular disease

People with untreated high blood pressure have a greater than normal risk of developing strokes, heart and kidney disease. If the blood pressure is high over a long period of time, then the constant force of the blood through the arteries means they are more likely to be damaged.

Controlling blood pressure

Several factors play an important role in controlling blood pressure. If you have high blood pressure, you need to do everything

EFFECTS OF HYPERTENSION

Hypertension, or high blood pressure, can cause damage to arteries in different areas of the body, including the brain, eyes, heart and kidneys. High blood pressure also increases the risk of atherosclerosis, coronary heart disease and stroke.

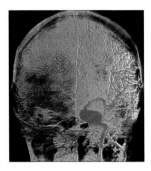

RUPTURED ARTERY
This arteriograph of the back of the head shows a ruptured artery caused by hypertension. This is one of the most common causes of stroke.

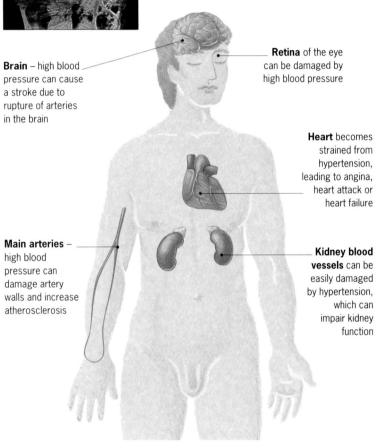

Brain – high blood pressure can cause a stroke due to rupture of arteries in the brain

Retina of the eye can be damaged by high blood pressure

Heart becomes strained from hypertension, leading to angina, heart attack or heart failure

Main arteries – high blood pressure can damage artery walls and increase atherosclerosis

Kidney blood vessels can be easily damaged by hypertension, which can impair kidney function

possible to reduce it as soon as possible. If you are even slightly overweight, you should go on a weight loss program. This is often the only measure needed to reduce blood pressure. If you must drink, then limit your consumption to no more than one glass of beer, wine or spirits per day. Follow a low-salt diet or use salt sparingly in cooking and eating (see page 51). Stop smoking immediately (see page 36). Develop mechanisms that may help you to deal with stress, such as learning to relax (see page 82).

Autogenic Training

Self-hypnosis is a very effective and simple way of reducing tension and stress by inducing deep mental and physical relaxation. People using autogenics regularly have been shown to have improved health and resistance to disease.

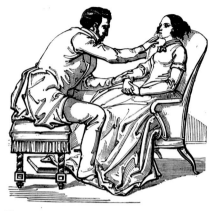

HYPNOSIS
Since the 1800s hypnosis has been used for various ailments. People often consult a hypnotist for help in quitting an addiction, learning to relax, or relieving pain. Those who respond well to being hypnotised will probably find autogenic training easy to learn and very beneficial.

The principle behind autogenics is the idea of 'passive concentration', which enables deep relaxation. Positive suggestions can then be introduced to reduce stress, change bad habits or encourage creativity.

How do you learn autogenics?
The training is usually taught in a group of eight to ten students, and the sessions will normally be weekly for a period of eight to ten weeks. During this period you will learn the basic relaxation techniques and how to apply them. More advanced training includes the use of specific positive affirmations or auto-suggestions, and meditations to increase health, well-being and energy levels. Although it is recommended you attend classes, it is possible to teach yourself autogenics by following a carefully laid-out course of home study. In this case it is important to be disciplined and to follow the instructions exactly, and not to be tempted to accelerate the course, or change the affirmations.

Where can I find a trainer?
Private clinics may specialise in autogenics but some hospitals have trainers on staff. They are usually qualified doctors, psychologists, nurses, or other health workers who have trained for a certificate in autogenics. Some natural therapists such as naturopaths may also be trained in autogenics.

What happens in the first session?
The trainer will give you a check-up to make sure you can do autogenic training safely. You will be asked questions about your medical history and personality. People with heart disease will only be trained under medical supervision.

The autogenic trainer will teach you the basics of autogenics in one or two sessions. You will choose a relaxing posture, and the trainer will talk you through the six basic exercises, asking you to visualise each of these: feelings of heaviness ('my left leg is heavy'), warmth ('my right arm is warm'), concentrating on the heartbeat, warmth in the stomach, calming the breath and coolness on the forehead.

The trainer will ask you to visualise each of these until every part of your body is relaxed. The trainer may then

Origins

Autogenic training, as a system of self-hypnosis, was developed by the German neuropsychiatrist, Dr J.W. Schultz, in the 1920s. It was later developed and expanded by Dr W. Luthe in Canada and brought to the UK by Dr Malcolm Carruthers. It is today widely employed as an aid to relaxation and to combat stress. Autogenics when practised regularly can also be used to target the unpleasant effects of many illnesses, as well as helping you to get in touch with your emotions. It can build creativity and enhance effectiveness in the workplace.

DR W. LUTHE
Luthe helped to develop the practice of autogenic training and introduced it to a large number of people.

introduce positive suggestions and affirmations, tailored to your specific needs and problems.

How often should you practise autogenics?

Regular practice is essential – your trainer will probably recommend practising three times a day initially. – morning, noon and night is the ideal. The advantage of autogenics is that it can be done in any quiet location, and as long as you remain uninterrupted. Any comfortable place is suitable, even the lavatory, if that is the only place available to you in a busy office! It is important to practise between sessions so that your trainer can monitor your progress and effectiveness.

How does autogenic training relieve stress?

For most people, the reaction to stress is partly physical and partly emotional. The effects of stress, such as the release of adrenaline and noradrenaline, also occur in pleasant situations, such as meeting a loved one or anticipating an exciting event. So, clearly, the stress reaction is not always undesirable, and indeed many people find a certain degree of stress stimulating. The autogenic trainer teaches you how to access a relaxed state at will and to move with ease and fluency from a state of excitement to a state of relaxation, so that the pains and strains built up by chronic stress are released as quickly as they form.

What problems respond well to autogenic training?

With practice you can learn how to formulate affirmations that are tailor-made to suit your problem. Autogenics is not a cure for physical problems, but attitude and emotions have been shown to be all important in fighting disease. In this respect, autogenic training can enhance the immune system, and help you to tackle problems such as addictions, high blood pressure, palpitations and persistent pain.

It can be used in conjunction with other treatments. Consult your doctor or autogenic trainer for further information on the compatibility of treatments.

How does autogenic training affect the emotions?

A release of stress will put you in touch with feelings that have been stored in the body, often as muscular tension. In autogenics, using a technique called 'offloading', accumulations of negative emotions can be released in a number of ways (see page 155). The trainer will teach you various vocal techniques, from singing to screaming, moaning or making baby noises, and physical techniques to release frustration, anger, and tension. Even sadness and anxiety may be offloaded like this.

Autogenics does not in any way deal with the analysis of emotion, and if negative feelings cannot be simply released using offloading, you are advised to use psychotherapy or counselling.

WHAT YOU CAN DO AT HOME

Do this exercise as many times as possible during the day: the more, the better. Sit in a comfortable chair, hands palm down beside you or resting on your thighs, eyes closed.

Step one: Scan your entire body in your mind, starting with your toes, then moving up the front of your body and then the back.

Step two: Take your mind to your dominant arm (right, if you are right-handed, left, if you are left-handed). Say 'My right (left) arm is heavy' and let your mind travel down its length. Your arm may go heavy, light, warm, tingly or do nothing at all. Just be aware of it. Repeat the phrase three times. Repeat with your other arm.

Step three: Clench both fists tightly, bending elbows briskly, then stretch your arms right out in front of you. Take a deep breath in. Open your eyes and breathe out. Repeat steps two and three, three times.

AUTOGENICS SESSION
You can participate in a session with up to ten people, or you can have individual training if you feel more comfortable.

Trainer will talk you through exercises

Sessions are often in groups of six to ten

THE IMPORTANCE OF CHECK-UPS

It is vital for individuals with a known high risk of heart disease to have regular check-ups. This particularly applies to all middle-aged and older people as the risk increases with age.

COUGHING
A bad cough can sometimes cause chest pain similar to angina.

HEARTBURN
Pain in the chest from indigestion may be confused with heart-related chest pain.

People are often worried unnecessarily about various symptoms which they confuse with heart-related problems. One of the most common of these is 'heartburn' – the feeling of burning in the middle of your chest – which is simply caused by indigestion and is treated with antacid tablets. Heartburn often occurs after eating and is made worse by very spicy food or fried food.

Chest pain is a cause for concern but it may be due to muscle strain or injury to the rib cage. Have you been in an accident, suffered a sports injury or had a severe cough? Any of these could be causing chest discomfort. Heart palpitations or a rapidly beating heart can occur when you are under extreme stress, feel fear or anticipation or drink a lot of coffee. Also, there are some common over-the-counter drugs such as sinus tablets that contain a lot of caffeine which can make your heart feel 'fluttery'.

If you are in any doubt at all, you should seek medical attention (see page 86 for symptoms related to heart disease).

HAVING A CHECK-UP

If heart disease is suspected, your doctor will do an extensive check-up. He or she will take a family history, look at your personal medical history and do a physical examination.

A cardiovascular physical examination includes measuring blood pressure, heart rate, various pulses, checking veins and any swelling, and listening to breathing and heart sounds (see page 20).

Routine blood tests, including cholesterol and other lipid testing, blood cell counts, oxygen levels and cardiac enzymes, may also be carried out (see page 90).

Depending on the results of this initial examination, the doctor may decide to send you for further tests, either non-invasive ones such as x-rays, ECG and stress tests, or more advanced, invasive tests in order to make a more definite diagnosis. These tests are explained in Chapter 5.

Tell your doctor

For a check-up to be most effective, it is important that you give your doctor as much information as possible. Before you go for your check-up, think about the following and write down anything that you might forget when you get there: all prior illnesses, accidents and hospitalisations; any allergies (to medications, foods and so on); any chronic illnesses, such as asthma; any medication you are taking (including the contraceptive pill); any bad lifestyle habits, such as smoking or drinking heavily; any medical problems that run in the family, such as high blood pressure, high cholesterol levels and heart disease; and any other relevant details.

It is also vital that you discuss all the symptoms that are bothering you and make sure you ask any questions you have.

You may decide after having a medical check-up that you would also like the opinion of a natural therapist (see page 99), such as a naturopath, a homeopath or a traditional Chinese medicine practitioner (who uses herbs and acupuncture). The above information is just as relevant to such therapists as they need to get a complete picture of you, your lifestyle and your habits. They may also ask additional questions concerning your moods and emotions, relationships and sources of stress, and your reactions to different situations and circumstances.

Middle-aged Woman at Risk

As people approach middle-age they tend to put on weight due to their metabolism slowing down and a lack of activity. Being overweight and under-exercised increases the risk of coronary heart disease, diabetes and hypertension. Regular check-ups are important to ensure that optimum health is maintained.

Alison, a 44-year-old accountant, is married to Jonathan, a solicitor. They have two teenage children, Tom and Sarah. Alison has just moved to a highly demanding job in a new partnership. She is sent for a routine medical check-up. The company doctor tells her she is 10 kg (22 lb) above her ideal weight and her blood pressure is too high – 150/95. The doctor suggests that she should try to lose weight by adopting a healthier diet and taking regular exercise.

Alison is worried about changing her lifestyle in any way as she has always been too busy with work to exercise and take much notice of what she eats. Her family, similarly, have busy lives and unfortunately also have unhealthy eating habits.

WHAT SHOULD ALISON DO?

Alison's busy life leaves little time for shopping or cooking, let alone regular exercise. Alison needs to manage her time more effectively to be able to eat more healthily and establish a regular exercise routine, and lower her stress levels. This will help her lose weight and lower her blood pressure.

She needs to learn about healthier foods, and form a plan which is realistic for her lifestyle and that of her family. She can get information about nutrition and exercise from the doctor's surgery and the local library. She needs to make long-term changes in her diet, eating healthy snacks and nutritionally balanced meals (see page 62 for the healthy heart diet).

Action Plan

WORK
Organise work schedule more efficiently and have a proper lunch break every day. Snack on fresh fruit. Park farther away from work and walk.

FAMILY
Ask family to support diet. Organise roster for the shopping and cooking and eat more healthy foods.

LIFESTYLE
Plan the family menu in advance. Cut down on own portion size. Buy an exercise bike and ride every evening for half an hour.

LIFESTYLE
Little exercise and a high-fat, high-sugar diet result in over-weight, and a higher risk for heart disease.

WORK
A high pressure job and long working hours can leave you tired and stressed and result in poor lifestyle habits, such as eating 'on the run'.

FAMILY
When the whole family is on the go constantly, poor eating habits may arise that are often difficult to change.

HOW THINGS TURNED OUT FOR ALISON

Alison and her family establish a shopping and cooking rota, and in time they come to enjoy healthy eating. After three months, Alison lost 5 kg (11 lb) and has more energy. Her doctor tells her that her blood pressure is normal. She is enjoying her job more as she does not feel so tired and stressed and she is pleased to see her family becoming more health conscious. When she occasionally breaks her eating plan she does extra exercise.

RULE OF THUMB FOR CHECK-UPS

Until you reach 40 years of age you should have a physical check-up every three to five years, then four times during your forties and five times during your fifties. Annual examinations are advised for people over 60. It is also important to go for a check-up if:

▶ *You are feeling unwell.*

▶ *You experience unusual symptoms.*

▶ *You smoke or drink heavily.*

▶ *There is a family history of heart disease or hypertension.*

▶ *You have diabetes, familial hyperlipidaemia, or hypertension.*

▶ *You are overweight.*

▶ *You are under great family or work stress.*

▶ *You are pregnant.*

STANDARD ECG
This test will be carried out on anyone who is suspected of having heart disease. It may be followed by an exercise ECG (see page 91).

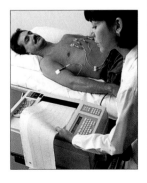

SCREENING POPULATIONS: REDUCING THE RISK

In both the UK and the US, coronary heart disease kills as many people as all other diseases put together. Government health strategies to reduce the number of deaths aim to tackle the three major risk factors: smoking, high blood pressure and high blood cholesterol.

Campaigns against smoking have decreased the number of deaths from coronary heart disease in recent years, as people have become more aware of the effects of smoking. Further reductions in deaths may be possible with more public education on reducing cholesterol levels by following a low-fat diet and in particular, reducing saturated fat.

Other campaigns focus on education at schools and in the workplace, placing emphasis on the importance of regular exercise, healthy eating and the avoidance of smoking and heavy drinking.

Government health departments in the US recommend that people 'know their cholesterol number' by having regular check-ups, and then act on it by changing their diet. This is particularly advised for people with an increased risk of coronary heart disease: who have a family history, or who have diabetes or at least two of the following risk factors – high blood pressure, obesity, inadequate physical activity and smoking.

CHOLESTEROL TESTING

Your doctor may decide to test your blood cholesterol levels when you go for a check-up, particularly if there is a family history of high cholesterol levels. Cholesterol tests may also be done during other screening checks such as breast cancer checks.

It is possible to buy home-testing cholesterol kits if you are interested in monitoring your own levels (see page 96).

A high reading does not mean that a heart attack is just around the corner. Your doctor will be able to balance the cholesterol measurement against all the other factors to properly assess your personal risk level. He or she will be able to advise you on changes you should make to your lifestyle and diet to minimise the chances of heart problems in the future.

BLOOD PRESSURE TESTING

Family doctors should routinely check blood pressure, especially if other risk factors for coronary heart disease are present. Adults should have their blood pressure checked at least once every three years. Women who are on the contraceptive pill should also have their blood pressure routinely measured when they receive a new supply of pills.

One high reading does not mean that you have high blood pressure – levels fluctuate in an individual, for example, when you are nervous. Therefore, to get a true picture of blood pressure levels, it is important to take a measurement after sitting quietly for a few

minutes. If the level is high, your doctor may take your blood pressure again at the end of your appointment. If it is still high you will be advised about further action.

Home blood pressure measuring kits are now available (see page 96), although these may give unrealistically high readings.

ELECTROCARDIOGRAPHY

Electrocardiography is the most commonly used test to diagnose heart disease. A machine records the electrical activity of the heart when electrodes (gel pads) are attached to each arm and leg and to six places on the front and left side of the chest. The test is painless and harmless.

The trace produced is called an electrocardiogram (ECG). It shows if there are any abnormalities, but sometimes it may suggest there are problems when the heart is perfectly healthy (see page 91). Further tests can be done to confirm or rule out a diagnosis (see Chapter 5).

Stress test

In many patients with coronary heart disease there are no symptoms at rest and an ordinary ECG is normal. But exercise may bring on ECG changes. So an exercise ECG, or stress test, is sometimes used to diagnose heart problems, especially angina.

The patient exercises either on a treadmill or on a stationary bicycle. The test usually takes around 15 minutes and ECG readings are taken both during and after the exercise routine (see page 93).

CHAPTER 3

EATING TO PROTECT YOUR HEART

You are what you eat is a phrase with particular
relevance to heart disease. About 30 per cent of the
people who die of heart disease do so partly because
of their diets. Since heart disease develops gradually
over many years, it is best to establish good eating
habits when you are young, and to follow them
throughout life. But even changes made late in life
can have a radical effect on the health of the heart.
Diet is one of the major 'natural' weapons
in the fight against heart disease.

DIET AND HEART DISEASE

As well as the foods you eat, the foods you avoid can play a crucial role in the prevention of serious diseases, such as coronary heart disease and stroke.

Medical researchers have looked at the eating habits of people in different countries to try to establish the link between food and heart disease.

THE DIET CONNECTION

Many of the early links between diet and heart disease were based on The Lipid Hypothesis proposed by the American Professor Ancel Keys in the 1950s and 1960s. Professor Keys found that countries whose native diets had a high fat intake, had a higher incidence of heart disease than those with a lower fat intake. A high fat intake, especially of the saturated fats (meat and dairy fats), was linked to raised blood cholesterol levels. During the 1970s and 1980s, further studies showed that high-blood cholesterol levels, often caused in part by a high-fat diet, were one of the most important risk factors for heart disease.

As a result, there has been an increased focus on healthier cooking methods and particular foods that seem to offer some protection against heart disease. There is evidence, for example, that it is not merely a lower fat intake by the Japanese or Chinese or by people in Mediterranean countries that results in a much lower rate of heart disease in these populations, but also the amounts and types of food that they eat. Based on such findings, many expert committees all over the world have put forward recommendations to help reduce the rate of diet-related diseases, particularly heart disease.

Fresh produce provides plenty of vitamins and minerals and no fat

Frozen foods usually retain all of their nutrients if they are frozen correctly

Tinned foods may have added sugar and salt, and a low vitamin content, but their fibre content is high

FOCUS ON FOOD
You should eat at least five servings of fruit and vegetables everyday. They can be fresh, frozen or tinned.

HEART DISEASE AND THE MEDITERRANEAN DIET

The rates of death from heart disease (per 100 000 of the population) and fat intake (as a percentage of total calorie intake) for different countries around the world are given here. The most striking fact shown by this chart is the relationship between the low-fat, high-fish and vegetable diet of the Japanese and their low rate of heart disease compared with Western countries.

However, the highest fat intake on the chart is for Greece (48 per cent of the total calories) yet their rate of heart disease is well below that of Finland (with only 37 per cent). This, and a similar result for France and Italy has been attributed to the special effects of 'the Mediterranean diet' (see page 56).

COUNTRY	CORONARY HEART DISEASE *	FAT INTAKE **
Scotland	779	40
Finland	629	37
England & Wales	595	40
Australia	514	42
USA	454	45
Germany	381	47
Greece	287	48
Italy	252	41
France	133	46
Japan	77	31

* Death rate per 100 000 population
** Percentage of total calorie intake

Eating for a healthy heart

Most people in the Western world eat too much fat – about 40 per cent of their total calorie intake. Since fat plays a key role in the development of heart disease, experts now recommend reducing total fat intake to around 30 to 35 per cent of total calorie intake (see page 53 for how to calculate your fat target). Recommendations also include making a specific reduction in the intake of saturated fats, which are found in animal products such as red meat, milk, cheese and other dairy products, as well as of trans-fatty acids (see page 53).

You need to eat more complex carbohydrates such as bread, potatoes, rice, pasta and low-fat, low-sugar breakfast cereals. These foods should make up around half of your daily calorie intake and form the main part of all your meals and snacks. To get the fullest benefit from the vitamins and minerals that are found in these foods, choose those varieties which are most high in fibre, such as wholewheat pasta, brown rice and wholegrain breads and cereals.

Fruit and vegetables also play a key role in the prevention of many diseases. Current guidelines recommend eating at least five servings of fruit, vegetables and salads every day. Fresh or frozen fruit and vegetables are best; the tinned varieties can be high in sugar and salt, and do not have the same level of vitamins and minerals – check the labels for added salt and sugar.

Other suggestions for a diet for a healthy heart include eating oily fish two or three times a week, reducing salt intake and drinking only moderate amounts of alcohol.

Developing good eating habits

Putting the advice of the experts into practice is often quite difficult when it comes to food. Most people eat for a number of reasons, not just because they are hungry or to stay healthy. Food provides pleasure and helps to ward off boredom or depression.

Changing from an unhealthy to a healthy eating pattern may take some time and organisation, so make a few gradual changes at a time rather than all at once. Start eating three regular meals a day, including breakfast or a mid-morning snack, a light meal and a main meal. Have your main meal during the day when you need energy, and only a light meal in the evening. Stick to the same eating patterns and follow certain dietary guidelines (see the food pyramid on page 62). Choose low-fat and low-sugar snacks (see box below).

Skipping meals altogether usually makes you so hungry later in the day that you can't resist unhealthy snacks. It is all too easy to choose fast foods: most – such as potato crisps, biscuits, hamburgers, chips and chocolate – are high in fat, salt and sugar. Fast foods can be eaten occasionally as part of the daily diet, but they should not make up a major portion of anyone's food intake, as they mainly provide 'empty calories' (calories without nutritional value).

Eating regularly also helps to control body weight. Studies show that many overweight people tend to skip meals, often compensating for this with high-calorie, high-fat foods.

Some people prefer to 'graze' – to eat smaller meals at more frequent intervals. As long as the foods chosen are healthy ones, this pattern of eating is fine. Eating more frequently can also stave off hunger and the effects of low blood sugar.

FILLING AND HEALTHY
Starchy foods are filling, contain fibre and vitamins, and are high in carbohydrates. Choose brown or wholegrain varieties of bread, brown rice or wholewheat pasta.

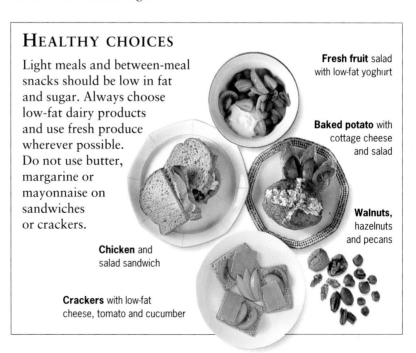

HEALTHY CHOICES

Light meals and between-meal snacks should be low in fat and sugar. Always choose low-fat dairy products and use fresh produce wherever possible. Do not use butter, margarine or mayonnaise on sandwiches or crackers.

Fresh fruit salad with low-fat yoghurt

Baked potato with cottage cheese and salad

Walnuts, hazelnuts and pecans

Chicken and salad sandwich

Crackers with low-fat cheese, tomato and cucumber

The Gourmet Traveller

Adopting a healthier eating pattern is challenging enough when you are at home. But people whose work requires extensive travel, and dining with clients and business colleagues in restaurants and hotels may find the prospect even more daunting, especially when health concerns indicate that a radical change in diet is necessary.

Chris is a 48-year-old civil engineer, and works for a large construction company that carries out projects all over the world. He spends approximately 70 per cent of his time overseas, which suits him as he has always loved good food and wine and enjoys the opportunity to try out the cuisines of many different countries.

At his last annual company check-up, he learned that he had a high cholesterol count, which alarmed him as he has a family history of heart problems. The doctor advised him to cut down on fatty foods. Chris does not have a sweet tooth, and is only a moderate drinker. He works out at least three times a week, at hotel health clubs, and he swims regularly.

WHAT CHRIS SHOULD DO

Chris must cut down significantly on his fat intake. He should eat less French food as it is often rich in cream, butter and eggs, and more Italian food which has low-fat pasta dishes (excluding the creamy sauces, of course). Middle Eastern food offers healthy meals based on grains and vegetables. Japanese food is another good choice, with its emphasis on rice and lightly-cooked or raw vegetables, fresh fish and very few dairy products.

Because he doesn't like sweets, Chris usually ends his meal with cheese. He should stick to the low-fat cheeses and wholegrain bread, and avoid using spreads, such as margarine or butter or, better still, he should eat fruit instead.

WORK
Business dinners in a foreign country can make it difficult to stick to a diet.

EATING
Starting the day with a healthy and satisfying meal reduces the temptation to snack later on.

DIET
A diet which is high in meat and dairy products and low in fruit and vegetables can cause a high cholesterol problem.

Action Plan

EATING
Do not skip breakfast. Eat fresh or tinned fruit, wholegrain cereal and bread and low-fat yoghurt. Avoid fried foods. Eat oat porridge for a hot breakfast.

WORK
Try to choose restaurants where there are some healthy dishes on the menu. If there is no choice, be extra careful the next day.

DIET
Cut down meat intake. Eat more poultry, fish, salads and vegetables. Use low-fat dairy products. Avoid creamy sauces and dressings.

HOW THINGS TURNED OUT FOR CHRIS

Chris kept a diary to monitor his consumption of saturated fats and to list restaurants which offered foods more suitable to his new diet. After trial and error with ways to cut fat and still enjoy food, he successfully reduced his fat consumption. At his next medical, Chris had lost 3 kg (6½ lb) and his cholesterol was at a healthier level, but he realised that he would have to remain vigilant to ensure that it did not climb back up again.

ARE YOU OVERWEIGHT?

A simple way to calculate whether you are overweight is using the Body Mass Index (BMI): your weight (in kilograms) divided by your height (in metres squared).

For example, for a woman whose height is 1.6 m and weight is 65 kg, the computation is:
65 divided by (1.6 x 1.6) = 25.4

A BMI of 20 to 25 indicates a healthy weight, between 26 and 34 is considered overweight and over 35 is obese. A BMI of below 20 indicates underweight and this too can cause health problems. Check the height and weight chart on page 97. Use the BMI as a guideline only as build and age need to be taken into account. Consult your doctor if you are concerned.

Obesity

Keeping to a healthy weight is important. Being overweight is believed to double the risk of developing heart disease. With around half the adults in many Western countries now classified as overweight, and 10 to 15 per cent as obese (their weight is 30 per cent higher than their ideal body weight), it has become increasingly vital for people to reduce their weight to healthy levels.

Obesity increases the risk of heart disease because it is linked with raised blood pressure and raised blood cholesterol levels. Too much body weight overworks the heart. And if you are carrying a lot of extra weight, you will be less likely, and probably less able, to exercise. Many overweight and obese people develop diabetes, which has also been linked to an increase in the risk of early heart disease (see page 32).

Beware of diets

Although it is important to have a healthy weight, be careful not to become obsessive about changing what you eat. Any dietary changes will need to be followed long term. Going overboard on any diet usually ends up in failure because the diet places too many restrictions and makes it impossible to lead a normal life. So your new diet should be practical and fit in with the way you live. Also, sudden dietary changes can cause extreme fluctuations in magnesium and potassium levels, which are essential for your heart's normal rhythm.

AVOIDING HIGH BLOOD PRESSURE

Raised blood pressure is a well-known risk factor for heart disease, as it can damage arteries that supply the heart muscle. It usually does not have one single cause – several factors, including diet, play important roles – but in people with moderately high blood pressure, dietary changes are often enough to keep the condition under control.

High blood pressure is particularly common in overweight people because of the strain on the heart. Losing excess pounds and maintaining a normal weight usually helps reduce blood pressure.

Drinking alcohol heavily also raises blood pressure. A modest intake two or three times a week may do no harm, but too much more can be dangerous (see page 119).

A high salt intake may be associated with high blood pressure. People who are salt sensitive because of damaged kidneys should have a very low salt intake. For most people, however, doctors recommend a moderate reduction. Do not add salt when cooking; always taste food before adding salt; try herbs and spices for flavour instead. Cut down on the amount of processed foods you eat. Over a period of time your taste buds will gradually adjust to a low-salt diet and you will find you do not miss it.

Some doctors prescribe salt substitutes such as potassium to help reduce blood pressure. High-potassium foods include fruit and vegetables, particularly dried fruit and fruit juices and bananas.

Many experts also recommend that people with high blood pressure should reduce their intake of fatty foods, both to lower blood pressure and help reduce the overall risk of heart disease.

CAUTION

Too much potassium can be harmful for people with kidney problems or on certain kinds of medication. Any salt substitutes should be used in moderation, and with your doctor's approval.

PROCESSED FOODS

Many ready-cooked or prepared foods are high in sodium (salt). Choose varieties with 'no added salt'. Avoid the following:

▶ *Processed meat such as ham, bacon, salamis and sausages.*

▶ *Smoked meat and fish, and meat and fish pastes.*

▶ *Tinned foods (unless the label specifies 'no added salt').*

▶ *Salted potato crisps, pretzels and nuts.*

▶ *Most cheeses.*

▶ *Condiments, bottled sauces and seasonings.*

▶ *Salted spices and stock cubes.*

▶ *Instant meals.*

THE PINCH TEST
If you can 'pinch an inch' of fat on your waist, you probably need to lose some weight. Check the weight chart on page 97. Consult your doctor before embarking on a weight-loss programme.

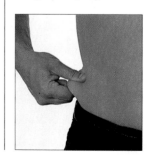

FATS AND HEART DISEASE

A diet that is good for your heart should be limited in both the total fat and the saturated fat it contains to keep your blood cholesterol levels down, and decrease your risk of heart disease.

Different fats

The saturation of a fat is determined by the amount of hydrogen bonded to its carbon atoms. If a pair of carbon atoms is free or not completely bonded to hydrogen atoms, a double bond forms between them.

SATURATED
The carbon atoms are all bonded to as many hydrogen atoms as possible.

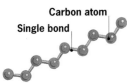

MONOUNSATURATED
All carbon atoms are completely bonded with hydrogen except one pair, which form a double bond.

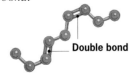

POLYUNSATURATED
Several pairs of carbon atoms are free and joined by double bonds.

Coronary heart disease results from two main processes, atherosclerosis and thrombosis. Atherosclerosis is caused, in part, by excess fat in the diet, and promotes thrombosis.

THE DEVELOPMENT OF HEART DISEASE

Atherosclerosis (or 'hardening of the arteries') is caused when plaques, made up of fatty material, are deposited on the inner linings of the arteries. Once they have formed, these plaques continue to grow, making the inner layer of the artery wall thicker and less elastic. The build up of plaque causes the channel of the artery to narrow, restricting blood flow; this raises blood pressure and puts a strain on the heart as it tries to force blood through the narrowed arteries. There is also a danger that part of the plaque will break away and cause a block elsewhere in the circulatory system. Atherosclerosis is especially serious when it affects the coronary arteries that supply blood to the heart.

Thrombosis (see page 125), the presence of blood clots, can block important blood vessels and lead to heart attacks and strokes.

The role of cholesterol

The amounts and types of fat in your diet are directly responsible for fluctuations in your blood cholesterol level. Early research into links between dietary fat and blood cholesterol levels looked at the incidence of disease in different countries and considered the effect of the local diet. Average blood cholesterol level was shown to be directly related to fat intake. Further, raised blood cholesterol levels were linked to increased risks of atherosclerosis and thrombosis.

But blood cholesterol actually exists in two main forms, low-density lipoprotein (LDL) and high-density lipoprotein (HDL). LDL is often referred to as the 'bad cholesterol' and HDL as 'good cholesterol'. People at a high risk from heart disease tend to have high levels of LDL and low levels of HDL. People with low LDL and high HDL levels tend to have a lower risk of heart disease.

Cholesterol tests should measure the total cholesterol content, as well as breaking down blood cholesterol levels into LDL and HDL cholesterol. By calculating the ratio of HDL to total cholesterol, the risk of heart disease can be determined more accurately.

TYPES OF DIETARY FAT

There are three main types of fat in the diet: saturated, monounsaturated and polyunsaturated fat. The difference between these fats is in their chemical bonding. The carbon atoms in saturated fats are linked by single bonds to each other as they are saturated with hydrogen on the other bonding sites; those in monounsaturated fats have one double bond in their structures and those in polyunsaturated fats have more than one double bond. Both of these have fewer hydrogen atoms. Fatty foods contain different combinations of all three fats.

Saturated fat, except for coconut oil and palm oil, is solid at room temperature. It is found in foods of animal origin, including meat and dairy products, although there is some in vegetables. Foods high in saturated fat include salamis and sausages, poultry skin, butter, cream, full-fat dairy products such as milk and cheese, and some vegetable fats such as palm oil, coconut oil and cocoa butter. Any dishes made from these foods will also be high in saturated fat.

A high intake of saturated fat tends to raise LDL cholesterol levels because saturated fat is turned into cholesterol by the liver. Saturated fats should make up no more than ten per cent of your total calorie intake.

Monounsaturated fats

These fats are liquid at room temperature. When these fats constitute the majority of fat in the diet, the level of HDL is increased and the level of LDL reduced. To protect your heart, monounsaturated fats should form the main source of fats in your diet and should contribute about 12 per cent of your total calorie intake. Monounsaturated fats are found in many foods, including olive oil, fish oil, and nut and seed oils (peanut, sesame, rapeseed).

Polyunsaturated fats

These are also liquid at room temperature. They tend to reduce total cholesterol levels but do not increase the 'good' HDL level. No more than six to ten per cent of your total calories should come from polyunsaturated fats. Higher intakes may be linked to an increased risk of cancer. Many vegetable oils, including sunflower, safflower, corn, soya bean and cottonseed oils, are high in polyunsaturated fats.

Essential fatty acids

Two of the polyunsaturated fats, linoleic and linolenic acids, are essential fatty acids. They are essential for growth and the regeneration of tissues as well as for normal metabolic processes. Neither of these fatty acids can be made in the body so it is important to retain some fat in your diet. These fats are converted in the body to omega-3 and omega-6 fatty acids, which appear to help lower blood cholesterol levels.

Fish, especially oily fish such as mackerel, herrings, kippers, sardines and tuna, are a good source of the omega-3 fatty acids, which appear to protect against heart disease. High intake of omega-3 fatty acids results in a reduction in blood fat levels, in blood pressure and in both the thickness of the blood and its tendency to clot, all of which can improve the health of the heart and reduce the risk of heart disease. Studies have also shown that those who suffer one heart attack but then increase their intake of oily fish reduce the likelihood of having another heart attack.

YOUR DAILY FAT TARGET

First you need to know your calorie limit (see page 142). Then read the table below to determine the maximum amount of total fat and saturated fat you can eat daily to maintain a healthy heart.

CALORIE LIMIT	TOTAL FAT INTAKE (grams)	SATURATED FAT INTAKE (grams)
1000	30	10
1200	40	13
1500	50	15
1700	55	18
2000	65	20
2500	80	25
3000	100	33

All figures are rounded off.

Trans-fatty acids

While some fatty acids are good for you, others, known as trans-fatty acids, may be harmful. These mono or polyunsaturated fats have been hydrogenated, or hardened, and are found in solid margarine and many processed foods, such as cookies, cakes and fried foods. Turning liquid oils into spreadable margarines, for example, produces high levels of trans-fatty acids. It appears that trans-fatty acids act like saturated fats, raising LDL and lowering HDL levels. Concern about trans-fatty acids has grown since a study that showed that women who had a high intake of trans-fatty acid also had a higher risk of heart disease (*The Lancet*, 1993). It is now recommended that no more than two per cent of your total calories come from trans-fatty acids. Check the list of ingredients on processed foods packaging for 'hydrogenated vegetable fats or oils'.

Triglycerides

These are the primary kind of fat in the body and diet, formed from three fatty acids and one glycerol molecule (an organic compound). Triglycerides are essential for the body's energy storing, but high triglyceride levels are believed to increase the risk of heart disease, as they play a role in the blood clotting mechanism. High levels are more common in overweight people, alcoholics, diabetics and women who take the contraceptive pill. Blood cholesterol tests usually give a separate triglyceride reading. Some people at high risk are advised to go on a triglyceride-lowering diet (see page 143).

IMPORTANT FATS
Oily fish are a good source of the essential fatty acids, omega-3 and omega-6. These are believed to have a protective effect on the heart by lowering blood cholesterol levels.

If you do not eat fish you can get both your essential fatty acids from seeds, nuts and vegetable oils, such as linseed, soya bean and rapeseed oil.

Measuring food energy

The energy value of food is measured in calories but as one calorie is so small, figures are usually given in units of 1000 calories, called a kilocalorie (kcal). This is also written as 'Calorie', although 'calorie' is now usually used to mean kilocalorie, as in this book.

REDUCING FAT IN THE DIET

Calculate your daily fat target (see page 53) and then monitor how much fat you eat everyday. More than likely you will have to reduce the amount of total fat and saturated fat in your diet, which may not be easy. While some fats are visible as in meat, cream, butter and margarine, most are hidden in less obviously fatty foods such as cakes, biscuits, pastry, potato crisps and chocolate. As a rough guide, 1 teaspoon of oil, butter or margarine contains around 5 grams of fat (45 calories) and 30 grams (1 ounce) of milk chocolate contains 9 grams of fat (81 calories).

By reducing the amount of fat you use in cooking it is possible to make a major impact on your total daily fat intake. One way to cut down on fat is simply to use less. Healthy cooking practices (see opposite),

like straining fat off gravy or cutting all visible fat off meat, are aimed at reducing fat in the diet. You can also use non-stick pans which do not need fat for cooking, or steam and poach food. Stir-frying in a wok needs only a little oil. Or, instead of cooking oil, try non-stick sprays, if available.

Low-fat dairy products

Dairy products, such as milk, cream and cheese, contain large amounts of total fat and saturated fat. On average, they contribute about 20 per cent of most people's total fat intakes. However, dairy products are nutritionally very important because they are major sources of protein, iron, calcium and other vital vitamins and minerals. You can still benefit from all these nutrients but avoid taking in too much fat by using reduced-fat products.

FATS IN DAIRY FOODS

Some dairy food products are very high in saturated fat and should be avoided. However, dairy foods are an important source of calcium, iron and protein. To ensure you get these nutrients, choose from the wide range of low-fat dairy products which give you the goodness without the fat.

DAIRY PRODUCT (100 gram/fluid ounce serving)	SATURATED FAT (grams)	MONO-UNSATURATED FAT (grams)	POLY-UNSATURATED FAT (grams)	TOTAL FAT * (grams)
Skimmed milk	0.06	Trace	Trace	0.1
Semi-skimmed milk	1.0	0.5	Trace	1.6
Dried skimmed milk	0.4	0.2	Trace	0.6
Whole milk	2.4	1.1	0.1	3.9
Single cream	11.9	5.5	0.5	19.1
Whipping cream	24.6	11.4	1.1	39.3
Double cream	30.0	13.9	1.4	48.0
Butter	54.0	19.8	2.6	81.7
Soft margarine	16.2	20.6	41.1	81.6
Low-fat plain yoghurt	0.5	0.2	Trace	0.8
Low-fat fruit yoghurt	0.4	0.2	Trace	0.7
Whole milk fruit yoghurt	1.5	0.8	0.2	2.8
Low-fat cottage cheese	0.9	0.4	Trace	1.4
Cheddar cheese	21.7	9.4	1.4	34.4
Brie cheese	16.8	7.8	0.8	26.9
Blue Stilton cheese	22.2	10.3	1.0	35.5
Soft cream cheese	19.4	9.0	0.9	31.0
Low-fat fromage frais	0.1	0.1	Trace	0.2
Plain fromage frais	4.4	2.1	0.2	7.1

* Where the total fat quantity is more than the sum of the fats listed, the difference is trace quantities of other kinds of fat, including trans-fatty acids.

CHOOSING HEART HEALTHY FOODS

Although it is sometimes easier to buy and eat processed or ready-made foods, they are usually high in fat and salt and low in nutrients. For a healthy heart, prepare meals using fresh and natural foods, and don't add salt or sugar.

BAD FOR YOUR HEART
High in saturated fat, sugar and salt, meals such as this one contribute to high cholesterol, high blood pressure and overweight.

Fried chicken and chips

Apple pie and ice cream

Hot chocolate and cream

GOOD FOR YOUR HEART
A meal of freshly prepared food such as this is high in protein, vitamins and minerals, and fibre, and low in fat, sugar and salt.

Fresh fruit salad

Herbal tea

Beans, vegetables and rice

Choose either skimmed or semi-skimmed milk. Skimmed milk is virtually fat free and semi-skimmed milk contains less than half the fat content of whole milk. These milks contain the same amounts of nutrients as full-fat milk, except for reduced vitamin A and D content. You can use them in drinks, on cereals and in cooking. Young children, however, need more fat than older children and adults, so they should not be given low-fat milk until they are five years old.

Choose low-fat yoghurt and fromage frais rather than cream or full-fat or Greek-style yoghurt. Yoghurt has many uses: it is ideal to use in cooking, for sauces, to extend mayonnaise and other salad dressings, on baked potatoes, with fruit and in desserts. If you like cream, choose a single or low-fat cream rather than double cream. Avoid coffee creamers and whiteners which are usually high in total fat and saturated fat.

Full-fat cheeses should not be eaten in large quantities, although eating 60 grams (2 ounces) of full-fat cheese a few times a week will not overload your saturated fat intake. Avoid eating cheese after a meal; you do not need the additional fat and calories if you have eaten a balanced meal. Low-fat cheeses like cottage cheese and low-fat soft cheeses can be substituted for the higher-fat variety the rest of the time.

Low-fat high-protein foods

Meat and meat products are major sources of total fat and saturated fat in the diet. They account for around a quarter of the total amount of fat most people eat. Reducing your intake of fats, particularly from these sources, is therefore an important part of a healthy diet.

As with dairy products, meat and poultry do not have to be avoided entirely as they provide a valuable source of protein, vitamins and minerals. To remain healthy, choose lean cuts of meat, such as chicken breast without the skin, or turkey and extra lean ham and beef. Bacon, duck, goose, salamis, sausages and heavily marbled steaks are full of fat and should be eaten sparingly. Always trim off any visible fat and add only minimal amounts of fat when cooking. When basting chicken, for example, use low-sodium stock instead of butter.

You will also reduce the amount of fat in your diet if you eat meat in smaller portions and less often. Around 115 to 170 grams (4 to 6 ounces) of lean meat per portion for a main meal is a good guide. When making snacks and sandwiches, use less meat and choose lean varieties.

Do not eat meat at every meal. Instead have poultry, fish or a vegetable dish in place of red meat at least four times a week.

LEAN MEATS
Always choose lean cuts of meats and trim off any visible fat.

READING FOOD LABELS
READING FOOD LABELS
Nutritional information is usually given as quantities per 100 grams (3½ ounces). It is important to check the total fat content as well as the breakdown of monounsaturated and saturated fats. Make sure the carbohydrates are mostly starch not simple sugars, as in this example. Compare different brands of a particular food to make sure you choose the healthiest option.

NUTRITIONAL INFORMATION	
Energy	1300 kJ/310 kcal
Protein	10.5 g
Carbohydrate	6.5 g
of which sugars	2.0 g
Fat	5.0 g
of which	
monounsaturates	4.0 g
saturates	1.0 g
Sodium	0.3 g
Fibre	8.5 g

MEDITERRANEAN-STYLE EATING
Adopting a Mediterranean diet means eating plenty of fresh fruit and vegetables, complex carbohydrates, legumes and the occasional glass of red wine.

You will not miss large helpings of meat as much if you eat something in their place. Pad out meals with more vegetables, salad and starchy foods such as bread, potatoes, rice and pasta. You can use less meat in recipes like lasagne or chilli by adding some pulses such as beans or lentils instead, which are also rich in protein and iron but low in fat.

Reading food labels

There has been a massive increase in the use of manufactured foods and ready-made meals in the last 20 years. Such foods are often high in fat and should not be eaten regularly. To choose which of these convenience foods are good for you and which are not, you need to understand labels.

The labels will show the breakdown per unit weight, usually per serving weight and often per 100 grams (3½ ounces) or other standard weight. You should translate the per serving information into how much of the food you will eat, then how the food fits in with your daily fat targets (see page 53).

Use the labels to choose foods with a low total fat, saturated fat and trans-fatty acid content. Labels can also help you choose low-fat alternatives, such as lower fat crisps, salad dressings, hamburgers and oven chips. But remember, lower fat does not mean low fat. A lower fat chip, for instance, can still contain a great deal of fat, so you should eat small quantities only.

The Mediterranean diet

Many of the recommendations for eating for a healthy heart are already a natural habit in the southern European countries that border the Mediterranean, for example Italy, Spain and Greece. These countries share a common pattern of eating. The typical diet includes large amounts of starch as a staple, whether it is in the form of bread, rice or pasta, as well as plenty of fresh fruit and vegetables. This is balanced by small amounts of meat, fish and dairy products.

Most of the fat in the diet comes from olive oil, which is high in monounsaturated fats. These Mediterranean countries all report a much lower incidence of heart disease than the countries of northern Europe. By analysing the diets eaten in those countries, experts have tried to explain the different disease rates. They now think that many of the health differences are due to dietary differences. They therefore recommend that the rest of Europe adopt some of the positive aspects of the Mediterranean diet to reduce the incidence of heart disease.

Changing to a Mediterranean diet means eating more fruit and vegetables, grains and legumes, complex carbohydrates such as wholemeal bread and pasta, moderate amounts of dairy produce, fish and poultry and only small amounts of red meat. Also, use olive oil as the main fat for cooking and in dressings, and drink the occasional glass of red wine with meals, unless your doctor advises otherwise. (People who do not drink

DID YOU KNOW?

In 1960, although the overall fat intake of people in Crete exceeded 40 per cent of their total calories, they were 20 times less likely to die of heart disease than Americans whose fat intake was less. The high level of mono and polyunsaturated fats in their diet was thought responsible.

CAUTION WITH FAT

You should never try to cut fat out of your diet completely as some fat is needed for good health. However, it is important to use unsaturated fats rather than saturated ones.

BUTTER
Butter contains mainly saturated fat, and should be used sparingly. Also avoid red meat, hard cheeses, palm and coconut oil, and cocoa butter (found in chocolate).

MARGARINE
Use margarine made from a mixture of mono and polyunsaturated fats. Avoid any spreads containing trans-fatty acids (hydrogenated vegetable fats).

OILS
Monounsaturated and polyunsaturated oils are recommended for salads and cooking. Monounsaturated oils include olive oil, peanut, sesame and rapeseed. Polyunsaturated oils include corn, soya bean, safflower and sunflower. Do not re-use oil for frying as the chemical structure becomes changed and saturated and the oil will turn rancid, which can make you ill.

Enjoy your food
No foods are banned forever. It is simply a matter of eating some foods more often and others less. Good food is a pleasure and eating with friends and family an important part of life. In many parts of the Mediterranean, where there is a low incidence of heart disease, family meals and food are held in great esteem. So, be sure to make time in your daily schedule to sit down and relax while you are eating – you will digest your food better and be more aware of what you are eating.

at all are not advised to take up drinking. You can make great changes to your heart health by changing your foods alone.)

There has been much controversy since the early 1990s among various government health departments about issuing a new 'Mediterranean food pyramid' to replace the UK accepted United States Department of Agriculture (USDA) pyramid (see page 62). The new pyramid specifies eating very little red meat, if any, eating low-fat cheese and yoghurt as the main dairy foods, olive oil as the main source of fat, and wine in moderate amounts. It is similar to the USDA pyramid in its recommendation that complex carbohydrates and fruit and vegetables form the main content of the diet. Those who oppose the new pyramid disagree with its exclusion of milk, saying people would not get sufficient calcium; its emphasis on olive oil, because it encourages a greater fat intake; and its inclusion of wine, as this encourages drinking.

Those who support the Mediterranean diet believe that it could help protect against heart disease, as well as other diseases such as cancer, because of the particularly high quantity of protective antioxidant vitamins, beta-carotene, vitamin C and vitamin E, and of flavenoids and monounsaturated fat (see page 53). This is also used to explain the paradox of the French diet.

The French paradox

Like the southern Mediterranean countries, France has a lower reported incidence of heart disease than the rest of Europe. This was puzzling to scientists, since the French actually eat a diet high in saturated fats, found in butter, cheese, cream and pastries.

This paradox of high total and saturated fat intake combined with a low heart disease rate is thought to be explained by the presence of certain foods found in the French diet. The French, like the southern Mediterraneans, eat a lot of fruit and vegetables that are full of antioxidants. They also tend to drink red wine with meals, which is thought to raise HDL cholesterol levels. (Red wine contains more antioxidant substances than white wine and is thought to be more beneficial for the heart.)

The benefits of the Mediterranean diet and the French paradox have made the whole discussion of diet and heart disease more complex, as scientists realise that eating less fat or more unsaturated fats, although important, is not the whole answer. It appears that there are nutrients that either promote heart disease, or protect against it. So, many dietary factors need to be considered when suggesting a diet that is best for the heart. In addition to eating less of some foods, you need to eat more of others, particularly fruit and vegetables.

Saturated fat and cholesterol
Most of the cholesterol in your blood is actually made in the body from the saturated fats you eat. The amount of dietary cholesterol you eat has very little effect on the blood cholesterol level in healthy people. So when you buy a food product, check that it is low in saturated fat, rather than low in cholesterol.

FOODS FOR A HEALTHY HEART

Foods that are good for your heart are quite varied and so, too, are the ways in which they work. Therefore, it is important to include a wide selection in your daily diet.

Better beta-carotene
Beta-carotene is the pigment in brightly-coloured fruit and vegetables, which is converted to vitamin A in the body. Unlike other vitamins you get more beta-carotene from cooked foods than raw ones. Cooking breaks down the food structure, releasing the beta-carotene. Shredding food does the same.

Probably the most important protectors against heart disease are the antioxidant vitamins that are found in fruit, vegetables, wine and even tea. Antioxidants help protect you against the harmful effects of free radicals – oxygen molecules that damage body tissues.

FREE RADICALS

Free radicals develop normally in the body as a result of several metabolic processes. Some free radical activity is needed to kill bacteria, but an excess can cause problems by setting up a chain reaction of destruction in the body tissues. Under normal circumstances the body has an elaborate defence mechanism to control the build up of these free radicals and to prevent tissue damage. Antioxidants are of major importance in this defence. Many destructive free radicals come from the environment, such as industrial chemicals, air pollutants, pesticides and cigarette smoke.

It is now widely accepted that free radicals play an important role in the development of atherosclerosis by reacting with 'bad' low-density lipoprotein (LDL) cholesterol. In a 1992 study the US National Institute of Health and the University of Mississippi's Atherosclerosis Research Laboratory found that giving people antioxidant vitamins raised 'good' HDL cholesterol and reduced LDL cholesterol, lowering the incidence of atherosclerosis. Increasing your daily intake of fruit and vegetables is the best way to get antioxidants and reduce free radicals.

High risk and low risk diets

According to a 1994 study by the World Health Organisation, both men and women in Glasgow are at a very high risk of heart disease, compared to the rest of the world, with Glaswegian women having a higher risk of dying from heart disease than any others. Factors such as smoking, obesity, lack of exercise, heavy alcohol intake and high cholesterol are important, but Glaswegians also have a very low intake of fruit and vegetables, and thus a high level of free radicals. European studies have found that high rates of heart disease are linked to a diet low in fruit and vegetables.

Vegetarians

The long recognised fact that vegetarians suffer less from heart disease than meat eaters is probably because they tend to have a healthier lifestyle than meat eaters. But many researchers also believe that the foods they eat play an important role in keeping them free of heart disease.

Vegetarians' lower risk is probably not due simply to avoiding meat, but to eating more foods that are high in antioxidants.

FREE RADICALS

Free radicals damage tissue by adding oxygen to cells. The damaged cells then become free radicals. Free radicals may also act on cholesterol causing atherosclerosis.

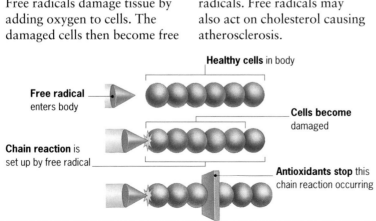

Healthy cells in body

Free radical enters body

Cells become damaged

Chain reaction is set up by free radical

Antioxidants stop this chain reaction occurring

They tend to eat more fruit, vegetables, nuts and seeds. To follow a diet that will benefit your heart, it is not necessary to give up meat. Instead, eat less fat and include more foods that are high in antioxidants.

Where are antioxidants found?

Many different nutrients and foods contain antioxidants. The main antioxidants are beta-carotene (which is turned into vitamin A in the body), vitamin C and vitamin E. Other antioxidants include minerals like selenium, and chemicals such as flavonoids, tannins and phenolics. There are also many other nutrients in fruit and vegetables that may play an important role in the prevention of damage and disease, including lycopene, the red pigment in tomatoes, and lutein, which is found in many of the same foods as beta-carotene.

The World Health Organisation recommends an intake of 420 grams (15 ounces) of fruit and vegetables every day. This quantity should include 30 grams (1 ounce) a day of pulses, nuts and seeds. At present, in the UK, the average is around 225 grams (8 ounces) a day. It is hard for most people to envisage 420 grams (15 ounces) of fruit

and vegetables, and it is impractical to weigh every morsel that you eat. To make this message easier to understand, health experts recommend eating 'five a day' – at least five servings of around 70 grams (2½ ounces), each of fruit and vegetables every day.

To ensure you are getting five helpings of fruit, vegetables and salads a day, include fresh, tinned, or dried fruit in your diet, as well as fruit juices. Vegetables can include frozen and tinned varieties as well as fresh. (Remember that tinned goods may have added fat, salt and sugar, and are often lower in nutrients.) Potatoes, while a good source of many nutrients, do not count as part of the five-a-day requirement. You should also include more wholegrain cereals in your diet, and eat foods such as nuts and seeds that contain vitamin E.

Some minerals have an antioxidant role in the body. The most important ones are selenium, manganese, copper and zinc. A good, varied diet, including food from all five food groups (see page 62) should ensure that you are getting an adequate amount. Supplements are not recommended and are usually not necessary if the diet is adequate.

FLAVONOIDS
The important antioxidants, flavonoids, are found in tea, red wine, onions, apples and other fruit and vegetables. A low dietary intake of flavonoids increases the risk of death from heart disease (The Lancet, 1993). Flavonoids can easily be included in a well-balanced diet.

ACE FOODS

The powerful antioxidant vitamins are beta-carotene (a form of vitamin A), vitamin C and vitamin E, and foods containing them should be included in your daily diet. Doctors advise dietary intake rather than supplements as these may interact with each other and reduce the overall antioxidant effects.

Beta-carotene sources include carrots, dark green leafy vegetables such as spinach and broccoli, tomatoes, sweet potato, red, yellow and orange peppers, mango, apricots and melon

Vitamin C sources include citrus fruits, strawberries, blackcurrants, kiwi fruit, potatoes, green leafy vegetables, green peppers, and raw cauliflower

Vitamin E sources include vegetable cooking oils, especially sunflower, soya and corn oil, wheatgerm oil, wholegrain cereals, green vegetables, almonds, hazelnuts and seeds

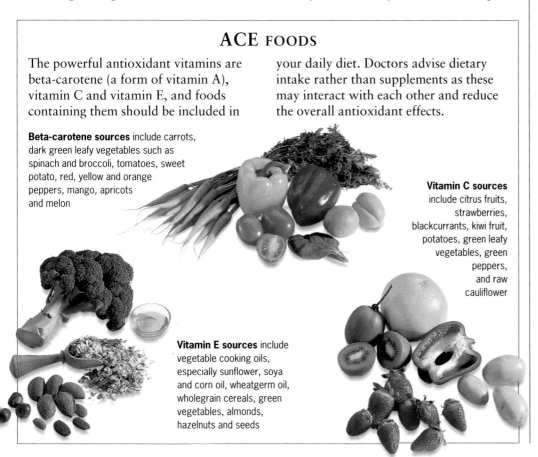

EASY WAYS TO GET FIBRE

If you follow the recommendations of the food pyramid, and eat five to six servings of complex carbohydrates and five servings of fruit and vegetables each day, you will get enough fibre. If you find this difficult, follow these suggestions.

▶ *Sprinkle oat or rice bran on breakfast cereal or yoghurt.*

▶ *Each time you feel the urge to snack, eat a piece of fresh fruit.*

FIBRE AND HEART DISEASE

Fibre, formerly called roughage, also plays a part in protecting your heart. Fibre is the part of food that is not digested or absorbed by the body. There are two main types of fibre in foods – those that are soluble in water and those that are insoluble. Both types are found only in foods that are obtained from plants.

Insoluble fibre is found in wholegrain bread, wholegrain breakfast cereals, brown rice, wholewheat pasta and any food made from wholemeal flour. This type of fibre is important in preventing constipation, as it holds water in the bowels making stools softer, and is an essential part of a healthy diet. It does not seem to have any effect on blood cholesterol levels and the prevention of heart disease.

Soluble fibre is found in fruit, vegetables, oatmeal and pulses such as beans and lentils. Unlike insoluble fibre, it does seems to play a role in helping reduce total blood cholesterol and LDL cholesterol levels. Diets rich in soluble fibre are now often recommended to lower cholesterol. However, consuming lots of soluble fibre will not compensate for a high-fat diet. To reduce cholesterol levels effectively, total fat intake must be reduced and fibre intake, both soluble and insoluble, must be increased.

If you are not used to eating fibre, you should introduce it into your diet gradually. Taking too much too soon can cause abdominal discomfort, flatulence and diarrhoea as it ferments in the intestine. Increasing your fibre intake slowly gives your body a chance to get used to it and process it more efficiently.

Excess fibre binds minerals such as zinc, magnesium, iron and calcium, decreasing their absorption in the body. Fibre supplements, which contain no other nutrients, are more likely to cause mineral deficiencies.

How soluble fibre helps your heart

Soluble fibre is thought to help lower blood cholesterol levels by interfering with the absorption of fats and bile acids in the small intestine. Cholesterol binds to the fibre and is excreted with it. Fibre may also affect cholesterol metabolism in the liver.

Bile acids are made from cholesterol by the liver and released into the intestine to aid digestion of fats. Many of these cholesterol-heavy bile acids are reabsorbed into the blood and used again. The presence of soluble fibre breaks this recycling process. It

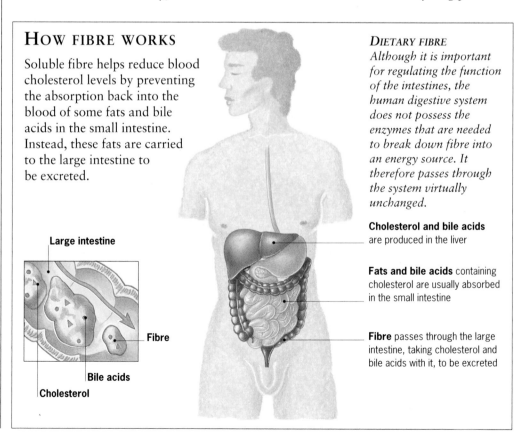

HOW FIBRE WORKS

Soluble fibre helps reduce blood cholesterol levels by preventing the absorption back into the blood of some fats and bile acids in the small intestine. Instead, these fats are carried to the large intestine to be excreted.

Large intestine

Fibre

Bile acids

Cholesterol

DIETARY FIBRE
Although it is important for regulating the function of the intestines, the human digestive system does not possess the enzymes that are needed to break down fibre into an energy source. It therefore passes through the system virtually unchanged.

Cholesterol and bile acids are produced in the liver

Fats and bile acids containing cholesterol are usually absorbed in the small intestine

Fibre passes through the large intestine, taking cholesterol and bile acids with it, to be excreted

SOURCES OF FIBRE

There are two main types of fibre, soluble and insoluble, that are found in different plant foods. Insoluble fibre helps improve your digestive system, while soluble fibre can help lower blood cholesterol levels, reducing the risk of heart disease.

INSOLUBLE FIBRE
The best sources are wholegrain breakfast cereals and bread, brown rice and wholewheat pasta.

SOLUBLE FIBRE
The best sources are fresh fruit and vegetables, oatmeal, beans and lentils.

enables cholesterol to be removed from the blood and excreted, which can lead to a reduction in total cholesterol and 'bad' LDL-cholesterol.

Fibre is also believed to be beneficial to diabetics as it slows down the absorption of nutrients in the blood, reducing blood sugar swings and the need for insulin.

How much fibre?

A healthy diet should include at least 20 grams (¾ ounce) of soluble fibre per day. You could get this from a daily intake of 3 tablespoons of oat bran or rice bran, which should be be added to various foods (such as cereal or yoghurt) rather than taken all in one go. However, a healthy diet should provide sufficient fibre. There is no need to worry about 'counting fibre' – simply eat lots of fresh fruit and vegetables, include beans or peas in your main meal and eat wholegrain breads, rice and pasta as part of your daily carbohydrate intake. Other foods high in fibre include pectin (found in citrus and other fruits) and guar gum.

Drinking plenty of water makes it much easier for fibre to pass through your digestive system. Lack of water and too much fibre may cause bloating.

Are oats still in?

A study at the University of Kentucky in 1990 added oat bran or beans to the diets of people with high blood cholesterol levels. Their total cholesterol was reduced by an average of 19 per cent. This massive reduction was probably due to the large amounts of beans and oats eaten by the volunteers and the consequent reduction in other forms of food, and also to the fact that the study involved people whose cholesterol levels were particulary high, making possible a greater drop. The study then concluded that oats are a useful cholesterol-lowering food when included as part of a balanced diet.

Further research has now confirmed a direct link between the amount of soluble fibre eaten and the reduction in cholesterol. Therefore, as a general rule, eating a low-fat diet that is combined with a diet rich in soluble fibre will reduce cholesterol.

Most people would not eat enough oats to reduce their cholesterol levels drastically, but eating smaller quantities over a long period of time is beneficial. However, it is best to get your soluble fibre from a variety of sources, to ensure that you get a variety of other nutrients.

continued on page 64

Is garlic that great?
Many studies have been performed to investigate the benefits of garlic. One is now underway with the British Heart Foundation.

The studies show that fresh garlic and some extracts, including garlic capsules and tablets, appear to lower blood cholesterol and reduce the risk of blood clots, the usual cause of heart attacks and strokes. The most beneficial dose appears to be 4 grams of fresh garlic daily (one to two cloves).

In Germany, garlic supplements are licensed drugs, and provided by their national health service. However, until further research is done, garlic is not considered a wonder cure for heart disease but can be included in a healthy diet.

GARLIC TOAST
Try the Italian way of eating garlic – toast some bread, sprinkle with a little olive oil, and top with crushed garlic and fresh herbs.

The Heart Diet

Some foods seem to fight off heart disease, others seem to cause it. By eating more of the foods that protect your heart and fewer of those that may harm it, you will keep your heart healthy. Eating a healthy diet is easier than you think.

EGGS
Eat a maximum of three whole eggs a week. However, you can eat as many egg whites as you like, as they are low in fat and cholesterol, but high in protein.

Foods are neither good or bad – it is the amount of each you actually eat that matters. Favourite foods do not need to be avoided entirely, just eaten moderately. Your daily diet should include foods from the five main food groups, as shown in the pyramid below. For meal ideas, the sample weekly menu gives a balanced and varied selection. Eating healthily will soon become natural as you find out how easy it can be.

THE HEALTHY EATING PYRAMID

This pyramid gives standard recommendations for a healthy balanced diet, ensuring that you get all the vitamins, minerals, protein, carbohydrates and fats that you need. This food plan should be followed by the whole family unless someone has specific dietary restrictions (such as diabetics or those suffering from familial hyperlipidaemia – see page 32). Children under five need to eat full-fat milk and dairy products.

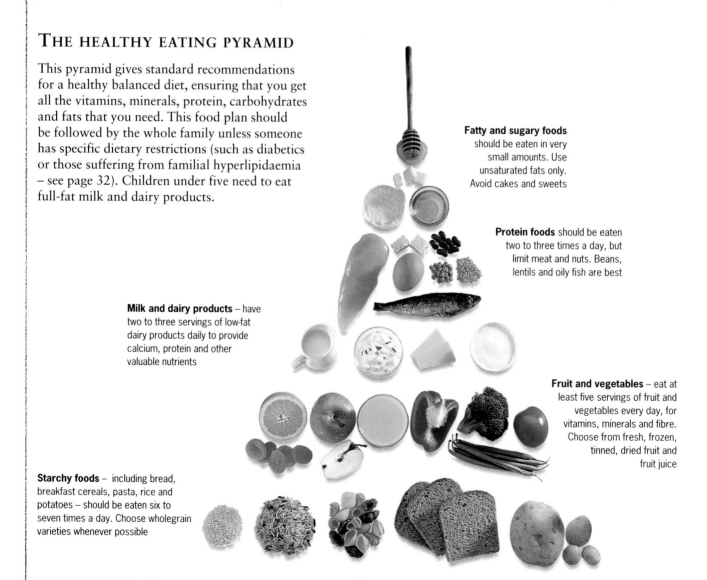

Fatty and sugary foods should be eaten in very small amounts. Use unsaturated fats only. Avoid cakes and sweets

Protein foods should be eaten two to three times a day, but limit meat and nuts. Beans, lentils and oily fish are best

Milk and dairy products – have two to three servings of low-fat dairy products daily to provide calcium, protein and other valuable nutrients

Fruit and vegetables – eat at least five servings of fruit and vegetables every day, for vitamins, minerals and fibre. Choose from fresh, frozen, tinned, dried fruit and fruit juice

Starchy foods – including bread, breakfast cereals, pasta, rice and potatoes – should be eaten six to seven times a day. Choose wholegrain varieties whenever possible

THE WEEKLY MENU

This menu gives suggestions only. Do not eat more than you need. For vegetarians, substitute beans, lentils or tofu for fish or meat. If you drink tea or coffee with breakfast, use skimmed milk and a sugar substitute.

Always use wholegrain varieties of bread, pasta, brown rice and low-fat dairy products. Make sure that your breakfast cereals are low in fat and sugar, and that tinned fruit has been prepared in juice not syrup.

BREAKFAST	LUNCH	DINNER
MONDAY		
Muesli with low-fat yoghurt; canned peaches; two slices wholegrain toast with low-sugar marmalade.	Vegetable pilaf with brown rice; fresh fruit salad; glass of skimmed milk.	Stir-fried chicken with peppers, onions and pineapple; fresh orange juice; banana.
TUESDAY		
Grapefruit; cooked oat porridge with skimmed milk; two slices wholegrain toast with peanut butter.	Salad: one hard boiled egg, lettuce, tomatoes, cucumbers, peppers and olives; two slices wholegrain bread; bunch of grapes.	Lentil soup with wholegrain bread roll; grilled vegetable kebabs; low-fat yoghurt with dried fruit.
WEDNESDAY		
Melon; two slices wholegrain toast with one poached egg and baked beans; glass of skimmed milk.	Salad: pasta, chicken, tomatoes, olives and sesame seeds; low-fat yoghurt with orange segments.	Chilli bean or beef casserole; baked potato; salad: spring onions, watercress and cucumber; blackcurrant sorbet.
THURSDAY		
Fresh orange juice; bran cereal with prunes and skimmed milk; two slices wholegrain toast with low-fat cheese spread.	Two baked potatoes filled with onions, tuna fish and tomatoes; skimmed milk banana shake.	Pasta with lean beef and tomato sauce; steamed broccoli and carrots; low-fat yoghurt.
FRIDAY		
Stewed apple; oat porridge with skimmed milk; two slices wholegrain toast with low-sugar marmalade.	Salad: low-fat cottage cheese, chives, onions, radishes and cucumber; two slices wholegrain bread; low-fat yoghurt.	Poached fish; steamed Brussels sprouts and cauliflower; mashed potato; stewed fruit.
SATURDAY		
Grapefruit; two slices wholegrain toast with low-fat cheese; glass of skimmed milk.	Salad: cooked chickpeas, avocado, onion, baby tomatoes and lemon juice; two slices wholegrain bread; fresh fruit salad.	Stir-fried chicken with mushrooms and mangetout; low-fat rice pudding.
SUNDAY		
Fresh fruit salad and low-fat yoghurt; omelette (one egg); one to two slices wholegrain toast with low-fat margarine.	Dry roasted chicken; steamed carrots, spinach and cauliflower; poached pears.	Pasta with tomato-based (not creamy) sauce; spinach and red onion salad; lemon sorbet.

VEGETABLE KEBABS
Skewer cubes of peppers, courgettes, baby onions and tomatoes. Marinate in low-sodium soya sauce and spices and grill until slightly brown.

POACHED FISH
Put fish in a fish kettle or large saucepan with carrots and onions, bay leaves and other herbs. Cover with water and simmer until fish flakes easily.

DRY ROASTED CHICKEN
Coat chicken in mustard, spices or a little honey. Roast on a rack to allow fat to drain away and cover with foil for the first part of cooking.

WHO SHOULDN'T DRINK?

The following people should avoid alcohol altogether:

▶ *Women who are pregnant or trying to conceive.*

▶ *Anyone planning to drive or undertake any activity requiring good concentration and/or muscle coordination.*

▶ *People who are taking antihistamines, sedatives, antibiotics or other medication.*

▶ *Recovering alcoholics.*

▶ *People suffering or recovering from illnesses that affect the liver (such as hepatitis).*

▶ *People under 18.*

COFFEE CONNECTION
Caffeine has no proven connection to heart disease, but nevertheless, it should be drunk in moderation because it can cause constriction of the blood vessels.

ALCOHOL AND YOUR HEART

Moderate drinkers are believed to have a lower risk of heart disease than those who do not drink.

Moderate alcohol intake is associated with higher HDL (good cholesterol) levels, and a reduced tendency for blood to clot, and therefore has a positive effect on the two main processes in the development of heart disease.

A study of alcohol intake and heart disease risk at Harvard University (1993) showed that drinking two standard alcoholic drinks every day for six weeks increased the HDL cholesterol by 17 per cent. This rise can be interpreted as a 40 per cent reduction in the risk of heart disease.

A 1994 study by H. Hendriks (the Netherlands), reported in the *British Medical Journal*, investigated the influence of moderate alcohol intake on the clotting mechanism. The alcohol was taken before and during the evening meal in the form of beer, red wine or gin. The results showed that all forms of alcohol activated reactions that may be beneficial, helping blood clots dissolve and preventing new ones forming.

How much to drink?

Experts at the British Medical Association, the American Heart Association and the World Health Organisation acknowledge the protective qualities of alcohol when taken in moderation, but they are quick to emphasise that this does not mean everyone should begin to drink more or that teetotallers should start drinking.

The experts do not encourage everyone to drink more because high intakes of alcohol tend to increase blood pressure, itself a risk factor for heart disease. Drinking a lot of alcohol, which is relatively high in calories, also tends to cause weight gain, again a risk factor for heart disease. Other problems connected with high alcohol intakes include liver disease, damage to other body tissues including the kidneys, brain and heart, an increase in road accidents, peptic ulcers, an increased risk of low birth weight babies and foetal alcohol syndrome.

Drink alcohol with meals to slow absorption. Do not drink instead of eating as you will miss out on important nutrients. And do not binge drink. A large intake at one time can overload the liver and other body organs such as the kidneys.

Safe levels of alcohol

In both the UK and the US, alcohol intakes are often expressed in terms of 'units'. One unit of alcohol is equal to one glass of wine, one single spirit measure, one half pint or one quarter litre of beer, or one small glass of sherry or fortified wine. In the UK, most doctors recommend a weekly maximum of 14 units of alcohol for women and 21 units for men. Current UK Government guidelines do not set a weekly maximum. Instead, they suggest a daily limit of 2–3 units for women and 3–4 units for men. All health experts recommend that you should spread your units over the week and allow for one or two drink-free days every week.

Is wine special?

Some studies – but not all – suggest that wine has a more powerful effect in protecting against heart disease than beer or spirits. If so, there may be two explanations for this: wine, especially red wine, contains an assortment of chemicals – phenolics, flavenoids, flavonols, anthocyanins and tannins – that have antioxidant effects as shown in a report in *The Lancet* (1993).

Alternatively, wine drinkers may simply have healthier lifestyles than beer and spirit drinkers. Some doctors believe that the difference is not so much what is in the bottle of alcohol, as who is drinking it. In the US wine drinkers tend to be women, non-smokers, better educated and moderate drinkers. All these factors are associated with a low risk of heart disease.

CAFFEINE AND YOUR HEART

Studies of the connection between caffeine and high blood pressure, and therefore the increased risk of heart disease, are inconclusive. However, doctors still recommend that people with hypertension restrict their intake of caffeinated drinks such as coffee and cokes. Caffeine increases adrenaline production which causes blood vessel constriction. Drinking two to three cups of coffee a day is unlikely to cause problems for your heart, but excessive caffeine may cause palpitations (see page 87) so people who have been diagnosed with arrhythmias should avoid caffeine drinks.

Coffee may raise the blood cholesterol levels if it is boiled for about 10 minutes, as practised in Scandinavia. Filter, espresso and instant coffees do not have this effect.

CHAPTER 4

EXERCISING TO PROTECT YOUR HEART

A daily exercise regime can be justified simply because it promotes fitness and well-being. But the benefits of a controlled programme extend even further – in its effects on the heart. The more regularly you induce the body's pump to work harder, the more you build up a defence against cardiovascular disease. Exercise programmes can be tailored to all levels of fitness and should be planned in consultation with your doctor.

EXERCISE AND YOUR HEART

A regular exercise programme can make an important contribution towards your well-being. Physical activity improves the functioning of your heart, lungs and circulatory system.

Falling heart rate

This graph shows the effect of regular exercise on a middle-aged man's resting heart rate.

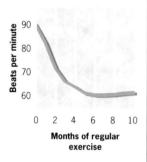

Cardiac output

A fit person uses oxygen more efficiently. As the demand on the heart increases, it does not need to pump as much blood per minute to meet oxygen requirements.

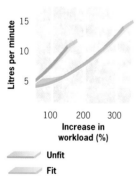

Among the many and varied causes of cardiovascular diseases, a sedentary life must be listed, and with modern labour-saving technology, people have less need to exert themselves physically. Low levels of exercise alone rarely strike down an otherwise healthy individual, but many studies make it clear that exercise can help in both the prevention of and recovery from heart and lung diseases.

Physical fitness plays a central role in many of the medical programmes designed to prevent heart disease. It is now regularly prescribed for people who already suffer heart problems. Patients who have had a heart attack or undergone coronary artery bypass surgery are often encouraged to begin medically supervised exercise programmes within two weeks of leaving hospital.

THE BENEFITS OF EXERCISE

The short-term benefits of exercise include greater physical and mental energy, relief of stress and more self-confidence.

For exercise to be beneficial in the long term it needs to be done regularly, and over a long period. If you quit after a few months, any benefits you have gained will rapidly disappear. You need to keep it up.

Regular physical activity may result in a lowered risk of early death, reduced chance of coronary artery disease and stroke, reduced blood pressure and cholesterol levels, prevention of osteoporosis, maintenance of a healthy body weight, relief of stress and enhancement of self-confidence.

Exercise and the heart muscle

During exercise the muscles require more blood to keep them supplied with energy and oxygen. The volume of blood into the heart increases and the heart has to contract more powerfully to eject it. With regular exercise, the heart muscle strengthens and its blood vessels proliferate (more capillaries grow), improving its ability to pump blood and making it more efficient. (This proliferation of blood vessels occurs in all muscles that are worked regularly.)

The healthier, fitter heart pumps more blood with each beat, and can decrease its work rate while sustaining the same level of flow, resulting in a lower resting pulse. As fitness increases, the exercise pulse rate also slows, and the pulse returns to its resting level more quickly.

Exercise and fat burning

Keeping your weight within recommended limits is important for the health of your heart – excess weight puts strain on the heart as it has to work harder to supply the extra tissue. Less body fat also means a reduced risk of disease-causing cholesterol accumulating in the arteries.

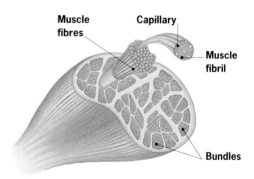

INSIDE A MUSCLE
During exercise the muscle fibres produce energy by burning fats and glucose using oxygen, all of which are supplied by the blood. As more blood is required, the number of capillaries increases.

Low-to-moderate intensity exercise, such as walking or swimming for regular periods of at least 20 minutes a session, uses energy from fat stores. With regular exercise your body becomes more efficient at accessing fat stores, and the fitter you are, the quicker it will burn fat.

High-intensity exercise, such as sprinting in short spurts, uses energy from glycogen stores in the muscles and, although it burns calories, it does not use up your fat.

Exercise also increases the amount of muscle tissue in the body. As muscle cells, even at rest, have high energy requirements compared to other cells, more muscle means a higher metabolic rate. This means you burn more calories even while resting.

WHAT IS FITNESS?

Fitness is a general term that encompasses an overall standard of strength, flexibility and endurance. Your body responds to an increase in the amount or intensity of exercise by adapting and maintaining itself in a more ready state, so that you can initiate and maintain an increased pace whenever the need occurs.

The most important type of exercise for the heart is that known as cardiovascular, cardiorespiratory or aerobic exercise. All of these refer to exertion which requires more oxygen usage by your muscles, which makes you breathe harder and your heart beat faster. Exercises for strength and flexibility may be no less vital to the body as a whole, but they are not as directly important to the heart's healthy functioning.

Assessing your fitness

Before you start an exercise programme, it is well worth getting advice from an exercise professional (see page 72). You can also get an exercise screen (from a personal trainer or health club), which looks at your way of life, medical background and previous exercise patterns, in order to assess your aims and needs in a fitness programme.

Starting with caution

An aerobic exercise programme should ideally be entered into only after a proper evaluation of any cardiovascular risk factors. These include levels of cholesterol and triglycerides in the blood, blood pressure, family history of premature heart disease and any chronic illness such as asthma.

Other types of exercise should be treated with even more caution: strenuous activities such as lifting and holding heavy weights, or squeezing muscles tightly for extended periods, may strain the skeleton and the heart and may elevate blood pressure to very high levels.

If your blood pressure is 140/90 or below then you can exercise safely. However, if it is higher than this you need to speak to your doctor about precautions you should take when exercising, and have your blood pressure checked regularly.

Also, you should speak to your doctor if you have recently suffered an illness or have not exercised for a very long time. It is important to feel confident that there will be no hidden problems that might suddenly develop when you begin exercising.

COMPONENTS OF FITNESS

The basic elements of any good physical fitness programme are exercises designed to increase endurance, flexibility, and strength.

HOW EXERCISE AFFECTS YOUR BODY
When you exercise, your body is put under physical stress. The central nervous system and adrenal glands produce the hormones noradrenaline and adrenaline which cause changes that ensure your body works as efficiently as possible.

Exercise really helps

The Framingham Study (USA) of 5000 people, which began in 1948 and continued for over 40 years, has confirmed that people who do little or no exercise are at greater risk of heart disease than those who do regular, moderate exercise.

Over a period of 12 years, researchers found that those people who had very low levels of activity were five times more likely to die from heart disease than very active people. In cases of sudden death from heart disease, there was a direct and consistent statistical relation to poor fitness levels.

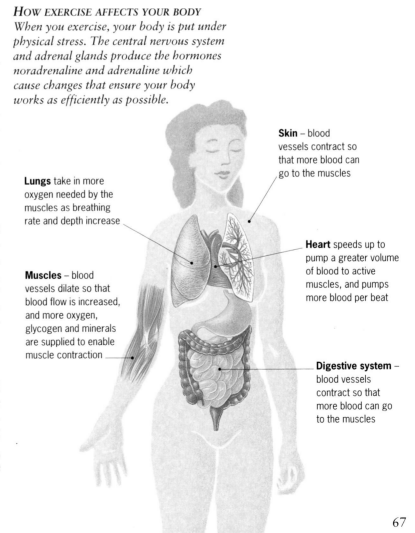

Lungs take in more oxygen needed by the muscles as breathing rate and depth increase

Muscles – blood vessels dilate so that blood flow is increased, and more oxygen, glycogen and minerals are supplied to enable muscle contraction

Skin – blood vessels contract so that more blood can go to the muscles

Heart speeds up to pump a greater volume of blood to active muscles, and pumps more blood per beat

Digestive system – blood vessels contract so that more blood can go to the muscles

The talk test

A good rule of thumb to test whether you are overexercising is to see if, during the activity or just after it, you are able to carry on a conversation with a companion. While working at 50–60 per cent of maximum heart rate, it should be possible to hold a normal conversation without undue disruption to breathing. At 70–80 per cent, your conversation will be punctuated by an increased breathing rate. If you are too winded to talk, you are probably overdoing it and should slow down your pace.

Dynamic or 'aerobic' exercise will increase endurance and has the most positive effect on the health of the cardiovascular system. High-intensity or strength exercises, which are often referred to as 'anaerobic', are important for overall fitness.

Endurance

Aerobic endurance, or stamina, refers to the capacity to postpone fatigue and keep going without gasping for breath or suffering other discomfort. To improve stamina you need to improve the efficiency of your heart and lungs by undertaking regular exercise that lasts for an extended period of time. Intensity of the exercise is important. You should measure your heart rate before, during and after exercising, aiming for your target heart rate zone (see page 70). This varies according to fitness. With regular exercise, as your heart becomes stronger, you can work towards the higher range of your target heart rate zone.

Flexibility

Stretching increases the range of movement in the body's joints, improves the elasticity of the muscles that work the joints, tightens and tones the joints themselves, and also shortens and strengthens the supporting ligaments. Stretching helps slow the decline in mobility that comes with ageing, relieves tension in tired muscles and can help reduce overall stress levels. Since stress is a contributory factor in heart problems, stretching is a useful part of an exercise programme and balances periods of exertion.

Stretching is carried out using safe 'static' techniques, which involve moving slowly into certain postures and holding them for 10–30 seconds.

Stretching is an excellent way to start the day or unwind at the end of a stressful day. Try stretching to soothing music for a very effective relaxation session.

Strength

To make muscles and bones stronger, carefully controlled strength exercises should form part of any exercise routine even though they do not directly affect the heart. Weight-bearing exercises play an important role in the prevention of osteoporosis (bone weakening disease), but sufferers of coronary artery disease or high blood pressure should approach them carefully.

THE FITNESS COMBINATION

A fully-balanced exercise programme should include an aerobic, stretching and toning component for maximum fitness and health. Refer to pages 78 to 81 for more exercises on stretching and toning various parts of your body.

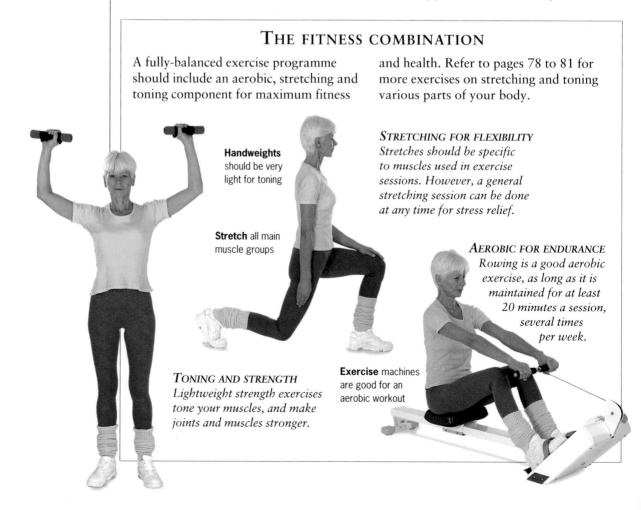

Handweights should be very light for toning

Stretch all main muscle groups

STRETCHING FOR FLEXIBILITY
Stretches should be specific to muscles used in exercise sessions. However, a general stretching session can be done at any time for stress relief.

AEROBIC FOR ENDURANCE
Rowing is a good aerobic exercise, as long as it is maintained for at least 20 minutes a session, several times per week.

TONING AND STRENGTH
Lightweight strength exercises tone your muscles, and make joints and muscles stronger.

Exercise machines are good for an aerobic workout

Exercises designed to improve strength can be performed either with your own body weight, 'free' hand wrist and ankle weights, or machines, and should target all the joints and muscles in a balanced way. They should be carefully prescribed and supervised and performed slowly and carefully, within a joint's normal range of movement. These exercises will not make you muscle-bound, since the weights used are light and because the time period is not sufficient to build-up any visible muscle tissue.

TEST YOUR FITNESS

Try these three tests to find out how fit you are. Keep a record of your scores and redo the tests after a month of regular exercise. If you are not improving at all you may not be trying hard enough. You may wish to seek the advice of a personal trainer (see page 72).

AEROBIC FITNESS INDEX RATING

Calculate your aerobic fitness index (AFI) and compare with the chart below to see how fit you are.

Poor	0–50
Fair	50–79
Good	80–99
Very good	100–119
Excellent	120+

ENDURANCE STEP TEST
Step up and down in time with the beat for 5 minutes. Sit down for a minute, take your pulse for 30 seconds. To calculate your aerobic fitness index (AFI): 30 000 divided by (your 30-second pulse x 5.5). For example, if your 30-second pulse count is 50, then your AFI equals: 30 000 divided by (50 x 5.5) = 109

Use a wide step about 20 cm (8 in) high. Set a metronome at 100–120 beats per minute

MUSCLE STRENGTH RATING

To score, count how many curl-ups you can do in 1 minute and match them against your age and sex.

AGE	20–35	36–50	51–70
WOMEN			
Poor	45	35	25
Fair	50	40	30
Good	55	45	35
Very good	60	50	40
Excellent	65+	55+	45+
MEN			
Poor	50	40	30
Fair	55	45	35
Good	60	50	40
Very good	65	55	45
Excellent	75+	65+	55+

STRENGTH CURL-UP TEST
Lie on your back, knees bent, feet flat on the floor. Keep your lower back pressed to the floor at all times. Place your hands on top of your thighs. Curl your shoulders forward off the floor so that your hands slide up along your legs towards your kneecaps. Uncurl. Repeat for 1 minute.

FLEXIBILITY RATING

To score, see where your fingers touch the tape and match the distance (in centimetres) against your age and sex.

Try to keep your back straight as you reach forward

FLEXIBILITY SIT AND REACH TEST
Lay a tape measure on the floor and secure it to the floor with tape at the 30 cm (12 in) mark and the 75 cm (30 in) mark. Sit astride the tape at the zero mark with legs outstretched and slightly apart.

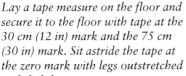

Slowly reach forward with both hands towards your heels. Hold for 3 seconds

AGE	20–35	36–50	51–70
WOMEN			
Poor	40	35	30
Fair	50	45	40
Good	60	55	50
Very good	70	65	60
Excellent	80	75	65
MEN			
Poor	30	25	20
Fair	40	35	30
Good	50	45	40
Very good	60	55	50
Excellent	65	60	55

Blood pressure and fitness

Regular exercise can help reduce high blood pressure. However, if you have very high blood pressure, you will have to avoid certain kinds of strenuous exercise, such as weight lifting.

You should have your blood pressure checked by your doctor. If it is 140/90 or below then you can exercise safely. However, if it is higher than this, ask your doctor to advise you about a safe exercise programme and have your blood pressure checked regularly.

MONITORING YOUR FITNESS

Most people are completely unaware of how fit their heart really is. If you are one of these, it is important to find out so that you can work to certain targets that will keep your heart healthy. There are a number of basic self-assessment tests.

Find out what your maximum heart rate potential and target heart rate zone are, and perform the tests that are shown on page 69 to get an idea of your endurance, flexibility and strength – the three components of fitness. You will need a stop watch and metronome in order to calculate your fitness level accurately. If you have not exercised for a long time, do these tests with caution, taking each stage gradually and be sure to stop immediately if you feel any discomfort. Repeat the tests every few weeks after starting your exercise programme to monitor your progress. Be sure to warm up properly before starting any exercise (see page 78).

Rate of perceived exertion

A simple way to check that you are exercising at the right intensity is to assess how it feels or how you perceive it. Rate of perceived exertion (RPE) is a very quick yet surprisingly accurate way of monitoring your exercise intensity.

It works on the assumption that if you perceive you are working hard then you probably are, and your heart rate is likely to be in the target zone. The scale runs from 6 (no exertion) to 20 (maximum exertion). By adding a zero to each number, you can get a rough approximation of your heart rate. For example, at a rate of perceived exertion of 13 (somewhat hard) your heart rate is approximately 130.

PERCEIVED EXERTION RATES

EXERTION LEVEL	RATING
No exertion at all	6
Very very light	7–8
Very light	9–10
Fairly light	11–12
Somewhat hard	13–14
Hard	15–16
Very hard	17–18
Very very hard	19
The limit of exertion	20

TARGET HEART RATE ZONE

Your target heart rate zone (THRZ) is 60–90 per cent of your maximum heart rate potential and is the range in which fit people should exercise. Unfit people should start at 50–60 per cent and increase their exertion over a few weeks. To check your THRZ, take your pulse half-way into your exercise session or use a heart rate monitor (see page 97).

AGE	MAXIMUM HEART RATE	60% LEVEL	90% LEVEL
20	200	120	180
25	195	117	175
30	190	114	171
35	185	111	167
40	180	108	162
45	175	105	158
50	170	102	153
55	165	99	149
60	160	96	144
65	155	93	140
70	150	90	135

Maximum heart rate

Any exertion that makes your heart beat faster is good exercise for your heart. To get the most from an exercise programme, however, you need to exercise at a rate that is a balance between being sufficiently difficult in order to give your heart a thorough workout, but not so difficult that you are forced to stop after only a few minutes.

Your maximum heart rate potential (MHR) is the uppermost level at which your heart can beat during exertion and varies according to age. The formula for the calculation is: 220 minus your age. So a 40-year-old person will have a MHR of 180. Never aim to exercise at your MHR as you will not be able to sustain this level of intensity and it is not healthy for your heart, but once you know your level you can calculate your target heart rate zone (see above) and make your heart work comfortably within it.

According to the scale above, a 40 year old of average fitness should aim to exercise at a heart rate of 108–162 beats per minute. A very unfit person should aim to exercise at 50–60 per cent of his or her MHR and build up gradually to 90 per cent.

AEROBIC EXERCISE
Riding at moderate speed for at least 20 minutes burns fat and is good for your heart.

AEROBIC AND ANAEROBIC EXERCISE

Aerobic exercise describes any prolonged activity, done for at least 20 minutes, which increases the heart rate, uses oxygen to produce energy for the muscles and breaks down fat for fuel. It includes walking, swimming, jogging, aerobics, dancing and cycling.

Anaerobic exercise refers to short, sharp bursts of strenuous activity in which the oxygen supply in the blood stream is not sufficient to provide energy quickly enough to the muscles, so the muscles use a chemical process without oxygen to break down carbohydrates, not fats. Sprinting, squash, tennis, skiing, team sports and weight lifting are all anaerobic exercises.

The benefits of aerobic exercise

Even a slight increase in intensity of exertion will require the heart to perform more work to pump blood around the body to the muscles and keep pace with the muscles' demand for oxygenated blood. Low-to-moderate intensity exercise allows the heart to increase its workload gradually and therefore allows you to work for longer. This is far better for your heart and muscles than short bursts of strenuous exercise.

Low-to-moderate intensity aerobic exercise is the key to a healthy heart and a healthy circulatory system. With regular participation in aerobic exercise, the heart, lungs and blood vessels are all called upon more frequently – they become more efficient and perform their tasks with less stress. So exercise which felt hard to begin with becomes much easier with practice.

For the full benefits of aerobic exercise you may wish to join a gym. Most offer a wide variety of classes, varying in intensity and level of difficulty. Step classes, for example, involve a routine of exercises done stepping up and down on a box. When you join a gym you should get a fitness assessment and be advised as to which level class you should start with and further advice on when you are ready to move up a level.

EFFECTIVE EXERCISE

The degree of pleasure that you get from exercising is likely to be important in determining how long you stick to it and thus its effectiveness. It is important, therefore, to choose your exercises carefully. The main determining factor is whether you want to exercise alone or in a group. For some, exercising alone is more attractive because of the privacy and the relaxing solitude it provides. The activity and location can also be tailored to individual tastes. Other people prefer the social interaction and mutual encouragement that a group activity offers. Simply exercising with a friend affords companionship and motivation.

What about sports?

Another important factor in choosing activities is what you want to achieve with the exercise. While aerobic activities can play an important role in keeping you healthy, sports such as tennis, squash, skiing, and team sports such as football may not. They are more an exercise for those who are already in good shape than an effective way of becoming fit. In particular, sports that demand high-intensity exercise, such as skiing and squash, or sporadic involvement in competition sports, require a good deal of physical preparation if they are to exercise the heart effectively.

Sporadic involvement in a high intensity exercise or sport, such as a game of football or basketball, will overstrain an unfit heart. A sound low-to-moderate aerobic exercise programme, supported by regular work on strength and flexibility, is more effective in restoring or maintaining basic fitness than any strenuous participation in sports. It is wise to bear in mind the motto: 'Get fit to play sport, don't play sport to get fit.'

ANAEROBIC EXERCISE
Squash is anaerobic and involves short spurts of very intense exercise, and therefore burns carbohydrates rather than fat for energy.

The Personal Trainer

If you are particularly concerned about improving the health of your heart, a personal trainer can devise a programme with that aim in mind. More and more people are enlisting a trainer's specialist skills when they embark on fitness programmes.

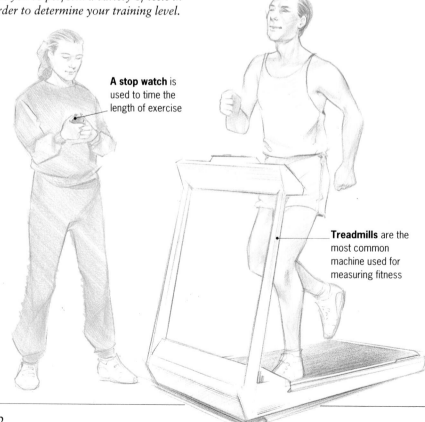

WHAT TO WEAR
Buy the appropriate shoes for your chosen type of exercise. Make sure they are supportive and well-cushioned. Wear comfortable clothing that allows you to move freely and will absorb perspiration. Cotton fabrics are usually best for this. Avoid pure lycra. Dress warmly if exercising in cold weather.

ASSESSING YOUR FITNESS
At the first appointment, the trainer may ask you to perform a variety of tests in order to determine your training level.

A stop watch is used to time the length of exercise

Treadmills are the most common machine used for measuring fitness

Personal trainers use their expert knowledge of fitness to devise and conduct exercise programmes that are tailored to the individual's special needs and levels of fitness. Check your trainer's qualifications: contact the National Register of Personal Trainers. Most personal trainers will also have completed a special course and therefore should have a personal trainer's certificate in addition to the basic qualification. Some trainers may also have a degree or diploma in sports science or exercise studies, although this is not essential. A trainer should have professional insurance and should be certified in Cardiopulmonary Resuscitation (CPR) or First Aid.

Why should I use a personal trainer?
Personal trainers are perfect for people who prefer individual attention and require extra motivation. A personal trainer can not only design a fitness programme for you, but also constantly adapt it to suit your personal circumstances, preferences and personality.

Having a personal trainer means that you can arrange sessions when you find it most convenient, at a time and place that suits you – for example, first thing in the morning, or in the evening and at home, in the office, in a gym or outside.

In addition to giving you advice on exercise, he or she may be able to suggest a suitable diet and advise you on the management of stress, all of which are essential for a healthy heart. Most importantly, the trainer will keep you constantly motivated and ensure that you keep up your programme, at the same time making sure that you exercise using good, safe techniques, so that you avoid injury and derive the greatest benefit.

What happens at the first consultation?
Your trainer will discuss your health, fitness goals and your lifestyle. You will be given a health questionnaire that covers your medical history, including any incidence of heart disease, high blood pressure (hypertension) or back problems.

This information is then used by your trainer to put together a suitable programme for you. Together you will both decide how many weeks you wish to commit yourself to and how you will achieve your goals. This first meeting also allows you and your trainer to get to know each other.

Will I need to take any tests?

This depends upon your aims. If your purpose is to lose weight then your trainer may just take some basic measurements such as your height, weight and body fat percentage (by measuring the thickness of a 'pinch of fat' on your upper arm against the circumference of your arm). This will be used as a yardstick to measure your progress. If your aim is to improve and monitor your fitness, he or she may decide to carry out a more detailed fitness assessment to check your endurance, flexibility, and strength.

How much will it cost?

Personal trainers' fees vary enormously, depending on where you live, whether you train at home or in a gym, and the reputation of the trainer. Although the cost is moderately high, many people feel that the money is well spent because of the improvements in their health. Ask for information from your local health club for an indication of fees, or check with your local fitness instructor's accreditation board.

How often do I need to see a personal trainer?

To achieve your goals and maintain your motivation, you need to have regular contact with your trainer. In your first consultation you will probably make an agreement to meet once, twice, or perhaps three times a week. How often you choose to meet will depend on the time you have available and also on what you can afford. Once a week is the minimum, in which case the trainer will also advise you to exercise on your own at least twice a week.

Whatever you choose, you should be exercising a total of at least three times a week.

How many weeks do I need to commit myself for initially?

Most trainers will ask you to commit to ten sessions to start off with. This could last between three and ten weeks, depending on how often you see your trainer. It is important to undertake this commitment so that you can see results. After this you may wish to renew the ten-session commitment. Although most trainers prefer a definite arrangement, some may be happy to see you for occasional sessions thereafter.

How soon will I see results?

Most beginners should see results within six weeks, perhaps sooner if you exercise more than three times a week. If you miss out on any of your sessions or train sporadically the improvements will come about much more slowly. Your trainer will monitor your progress and change your programme as necessary. If your rate of improvement slows, the trainer may increase the frequency or duration of each session, or raise their intensity.

What happens if I want to discontinue my personal training programme?

It is rare for people to discontinue their programme altogether, but sometimes, for financial reasons or because of work obligations, they may have to reduce the frequency of their training sessions. Nevertheless, your trainer will be able to keep you motivated, and make sure that you maintain your fitness level, even if you have less time available. Once you have embarked on your programme, you must complete your ten-session agreement. Of course, if you are not happy with your trainer for any reason, you may wish to make a change after this or to continue your training alone.

WHAT YOU CAN DO AT HOME

Team up with a friend and act as each other's personal trainer, for motivation and encouragement, or be your own trainer. If you have any heart or other health problems, be sure to consult your doctor first and have regular check-ups. To get started, do the following:

▶ *Write down your long-term fitness goals, then divide these into a series of short-term attainable goals.*

▶ *List the benefits that will help keep you motivated.*

▶ *Think of a solution to any problems you have fitting exercise into your life.*

▶ *Create an exercise plan, listing activities either on a day-by-day or week-by-week basis.*

▶ *Keep an exercise diary, noting down exactly which and how much exercise you did and your improvement in fitness levels at each session.*

EXERCISING ON YOUR OWN
Videotaped exercise routines are useful for motivation as well as for showing you different exercises. Set aside specific times for using the tape, and ask your family not to disturb you.

MAKING EXERCISE PART OF YOUR LIFE

Many people claim to hate exercise or are just too busy for it, but developing an interesting and timely programme is not too difficult if you are aware of all the options.

Exercise should be a natural part of your weekly routine, particularly if you want to keep or achieve a healthy heart. The many aerobic exercises (see page 71) are equally beneficial, but it is a good idea to perform a range of activities.

For instance, you could walk three times per week, swim on Monday, cycle on Wednesday, and do an aerobics class on Friday. This way you will be able to exercise all your muscle groups without becoming bored or overstraining muscles and joints with repetitive movements. And when you feel like a rest, just do a stretching routine (see page 78).

CHANGING HABITS

Adding new layers to your routine or altering the familiar pattern of your day rarely come easily. If you have not exercised for a long time and are quite unfit, you could start off with a regular short exercise, lasting up to 5 minutes and build up to the recommended time step by step.

Even over this short period of time, the benefits to health are almost immediate. Previously sedentary people embarking upon an exercise programme for the first time will achieve impressive improvements in aerobic fitness by exercising at the very modest intensities of around 50 per cent of

THE FITNESS AND WEIGHT LOSS PROGRAMME

Any fitness programme aims to improve your cardiovascular health, burn off body fat, aid weight loss and enhance your overall well-being. Use the one below as a guide only and check it with your doctor. 'Aerobic' refers to supervised classes; as an alternative, do circuit training at home (see opposite).

MONDAY	TUESDAY	WEDNESDAY	THURSDAY	FRIDAY	SATURDAY	SUNDAY
WEEK ONE						
Walk 10 min.	Rest	Cycle 10 min.	Rest	Walk 10 min.	Rest	Rest
WEEK TWO						
Cycle 15 min.	Rest	Walk 15 min.	Rest	Swim 15 min.	Rest	Rest
WEEK THREE						
Rest	Walk 25 min.	Rest	Step 45 min.	Rest	Cycle 25 min.	Rest
WEEK FOUR						
Walk 20 min.	Rest	Aerobic 45 min.	Rest	Cycle 20 min.	Rest	Swim 20 min.
WEEK FIVE						
Swim 25 min.	Rest	Step 45 min.	Rest	Walk 25 min.	Rest	Cycle 25 min.
WEEK SIX						
Walk 30 min.	Swim 30 min.	Rest	Aerobic 45 min.	Cycle 30 min.	Rest	Walk 30 min.

CIRCUIT TRAINING

Performing activities in rotation – as shown below – is ideal for cardiovascular fitness and for strengthening different muscle groups. Join a circuit class at the gym or set up your own circuit at home. Your workout should use different muscle groups and include an aerobic component. Spend 30 seconds to one minute on each exercise. Keep repeating the circuit for at least 20 minutes.

1 Run on the spot: You could also run around the garden as part of your circuit, or up and down the street.

2 Step-ups: For aerobic exercise, step up and down on a box without stopping. If you are very fit, make the step higher.

3 Sit-ups: These are good for stomach muscles. Keep your neck straight. If your neck aches when doing sit-ups then you are not using your stomach muscles.

4 Skipping: Do not lift your feet too high as this may strain your knees. Skipping is beneficial to your heart, but it uses only a few of the muscle groups.

maximum heart rate. Sedentary individuals can increase their aerobic capacity by up to 20 per cent over an eight-week period by running for 20 to 30 minutes three times a week at 50 per cent maximum heart rate.

For regular exercisers who have made improvements, but have then noticed that the rate of these improvements is slowing down, an extra stimulus is required to take them further. This can be achieved by making the exercise more intensive or by increasing its duration.

YOUR EXERCISE PROGRAMME

A cardiovascular exercise session should begin with a 5 minute warm-up, muscle stretching, aerobic exercise for at least 20 minutes, and then a cool-down session.

Warming up

It is essential to warm up to protect muscles, tendons and ligaments. March briskly on the spot or up and down in a small area. Circle hands and feet in both directions to warm up the joints, making them more mobile. Gently stretch the muscles that are going to be used in the activity to follow. In cycling, for example, the ankles and hips need special attention; in swimming, the shoulders, ankles and hips. (See page 78 for stretching exercises.) This should take up a further 5 minutes. Your body should feel warm after you start to exercise. Start your chosen exercise slowly and then gradually increase the pace.

Cooling down

Following the hardest part of the exercise session, which should last a minimum of 20 minutes, a cool-down period should be included in the schedule to allow for the heart rate to return to normal, sweating to be reduced and to prevent muscle cramps and stiffness.

Gradually slow the pace of your exercise, then walk around for a few minutes until your breathing is normal. To slow your breathing, take a deep breath in as you raise your arms up above your head, and breathe out as you bring them down next to your

---

IF YOU HAVE A HEART CONDITION

For those with diagnosed heart disease, be sure to follow these rules:

▶ *Get your doctor's approval to exercise.*

▶ *Start your exercise programme at a slow pace and build up gradually.*

▶ *Do not exercise in extreme weather.*

▶ *Do not do any strenuous exercises.*

▶ *Do not exercise for at least 2 hours after having a bath or eating a meal.*

▶ *Stop exercising immediately if you feel dizzy or faint, experience chest pain, nausea, severe breathlessness, severe palpitations, fatigue, or extreme pain.*

AN EXERCISE SESSION

ACTIVITY	MINUTES
Warm up	5
Stretching	5
Aerobic activity	20–30
Cool down	10
Total session	40–50

sides. Repeat the loosening exercises and stretches you did in your warm up, paying special attention to the muscles you have used the most.

Pace yourself

If you are considering embarking on an exercise programme without the supervision of a trained fitness instructor, it is very important to begin slowly. Even the most gentle exercise causes some muscle damage if you are unaccustomed to it and can make you very sore in the days to follow. If you have not exercised for three to six months, take things very slowly and do not feel bad if you cannot do much at first. Even a 20 minute walk three times a week will benefit your heart.

Try the fitness and weight-loss six-week programme on page 74. This is intended as a guide only. Remain flexible in your approach and be prepared to adapt and modify the programme according to specific situations in your daily life and the kind of aerobic exercise you prefer. If your schedule is too rigid it will only dampen your motivation. More importantly, you should not exercise if you are injured or ill, for example if suffering from a bad cold or flu.

Vary your choice of exercise since a selection of different aerobic activities can help reduce repetitive strain in joints that may occur when just one activity is practised. No single aerobic exercise is superior to any other for improving the health of the cardiovascular system.

Always try to exercise at a minimum of 50–60 per cent of your MHR (see page 68). If you have been exercising regularly for at least six months, you may wish to exercise at 60–70 per cent of your MHR. And for those in good shape, aim for 60–90 per cent of your MHR.

On days where no aerobic exercise is specified, or if you are feeling very tired, why not do some stretching or toning exercises (see pages 78–81) or simply do some relaxation exercises (see page 82).

EXERCISE EQUIPMENT FOR THE HOME

Exercising at home can be as fun and varied as going to a gym or health club and perhaps more comfortable. The equipment below will ensure that you get a good cardiovascular workout. Always read the instructions for the machine and exercise carefully. Place your exercise machine where you will be certain to use it.

STEP MACHINE
This works the legs and bottom and gives your heart a workout.

TRAMPOLINE
Cheapest and most portable of home equipment items, this gives many aerobic benefits.

EXERCISE BICYCLE
Cycles are great for heart and lung fitness, thigh muscle toning and fat burning.

TREADMILL
This allows you to go for a walk or run regardless of weather conditions.

The Angina Sufferer

Angina patients often think they cannot exercise without provoking an attack. However, regular exercise of the right kind and intensity can actually make the heart fitter and reduce the number of pain episodes. Being fitter will also improve general health. Undertaking exercise is one of several lifestyle changes that angina sufferers need to make to improve their condition.

Greg is a 51-year-old bank manager married to Sue, a teacher. They have two children. Greg's lifestyle does not lend itself to keeping fit – he has working lunches in restaurants almost every day. Partly because of all the rich food, his weight has crept up over the past five years. At work there have been rumours of branch mergers and redundancies of senior staff, which has caused Greg to have frequent tension headaches. He has also been feeling uncomfortably breathless after climbing stairs, and he has a tight feeling around his upper chest after walking a short distance. Anxious about his health, as his father died from a heart attack in his sixties, he visits his doctor who diagnoses angina.

WHAT SHOULD GREG DO?

Greg's doctor has prescribed medication which Greg needs to take during his attacks, but he must also act to reduce all the factors that contribute to his angina.

Greg has a moderately raised blood cholesterol level so he needs to follow a low-fat balanced diet, as well as to lose some weight. In addition, he needs to exercise to lose weight, prevent high blood pressure and improve his cardiovascular health in general.

Greg should also find some means of reducing his stress levels and increasing the amount of time he spends relaxing. Getting his family's support in losing weight and exercising more will be vital as will assessing his work future.

Action Plan

EXERCISE
Establish a weekly programme – some solo activities, some with Sue and the kids. Possibly join a health club.

STRESS
Talk to area manager about fears for the future. Think about options if the news is not good. Increase relaxation time.

DIET
Check out low-fat and low-calorie options. Cut down on alcohol consumption. Check cholesterol levels in three months.

DIET
Being overweight increases the risk of heart disease. A low-fat diet is essential for a healthy heart.

STRESS
Tension and anxiety increases a person's heart rate and can precipitate an attack of angina.

EXERCISE
Physical exertion can help angina as it improves heart rate, blood pressure, volume of blood per heartbeat and oxygen supply to the heart.

HOW THINGS TURNED OUT FOR GREG

Greg buys bicycles for the family and they cycle together at weekends. He and Sue go swimming every week. A talk with his manager reassures him that his job is not presently at risk. This reduces his stress levels considerably. He also begins to improve his management techniques to ensure his position. He has lost 6.4 kg (14 lb) in three months, his cholesterol levels are lower and he has only had one angina attack.

Stretching

Before undertaking any aerobic or strength exercise, and after all exercise sessions, it is essential to stretch the muscles to avoid injury. Stretching is also beneficial for improving flexibility, easing stiffness, reducing stress and promoting relaxation.

NECK ROTATION
Start your routine with a neck stretch. Begin with your chin on your chest. Turn your head to the right, aiming your chin to your right shoulder, then rotate to the left, aiming to your left shoulder. Never roll your head back on your neck.

Get your body warm by walking briskly round the block or a park, increasing your stride length and swinging your arms. Alternatively, march on the spot, lifting your knees and pumping your arms.

Move into each position in a slow and controlled way. Do not force yourself, or bounce or jerk your

body. Go as far as you comfortably can. The stretches should not feel painful. Learn to relax into each position and breathe normally.

Perform the complete routine twice. As you become more flexible, hold the stretches for a few seconds longer, eventually building up to 10–30 seconds for each one.

STRETCHES FOR THE UPPER BODY

Make sure you feel warm and relaxed. Start with feet shoulder width apart and back straight. Do not keep knees or elbows rigid.

Clasp fingers with palms facing downwards

UPPER BACK
Bend knees slightly. Raise both arms above your head as you breathe in, interlock fingers and stretch arms upwards fully. Hold for 10 seconds, then exhale as you release.

Reach arm up and over to the side

Circle arms both forwards and backwards

Pull arms back to feel a stretch in the back

SHOULDER CIRCLES
Raise your arms straight in front of you. Move your arms slowly backwards six times, then forwards six times, making a circle each time.

WAIST STRETCH
Reach up with your right arm then bend to your left, placing your other hand on the side of your thigh. Hold for 10 seconds, then repeat on the other side.

CHEST STRETCH
Clasp your hands behind your back, elbows slightly bent, pulling your shoulders backwards. Hold for 10 seconds.

STRETCHES FOR THE LOWER BODY

Muscle strain is most common in the legs, so stretching leg muscles is essential before and after jogging, cycling, skiing, dancing, tennis, squash and field sports. Gentle stretching of the lower back is also important before and after exercise, but should be done with caution.

INNER THIGH STRETCH
Stand with feet wide apart and place both hands on thighs. Bend your right knee so it makes a right angle over the foot, keeping your left leg straight. Make sure your right knee is in line with your right foot. Hold for 10 seconds, then repeat on other side.

Keep back flat on floor

LOWER BACK STRETCH
Lie on your back. Keeping your shoulders down on the ground, hug your knees close to your chest and hold for 10 seconds.

C A U T I O N
Take care not to overstretch. Do not bounce or jerk. Hold a stretch in position then release. Stop if you feel any pain while stretching.

Bend knee at right angle

Keep foot flat on the ground

Reach towards toes, do not bounce

Keep back straight

Hold foot or ankle

Keep knees together

Front leg should be relaxed

Keep foot facing forward

HAMSTRING STRETCH
Place right heel on a chair, keeping leg straight. Bend forward at the waist towards the leg until you feel a stretch in your hamstrings. Hold for 6–10 seconds then repeat with the other leg.

FRONT THIGH STRETCH
Bend your left leg back, and hold onto your ankle or foot. Keep thighs parallel and hold for 6–10 seconds. Repeat with the other leg.

CALF STRETCH
Place both hands on a wall at shoulder height, with arms straight. Move your feet back until your legs are at a 45 degree angle to the floor. Bring left foot forward, keeping right leg straight. Adjust distance between feet until you feel a stretch in your right calf. Hold for 6–10 seconds then repeat with other leg.

Toning

A toning programme firms your muscles, strengthens your body, and improves your overall shape and posture. An exercise programme needs to include a toning component as well as stretching and cardiovascular activities.

WARMING UP
Walk briskly on the spot or around the room until you feel warm. Circle your joints. Stretch for 15 minutes until muscles feel loosened.

Increased muscle means a higher metabolic rate and more efficient energy burning in your body, even if toning does not contribute directly to cardiovascular health.

If you have high blood pressure or a diagnosed heart condition, you should consult your doctor before doing these exercises. Always warm up before toning to avoid injury.

Handweights are used in some of the exercises shown below. Choose very light ones (they start from 1 kg/2 lb 4 oz). There is no need to lift anything heavier, as the aim is to tone not build muscle bulk.

TONING EXERCISES FOR THE LEGS

Always keep your back straight when doing these exercises. Do only as much as you feel comfortable with. Stop if you feel very tired.

Keep shoulders relaxed

LUNGES FOR LEGS AND BOTTOM
Take a large step forward with your right leg, bending both knees so that your right knee is at a 90 degree angle. Keeping your back straight, push back with the right leg and return to starting position. Repeat ten times for each leg.

Knee should be over ankle

SQUATS FOR LEGS AND BOTTOM
Stand with feet just over shoulder-width apart. Hold handweights in each hand. Squat down, keeping knees in line with toes. Return to starting position. Repeat 20 times.

Thighs should be parallel to floor

CAUTION
If you have not done squats before, do not use handweights; bend legs only halfway down to avoid straining your knees.

TIPS FOR TONING

Do not use handweights if you have been diagnosed with high blood pressure.

Handweights are optional, but they should always be light enough to do at least ten repetitions without causing muscle strain. When your strength improves, increase the number of repetitions rather than using heavier weights. It is also more important to do each exercise correctly than to strain to increase repetitions.

Always breathe out as you go into the exercise, and breathe in as you relax out of it.

UPPER BODY TONING

Raise arms together

Keep handweight close to body as you lift it up

Front knee should be bent

Keep knees slightly bent

Keep elbows still as you raise hands

ONE ARM ROWS FOR UPPER BACK
Hold weight in left hand. Step forward with right foot. Start with left arm hanging down, then pull weight up towards waist, bending at elbow. Slowly lower. Repeat 20 times with each arm.

SHOULDER PRESS
Stand straight with feet facing forward. Hold handweights at shoulder level, palms facing forwards. Straighten arms as you push the weights upwards then slowly lower them. Repeat 20 times.

BICEP CURLS
Hold handweights by your sides. Slowly curl up the weights, bringing hands towards your shoulders. Keep your upper arms still. Return to starting position. Repeat 20 times.

Keep back flat

PRESS-UPS FOR CHEST AND TRICEPS
Start on all fours. Place hands apart just beyond shoulder width. Slowly lower trunk until elbows are bent at a 90 degree angle, but do not rest on the floor. Push yourself up using your arms. Keep abdomen taut. Repeat 20 times.

BENCH DIPS FOR TRICEPS
Sit on the edge of a chair, hands beside you, fingers forwards. Keep feet flat on floor and knees bent. Move your bottom forward just free of the chair. Lower yourself as you bend your elbows to a 90 degree angle, taking your body weight on your arms. Straighten your arms back to starting position. Repeat 20 times.

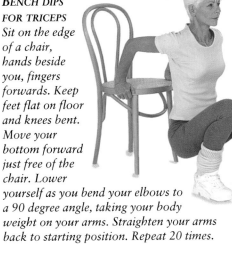

ABDOMINAL TONING

CURL-UPS FOR ABDOMINAL MUSCLES
Lie on the floor, knees bent, feet flat on floor. Place hands by your temples. Curl your head and shoulders off the floor as you breathe out, hold for 1 to 2 seconds, slowly uncurl. Keep lower back on the floor at all times. Repeat 20 times.

COOL DOWN
Stretch all the main muscle groups (see page 78) and walk around slowly until your body has cooled down.

81

THE ART OF RELAXATION

Relaxation exercises can relieve the symptoms of stress, thereby reducing your risk of high blood pressure and heart problems, as well as improving your quality of life.

A quick relaxation technique

Lie down on the floor and, starting with the toes, tense each set of muscles as you breathe in, hold for 2 seconds at maximum tension, then release gradually as you breathe out. Using the same technique, move up to the ankles, calves, knees, thighs and so on – even your scalp and ears can hold tension. Do not do the whole routine with an intense scowl of concentration on your face. Repeat the entire exercise two or three times to promote relaxation, as well as to increase circulation to tense areas.

Anxiety often manifests itself as headaches, knitted brows, aching neck and shoulder muscles, and back pains. The Framingham Heart Study (USA), which from 1948 examined risk factors in 5000 people, monitored the psychological profiles of more than 1000 volunteers over a period of 40 years. Their results suggest that stress does not stop at causing minor aches and pains but that through the long-term and less tangible effects of hypertension, also known as high blood pressure, its effects have more life-threatening implications. The mechanism is still unclear. However it is known that stress and tension raise the level of adrenaline in the blood, which causes blood vessels to contract and forces the heart to pump all the harder, thereby raising blood pressure. In addition, increased adrenaline levels may cause raised cholesterol levels. Stress is thereby associated with a raised chance of heart disease as prolonged hypertension and raised cholesterol are major factors in coronary heart disease.

RELAXATION
Find a quiet place to lie down and relax. Your back should be flat and straight and your neck only slightly raised on a pillow. Make sure you are not too hot or too cold, and that no one will disturb you.

COMBATING DISEASE WITH RELAXATION
Recent studies conducted in the United States show that relaxation is one of the most important safeguards against hypertension and heart disease. Another study, by C. Patel in 1981 reported in the *British Medical Journal*, showed that heart patients who were trained in relaxation techniques stayed healthier for considerably longer periods than untrained patients on hypertensive medication. Whether as a prevention or as a cure, following a regular relaxation programme is therefore a sound step in promoting the health of the heart.

In addition to fighting stress and hypertension, the power of the mind can also be used to ward off other illnesses. In 1991 Dr Karen Olness, professor of paediatrics at Ohio's Case Western Reserve University, taught a group of haemophiliacs to reduce bleeding after an injury. By using relaxation techniques, they were able to lower their blood pressure, thereby slowing blood loss. Some members of the group also used visualisation (see page 83) to control their bleeding. One child in the group imagined tiny airplanes flying through his veins dropping clotting bombs to stop the bleeding.

Despite such promising findings, some doctors are still not convinced that relaxation and visualisation can really help control disease. Relaxation exercises, however, have certainly been found to ease the physical discomforts of minor illness which drain your energy, and creative visualisation exercises may be helpful in fighting illnesses caused by stress, including heart disease.

Some people believe that they do not have much of an imagination and expect visualisation to be hard. In fact, everyone uses

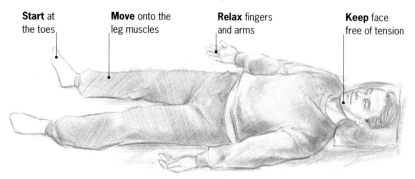

Start at the toes

Move onto the leg muscles

Relax fingers and arms

Keep face free of tension

their mental abilities to create images all the time. If you are asked to think of how to get to the supermarket, your imagination will make a series of pictures showing you the way. If you are asked what clothes are in your wardrobe, in your mind's eye you can take out each item and describe it. You can use this same skill to look at the tension spots in your body, and to focus on high blood pressure.

VISUALISATION

The first step in using visualisation is to take the time to examine mentally how your body feels – do you have any pain or tension anywhere, are you feeling stressed mentally?

Next, imagine that you are able to visit the tension within your arteries and in some way get rid of it, perhaps by facing it down. Take three slow, deep breaths right down into your abdomen and imagine yourself shrinking until you are small enough to travel through your arteries. Now, with your new, very small self, find a way into your own body, perhaps in through your mouth, and set off on a journey of exploration. Think of your bloodstream carrying you towards any tense spots gently and unhurriedly, but inexorably.

When you arrive, think about what the artery looks like. Is it blocked, or are the muscles constricted? Now look at the artery and consider what form or colour it is. How do you feel about it – are you resigned to it, angry and impatient with it, surprised to find it there at all?

Next, consider what would need to happen for the artery to get better. For example, you might be able to dismantle it bit by bit, dissolve the blockage, scrub the artery walls, or thin the blood. Finally, come back out of your body the way you came in and take a few deep breaths.

Initially you may find this process a little strange and difficult, but with practice you will be able to do it much more quickly and easily, and you will be able to start taking active steps towards relieving high blood pressure, or using this technique to reduce tension anywhere in your body.

Find your place in the sun

A relaxation exercise called 'Journey to the Golden Sun' can boost your circulation and sense of well-being. Lie down and relax completely by taking half a dozen slow,

FLOAT TO RELAX

If a relaxed mind leads to a fit body and a healthy heart, taking some time out to float peacefully in a flotation tank is an ideal way to let go of the stresses of modern life.

Little bigger than a bath, this totally enclosed tank is filled with very salty water on which you float effortlessly. Inside the tank there is no light to disturb the imagination and no sound to intrude, and all you will feel is a slight caressing where the surface of the water touches your skin. Virtually all of the input to the brain comes via the sensory nerves, so by shutting out sensation, the flotation tank provides the ultimate relaxation experience.

Most people spend up to half an hour inside the tank, almost unaware of the passage of time.

The tank can be opened from the inside if you wish to leave, but most people are surprised when the tank is opened at the end of the session. You will soon get used to having nothing to do, nothing to look at and nothing to hear.

BACK TO THE WOMB
By mimicking the first nine months of forgotten bliss, the womb-like effect of a flotation tank promotes relaxation in a way nothing else can approach.

IDEAL STRESS RELIEF
Gradually allow your attention to drift to your body and how it feels. Become aware of each part of your body. Relax any areas of tension.

Wear a cap and ear plugs to protect hair and ears from salt

deep breaths, right down to the bottom of your lungs. Each time you breathe out hold for the count of three at the end, and let all your tension drain away.

Then start to imagine a golden sun above you. In your mind, build up the picture until the sun is beautiful, bright and warm. Imagine that a beam of light drops from the sun and collects you up, transporting you to the very centre of the sun. Your arms and legs are spread to let the sun fill your entire being with gold. Really feel the energy going into your body. If you like, you can add a series of suggestions at this point. For instance, you might tell yourself: 'I can feel the energy from the sun passing into my body, drawing all the energy it needs and soothing away all my tensions. The sun's energy will revitalise my entire body, passing into every cell and every organ of my body.' Stay in the light and warmth for as long as you like, and then return slowly with the sun's golden rays still coursing through your veins. Feel your blood flowing with vigour and power.

Your own haven

A lot of people have their own 'safe place' which they 'visit' in their visualisation exercises. It could be a place you have actually been to or an entirely imaginary one: a beautiful beach, a hut in the mountains or a clearing in a forest. Be creative with inventing your haven – are there trees, a stream, a waterfall, a special seat to relax in or clothes that you like to wear whilst there?

Whenever you are feeling stressed or anxious about something, close your eyes and transport yourself to this place. If you are having problems with someone at work or with a personal relationship, take that person with you into your haven in your visualisation exercise and imagine that you are sorting out the problem. This often has the effect of making you more relaxed around the person and creates a better atmosphere for resolving things.

A QUICK ESCAPE
Visualising an idyllic setting can be extremely relaxing and a good way to remove yourself from a stressful situation. Decide on your own ideal place and use it as your haven – move your mind there whenever you feel the need to relax.

POSITIVE THINKING

When you know how to relax your body, you are likely to find that negative moods disappear and that you have a sense of well-being and a more positive viewpoint on life.

To enhance your positive feelings about yourself and your life, take a moment to watch what is happening in your mind. Do you tend to get stuck in thought patterns which are going nowhere? Or do you feel helpless or powerless in some parts of your life? If you can sum up your negative feelings in one sentence, you can change your feelings into a positive statement which will support you, and generate good feelings instead of bad. For instance, if you feel crestfallen when your boss finds fault with you, you could try repeating to yourself 'I am sensible and intelligent and good at my job'. If you feel at a loss when dealing with a difficult family member, try saying: 'I am patient, capable and resourceful.' Just as repeated negative statements can undermine self-esteem, so positive thoughts can generate good feelings. If you repeat these to yourself on a regular basis you will soon begin to feel better about yourself. Write positive affirmations in large letters and stick them on your bedroom walls so that you see them as soon as you get up in the morning and just before you go to sleep at night. You may even want to make a tape of affirmations, repeating your positive characteristics over and over again.

Some people like to keep a journal to record both negative and positive thoughts. This is very useful for analysing what kind of situations get you down and what makes you feel on top of things.

An extended stroll in the open air, a long, lazy soak in a warm bath, or the absolute tranquillity of a flotation tank are ideal moments to explore and elaborate some positive statements about yourself, and to begin your 'reprogramming' into a more positive attitude about your life.

CHAPTER 5

DIAGNOSIS AND TREATMENT OPTIONS

Symptoms of heart problems are an early warning system to alert you to seek help. Techniques and equipment for investigating heart and circulatory disorders are better than ever and can usually provide an accurate diagnosis. Natural therapies provide further diagnostic techniques which complement the conventional ones, as well as natural treatment options to aid recovery.

SIGNS AND SYMPTOMS

Although some heart and circulatory diseases may be doing their damage 'silently', there are usually warning signs and symptoms that, if recognised early enough, could save your life.

First aid for an angina attack

Help the person to sit down and ensure that he or she rests. If the person is already on medication for angina, assist him or her to take it. Calm the person down.

If symptoms persist for more than 20 minutes after these measures, call for medical help.

There are a wide variety of symptoms that accompany heart or circulatory disease. Having one or more of these does not necessarily mean you have heart disease, but you should visit your doctor to rule out it or any other problem.

CHEST PAIN

Causes of chest pain that need to be eliminated before a diagnosis of heart disease is made include indigestion or heartburn (excess acid from the stomach), which can occur after eating; strained muscle, broken rib or trapped nerve; an inflammation of a rib joint; or a lung infection (chest pain related to lung disease is usually most severe on each in-breath). If, however, the chest pain is due to coronary heart disease, then the pain is very distinct. It can be just a twinge or quite severe. The centre of the chest feels very tight and heavy or gripping, and this feeling may spread to the left or sometimes right shoulder, arm, neck, throat or jaw. It usually lasts five to ten minutes, and angina medication sprayed or sucked in the mouth can relieve it within a minute.

If attacks of chest pain last longer than 20 minutes or do not respond to medication, and recur over several days, seek medical help urgently.

Angina attacks

Angina pectoris or angina is the name given to the pain that results from the narrowing of one or more of the coronary arteries due to atherosclerosis, which severely reduces the blood supply and oxygen delivery to the heart muscle. During exercise, stress or emotional upset, the heart muscle has to work harder than usual and needs more oxygen to function properly, hence angina is usually brought on by these situations. Attacks are more likely when you are walking uphill or quickly, or when you are tense or excited. In some cases, though, an attack of angina can come on when resting. Slowing or calming down usually eases the pain and no permanent damage to the heart is done, although angina can signal that you are at risk of a heart attack.

Conventional treatment

A doctor will carry out various tests, such as an exercise ECG (see page 93), to determine the severity of your angina and its causes, then drugs may be prescribed to prevent or treat the attacks. The doctor will also advise dietary changes (such as reducing fat intake) and stress management. If your arteries are badly blocked, the doctor may recommend bypass surgery or balloon angioplasty (see page 111).

SYMPTOMS OF HEART DISEASE

The most common and immediate symptoms of heart disease are indicated here. Less common and more long-term symptoms include skin changes and changes in coordination and sensation.

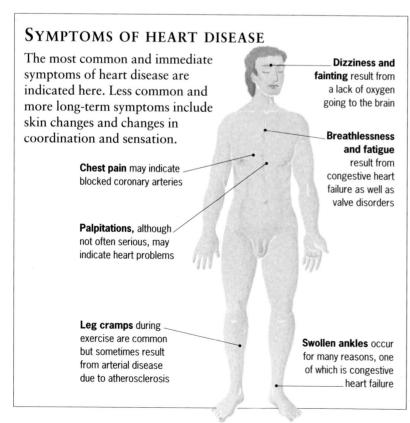

Dizziness and fainting result from a lack of oxygen going to the brain

Breathlessness and fatigue result from congestive heart failure as well as valve disorders

Chest pain may indicate blocked coronary arteries

Palpitations, although not often serious, may indicate heart problems

Leg cramps during exercise are common but sometimes result from arterial disease due to atherosclerosis

Swollen ankles occur for many reasons, one of which is congestive heart failure

Treating angina naturally

For regular sufferers of angina, a trained herbalist may help relieve symptoms. He or she may prescribe teas or infusions. Those herbs said to help angina include hawthorn berry and lily-of-the-valley, which dilate the arteries, and motherwort, a relaxant that is believed to strengthen the heart. Other useful herbs include garlic, bromelain (from pineapple), and lime blossom, all of which have anticoagulant properties.

Acupuncture has long been used in the East to treat angina, but orthodox doctors in the West do not recommend it as an exclusive treatment and suggest it is used in conjunction with prescribed medication. Acupuncture is beneficial for relaxation and pain relief, both of which make angina much easier to deal with.

Some natural therapists prescribe nutritional supplements, such as the antioxidant vitamins (see page 59), as these may help clear blocked arteries.

DIZZINESS AND FAINTING

Most attacks of dizziness – feeling light-headed and unsteady for a few seconds – are not serious. Low blood pressure is a common cause. If these attacks recur frequently with no known cause, however, they could be an indication of heart or circulatory disease. Recurrent dizziness may be a sign that not enough blood is getting to the brain and that there may be a blockage in the heart.

Fainting (also called syncope) is a temporary loss of consciousness due to a lack of oxygen reaching the brain. Again, fainting attacks are usually harmless and may occur simply because you have been standing for too long in a hot or stuffy atmosphere such as a packed train carriage. But in rare cases, fainting attacks could indicate a blockage in the heart, transient ischaemia to the brain (temporary stroke) or heart rhythms which are too fast or too slow. Consult your doctor if you faint frequently.

PALPITATIONS

Fluttering or thumping sensations in the chest or neck are known as palpitations. You perceive your heart missing beats or beating rapidly or thumping in the chest.

Emotional upset, stomach upsets, exercise, fever, anxiety and fear can all speed up the heartbeat and induce palpitations, and elderly people may experience palpitations

Pathway to health

Palpitations, even when harmless, can be unnerving, but a herbalist may be able to help you ease them. He or she may recommend that you drink calming, sleep-inducing herbal teas such as camomile and valerian. Other teas recommended for palpitations include bugleweed, mistletoe or hawthorn berry which are believed to help strengthen the heart. Night blooming cereus is used in treating irregularities in heart rate and rhythm.

You should, however, consult a trained herbalist for the best treatment for your symptoms, as some herbs can be harmful.

even if their hearts are normal. Although palpitations can feel very frightening they are rarely serious and, unless they are persistent, should not cause concern.

Palpitations caused by heart disease, on the other hand, feel like the heart is beating very rapidly or very slowly, and are usually accompanied by other symptoms such as sweating, faintness, chest pain and dizziness. These kind of palpitations usually occur unexpectedly and are a sign that the heart's rhythm is seriously disturbed – the sinoatrial node is at fault. A heartbeat that has an irregular rhythm or rate is called an arrhythmia and these have several causes.

Atrial fibrillation

This is an arrhythmia that occurs when the muscles in the atria do not contract together but instead flutter continuously, making the heart beat fast and irregularly. Atrial fibrillation causes palpitations and sometimes

WHAT TO DO IF YOU FEEL FAINT
Place your head between your knees and take deep breaths. If the feeling of faintness persists, lie down in a cool place with plenty of fresh air, and raise your legs on a cushion to restore blood supply to the brain. Loosen any restrictive clothing. Rest until you feel better. If breathing is difficult, get medical help.

Acupressure: apply pressure to the point that is two-thirds of the way between the middle of your top lip and your nose.

Substances that cause palpitations
Many substances can provoke a rapid heart-beat, such as various prescribed drugs, nicotine from smoking, and alcohol and caffeine. This is rarely serious. However, if you do experience severe palpitations you should stop intake or use of the substance responsible (if you can identify it).

Ectopic heartbeats

Irregular or ectopic heartbeats feel like a missed beat or a thud in the chest, because they have originated in the wrong part of the heart instead of the sinoatrial node, which normally regulates the heartbeat (see page 20). This makes the sequence of the electrical currents go out of order. Though unnerving to most people, these heartbeats are not dangerous and almost everyone will experience them once in a while. Drinking coffee or alcohol are common causes.

chest pain, breathlessness, light-headedness or fatigue. Blood in the atria does not flow normally so clots may form. These may break free and cause a stroke, heart attack or damage to other organs.

Tachycardia

When the heart beats too fast – over 100 beats per minute compared with a normal rate of 70 to 80 – you may feel weak, become short of breath and sweat a great deal. Most tachycardias are totally harmless. Very occasionally, however, they are an indication that something is wrong with the ventricles (the lower chambers of the heart) and can result in serious injury to other vital organs such as the brain, lungs or liver.

High or low concentrations of minerals such as potassium and magnesium can cause tachycardia. These minerals are often used as salt substitutes by people who have high blood pressure. The levels of these minerals in the blood can also be affected by certain drugs, including diuretics. If you are taking any medication and experience palpitations, consult your doctor immediately.

Bradycardia

This is a very slow heartbeat. During sleep and in super-fit people the heart rate is usually slow. But in other cases if it goes below 50 beats per minute, you will feel tired and dizzy, and this is a sign that something may be wrong with your heart.

BREATHLESSNESS AND FATIGUE

During strenuous exercise it is quite normal to feel out of breath if you are unfit, because the lungs can't keep up with the heart's demand for oxygen. But feeling breathless or extremely tired when you are at rest or doing low-intensity exercise may mean that your heart is not pumping properly or that its valves are faulty. In these cases, blood seeps back into the lungs, making them congested. Extreme fatigue may occur as tissues become starved of oxygen-rich blood.

Breathlessness and fatigue may simply indicate that you are stressed or run down or have a minor illness. If breathlessness occurs only at night, however, or when you are lying down, it may signal heart failure. To relieve breathlessness when lying down, prop yourself up on pillows. If breathlessness persists, consult your doctor.

LEG CRAMPS

When the circulation of blood to the legs is partially or totally blocked due to a narrowing of the arteries, the muscles do not get enough oxygen and muscle spasms may occur. Leg cramps are quite common during strenuous exercise or when you are unfit, but if you have them after a short walk or when you are walking very quickly or uphill (and they stop as soon as you rest), then you may have a leg arterial disease called intermittent claudication (see page 129).

Leg cramps caused by arterial disease may also be brought on by extreme cold, or medication that causes the constriction of the blood vessels. The location of the blockage in the arteries will determine which part of your leg gets cramped. Consult your doctor if you have persistent cramps.

SWOLLEN ANKLES

Swelling or oedema occurs when fluid leaks from the blood into tissues. Excess tissue fluid in the lower limbs can be the result of several conditions, including kidney damage, premenstrual fluid retention, starvation and vitamin B deficiency.

EASING LEG CRAMPS

It is important to find out the cause of continued leg cramps as they may indicate arterial disease. To relieve the immediate discomfort, ask someone to massage your leg. If you have no one to assist you, have a warm bath to relax, then gently stretch your leg muscles and apply self massage.

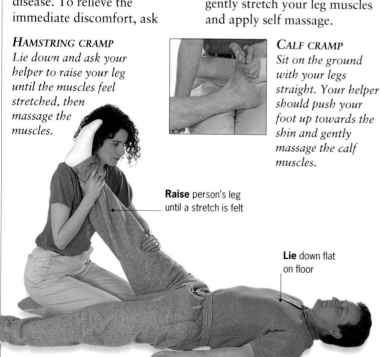

HAMSTRING CRAMP
Lie down and ask your helper to raise your leg until the muscles feel stretched, then massage the muscles.

CALF CRAMP
Sit on the ground with your legs straight. Your helper should push your foot up towards the shin and gently massage the calf muscles.

Raise person's leg until a stretch is felt

Lie down flat on floor

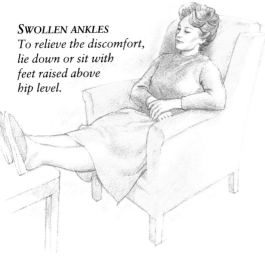

SWOLLEN ANKLES
To relieve the discomfort, lie down or sit with feet raised above hip level.

Gravity may often contribute to oedema, particularly in obese people. But even people of normal weight can get swollen ankles from standing for long periods, living in hot climates or on long journeys on airplanes. A blood clot can cause oedema if it blocks a vein. Pregnant women and convalescents often suffer from swollen ankles.

Swelling may be attributable to heart failure when the heart is unable to pump blood out effectively so incoming blood banks up in the veins and leaks into tissues. Swelling in the ankles is the most common symptom, but the fluid build-up can also cause abdominal discomfort and breathlessness. Consult a doctor if you have persistent swelling in the ankles and legs, and you

have a family history of heart disease or other major risk factors. As a test, press the swelling. If this leaves a dent on the skin's surface (called 'pitting oedema') it is more likely to be related to heart disease.

To relieve swollen ankles, wear loose, comfortable clothing. Support stockings may be necessary. Do not sit with your legs crossed, and avoid standing still for long periods. Sit or lie with legs raised above hip level to relieve swelling. If you are travelling by airplane, walk up and down the aisle as often as possible. Cut down on salt as it causes fluid retention. Gently massage your ankles to stimulate blood flow, using a massage oil such as tea tree or eucalyptus. Drink diuretic herbal teas such as dandelion, yarrow and lily-of-the-valley.

SKIN CHANGES

Unusually white, bluish, reddish or black skin, or recurrent sores that do not heal, may indicate cardiovascular problems. The usual cause is a blockage in arteries or veins.

SUDDEN CHANGES IN SENSES

Vision or speech disturbances, paralysis, weakness and numbness may all indicate a stroke or transient ischaemic attack (temporary stroke). These are usually the result of arterial blockages because of a clot that impedes blood flow to the brain.

SHOCK

Shock is a combination of symptoms, including very low blood pressure, loss of consciousness (sometimes), cold, clammy skin, pale face and poor breathing, which may be induced by a heart attack. If someone is in shock:

▶ *Lie the victim down so the head is below the level of the heart.*

▶ *If the victim is not breathing, give mouth-to-mouth resuscitation (see page 116).*

▶ *Raise the victim's legs if this does not interfere with breathing.*

▶ *If the victim appears unconscious, place in a comfortable position on his or her side. Call medical help immediately.*

HELP FOR A HEART ATTACK

The main warning sign of a heart attack is persistent, crushing pain in the centre of the chest, which may spread to shoulders, neck, arms, throat, jaw, back or abdomen. The victim may also feel breathless, faint, frightened, sick, weak or sweaty. An attack requires immediate medical attention and first aid if possible.

1 *Call for medical help immediately if you suspect that someone is having a heart attack.*

2 *Sit the person in a comfortable position if conscious. Reassure him or her and keep calm. Loosen clothing.*

3 *If the person is unconscious, has stopped breathing due to a cardiac arrest and you are properly trained, give cardiopulmonary resuscitation (see page 116). Otherwise, wait for medical help.*

DIAGNOSTIC TESTS

Some symptoms of heart disease are also those of less serious health problems. Doctors use a range of tests available to confirm or rule out a diagnosis of heart disease.

A doctor can learn a great deal about someone's heart just by paying careful attention to a description of the symptoms and by making a physical examination. What is learnt, together with the person's medical history and lifestyle risk factors, such as smoking, may indicate the presence of heart disease. But further tests are usually necessary for a diagnosis.

Listening to the heart through a stethoscope is a simple procedure, but it elicits valuable information if there are abnormal sounds that can indicate a heart disorder. All doctors are trained to do this. More specialist training, however, is required to carry out and interpret electrocardiograms, chest x-rays, Doppler scanning, nuclear scanning, CT and PET scans, MRI and cardiac catheterisation. Your symptoms will determine which tests you have.

LISTENING TO THE HEART

The sound of the heartbeat comes from the closing of the heart's four valves (see page 20). Using a stethoscope, a doctor will listen for abnormal sounds when the valves open and as blood flows through them. If there is an abnormal sound, such as a snap, click or murmur, the valve may be damaged. For instance, a snapping noise indicates that a valve is abnormally narrow (stenosed). A clicking sound suggests that a heart valve is faulty. The click is caused by the sudden closing and opening of the abnormal valve.

A murmur is a whooshing noise that is heard between normal heart sounds, when blood leaks back through a valve or passes through a narrowed valve or into the wrong part of the heart.

Doctors also listen for other sounds such as whoops, knocks, rubs and gallops, all of which indicate various abnormalities. As the murmur may change with position and breathing, your doctor will ask you to breathe in and out and adopt different positions in order to listen to your heart.

BLOOD TESTS

Analysing blood and other body fluids provides further information about the heart. Blood tests are used to check the blood cell count, oxygen, lipid and enzyme levels, the presence of anaemia (which may be made worse by heart disease), and clotting factors. Blood tests can also be used to assess the function of the kidneys and liver. Irregularities in either can be caused by damage to the organ, due to heart disease.

PHYSICAL EXAMINATION

During a physical examination, your doctor will check the following:

SOUNDS

The doctor will listen to your breath sounds to tell if there is excess fluid in your lungs; to your heart for abnormal sounds; and to your blood vessels for whispering sounds that indicate obstruction.

VENOUS PULSE

The doctor will watch your jugular vein to see if the right heart is pumping normally.

HEART RATE AND RHYTHM

The doctor will feel your pulse at various places to assess these. The places where the pulse is measured include wrist, neck, groin, inner elbows, behind knees, abdomen, top of feet and ankles.

BLOOD PRESSURE

The doctor will measure your blood pressure to get information on the pumping ability of your heart and arterial resistance. If your blood pressure is high your heart will be overworking.

SWELLING

Your ankles, shins, thighs, lower back, abdomen and hands will be checked for fluid retention.

HOMEOPATHIC DIAGNOSIS

Homeopathy is the use of dilute but powerful natural remedies to treat illness. It is a holistic therapy because it takes all aspects of the patient into account: body, mind and spirit. Because of this approach, homeopathy is very beneficial for overall health as well as the health of the heart.

At the initial consultation a homeopath will ask you questions about your physical symptoms as well as your reactions to work, other people, stress, environment and the weather; your moods, dreams and hopes, fears and major events in your life; your childhood and adolescence; and any relevant family history. Based on this information, a homeopath will arrive at a diagnosis and prescribe the appropriate remedies.

It is always advisable first to seek the opinion of your doctor concerning the health of your heart, but homeopathy can complement the techniques of orthodox medicine.

Lipids

Your blood will be tested for low-density lipoprotein (LDL) and high-density lipoprotein (HDL) cholesterol levels as well as triglycerides (see page 53). Lipid tests are inaccurate by up to five per cent so your doctor may test you on two different occasions. You may have to fast the night before your blood lipid test.

Enzymes

After a heart attack, certain enzymes, called cardiac enzymes, are released into the bloodstream by the damaged heart muscle. Measuring the levels of these enzymes gives an indication of how much muscle has been damaged, and also helps to narrow down possible diagnoses. It may take one to two days after a heart attack for these enzyme changes to be detected in the blood.

Oxygen levels

The oxygen content of your blood may be measured at different sites of your body, and may be taken from both veins and arteries. This will identify which part of the heart is inadequate at pumping blood.

Clotting

Blood can be tested for how long it takes to clot. People whose blood clots abnormally quickly, and are therefore at risk of clots in their arteries, may sometimes be put on medication to 'thin the blood'.

ELECTROCARDIOGRAPHY

Electrocardiography (ECG) is probably the most frequently used test for diagnosing heart disease. Together with the exercise ECG (stress testing), it is used for assessing all types of heart rate and rhythm disturbances and for distinguishing coronary heart disease from other types of heart disorders. It is a safe, quick and painless test that records the electrical activity of the heart. As no electricity actually goes into the patient from the machine, there is no danger whatsoever of an electric shock.

How an ECG works

Electrocardiography detects the flow of electricity through the heart associated with each heartbeat. The machine used in this test records the pattern of electrical impulses on a continuously moving strip of paper or a monitor. The image it produces is called an electrocardiogram. Different waves on the graph represent the electrical impulses as they travel to different parts of your heart.

If the heart muscle is damaged, then the electrical impulses become altered and an abnormal pattern is detected.

During the test, the person either sits or lies down. Electrodes (gel pads) are taped to each of the arms and legs and to six places on the front and left side of the chest. Jelly is placed on the skin where the electrodes are attached to ensure good contact. These electrodes are connected by 12 wires to the ECG machine which amplifies the electrical impulses before recording them.

What the ECG is used for

A standard ECG test is usually used to pick up abnormalities of heart rhythm and to identify defects in the conduction of electrical impulses through the heart. It can also detect old and recent heart attacks and give an indication of whether the heart is enlarged or not pumping properly.

The standard ECG test, however, does have its limitations. Sometimes it shows 'abnormalities' when the heart is healthy. At other times it suggests nothing is wrong

ECG readings

Electrocardiograms give useful information about the health of the heart. Different shapes show different heart problems.

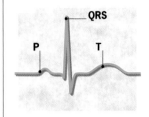

This ECG graph shows a normal heartbeat with regular P, QRS and T wave patterns (see page 21)

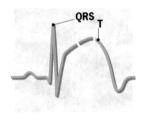

The peak between the QRS complex and the T wave indicates that a heart attack is occurring

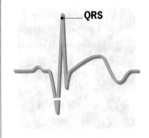

The deep part of the QRS complex shows that a heart attack might have occurred in the past

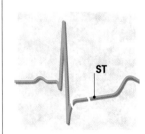

The lowered ST segment suggests that the heart is not receiving enough blood, indicating that angina may be occurring

The Airline Pilot

A middle-aged man's risk of heart disease is greatly increased if his lifestyle is characterised by a variety of unhealthy habits and if there is a family history of heart disease. Any symptoms that signify heart disease need to be checked out immediately and action taken to minimise all risk factors.

Alan is a 38-year-old commercial airline pilot, married to Judy, who looks after their two young children, Caroline and David. A steady diet of airline food and a large intake of alcohol to help him wind down after the stress of flying have not jeopardised his compulsory yearly medical check-ups, although the company doctor advised him to stop smoking. For the last month, however, he has noticed an uncomfortable pain in his chest at various times of the day which lasts for a few minutes. Alan is concerned as he is slightly overweight and does not exercise regularly. His father and grandfather had heart attacks in their fifties, and he and Judy fear he is suffering from angina. They are really worried he will lose his job.

WHAT SHOULD ALAN DO?

Alan must see his doctor and find out the cause of his chest pain as soon as possible. If there is any suspicion of heart disease, he has to inform his company that he cannot continue to work as a pilot until a diagnosis is made.

He and Judy also need to discuss the possibility that he will lose his job and be prepared for dealing with this situation.

Alan must realise that he needs to have a healthier lifestyle, regardless of the outcome – he has to quit smoking, improve his diet and lose weight, exercise regularly and reduce his stress levels by learning to relax. Alan also needs to moderate his alcohol consumption quite substantially.

Action Plan

FAMILY
Talk to Judy about making plans for the future in terms of job and family. Maybe Judy could work part-time. Take out a life insurance policy.

WORK
Inform company about undergoing medical tests. Arrange for holiday leave to relax and recover from the investigations.

HEALTH
Stop smoking and drink less. Eat more fruit and vegetables and cut down on fats. Join a weekly yoga class to relieve stress.

WORK
When loss of a job is threatened by heart disease, stress is compounded and may worsen symptoms.

FAMILY
A family history of heart disease greatly increases a person's risk and is a source of concern.

HEALTH
Stress, smoking, high alcohol consumption, poor diet and lack of exercise are all preventable heart disease risk factors.

HOW THINGS TURNED OUT FOR ALAN

Alan's GP sent him for a standard and exercise ECG, neither of which showed any heart abnormalities. However, in view of his family history, the GP referred Alan for a coronary angiogram. The test was normal, ruling out heart disease. The GP concluded that Alan's chest pains were due to stress. On her suggestion, Alan took a holiday and also started practising relaxation exercises. He also cut down on smoking, and his alcohol consumption.

with the heart when it is. Further testing will be done to confirm the results. False readings occur at random, although they can also be affected by the medication or drugs that the patient is taking. The ECG is therefore most useful to confirm suspected heart disease, but it is always interpreted in context, that is, in the presence of heart-related symptoms.

Exercise ECG (stress test)

A standard ECG test is not wholly efficient at diagnosing conditions related to insufficient blood supply, such as angina, which are most likely to occur during exercise or periods of unusual or prolonged stress. The exercise ECG, also known as 'stress testing', was therefore developed.

The person is monitored with electrodes (as in the normal ECG) while walking on a treadmill or pedalling on a stationary bicycle. The exercise begins at a leisurely pace but gets harder and harder. Blood pressure measurements are taken at various times during the test.

The test ends when the patient experiences pain, becomes really tired or very short of breath, or significant changes are recorded by the ECG. On average, the test takes 15 to 30 minutes.

Although exercise testing is an improvement on a standard ECG, it is not 100 per cent accurate, and is more inaccurate for women than men for unexplained reasons.

Holter (ambulatory) ECG monitoring

This is a continuous ECG recording that is used to detect intermittent abnormal heart activity. It is useful for diagnosing palpitations. The person being tested wears a portable device called a Holter monitor for 24 hours while going about his or her everyday activities (except taking a bath or a shower!). Recording leads are stuck to the front of the chest and wires are connected to the attached monitor. The person being tested has to keep a diary to record times and types of activities. Changes on the ECG can then be interpreted in the light of when certain activities occurred.

IMAGING TECHNIQUES

There are many different ways of 'looking' at the heart – its shape and size, pumping action, the flow of blood in and out of its chambers, and the size and shape of its valves. These techniques will show up structural abnormalities and help a doctor make a correct diagnosis.

EXERCISE ECG
Because angina is often exercise-induced, exercise ECGs are commonly used to test for it. The test is quick and non-invasive.

TRADITIONAL CHINESE MEDICINE

Traditional Chinese medicine takes a holistic view of health, looking at the body as a system, with all the parts working in harmony. The main focus is prevention rather than cure, but there is a wide range of treatments available when things go wrong. These include acupuncture, dietary changes, herbs, massage and exercise programmes. The Chinese medicine practitioner has four main methods of diagnosis:

▶ *Looking at the general appearance, complexion and tongue, and listening to the voice. The tongue is examined for unusual colours and bumps. On different areas of the tongue these may indicate different organs of the body.*

▶ *Taking notes on and considering the patient's medical history, including family history and lifestyle factors.*

▶ *Smelling for unusual body odour, breath and excretions.*

▶ *Feeling the pulse at both wrists, the abdomen, and at meridians (invisible lines which store chi or energy and connect the body's organs) and the acupuncture points.*

The practitioner uses a pulse diagnosis to assess the health of various body organs and the flow of 'chi' or the life force that passes through and around them. When there are blockages in the path of the life force (or energy), the body becomes more prone to illness. Acupuncture releases these energy blockages and restores the flow. The pulse assessment is the Chinese doctor's most important tool in the diagnosis of heart problems.

Chinese medicine can successfully treat both high blood pressure and angina through acupuncture, as well as helping to relieve stress. It is thought that acupuncture stimulates the production of the body's own pain-killing hormones, called endorphins.

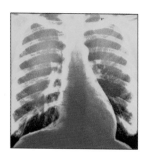

HEALTHY HEART
This coloured x-ray shows a heart with a normal shape and size (the red pear shape in the centre).

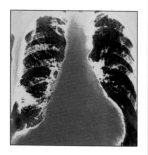

ENLARGED HEART
The heart in this x-ray (the large pear shape bulging to the right of the picture) is abnormally enlarged due to hypertension. This could lead to heart failure and other complications.

CHEST X-RAY

This is usually the first imaging technique a doctor uses. It is quick and painless and shows the size, shape and position of the heart. A chest x-ray can detect whether the heart is enlarged and confirm that the heart is failing to pump properly. It can also reveal calcium deposits in the coronary arteries, valves and heart muscle, and can be used to see the condition of the lungs (fluid in the lungs indicates possible heart failure).

ECHOCARDIOGRAPHY

This is a safe and painless test that is based on ultrasound. High frequency sounds are transmitted onto your internal organs by the scanning head, called a transducer. They are then reflected back into the transducer, which converts the echo into electrical signals. The pattern created by the sounds is interpreted by a computer and displayed on a screen. Using this technique, it is possible to get an image of the moving heart. Echocardiography is used to investigate disorders of heart valves, congenital heart defects, heart muscle shape and size, and blood flow patterns.

During the test, the person lies on his or her back or side. Gel or oil is rubbed onto the chest to improve sound wave transmission and the transducer is moved around the chest. The echoes picked up form a picture on a nearby monitor screen.

Specialised echocardiography

A development of this technique, Doppler echocardiography measures the speed of the blood flow in different parts of your heart. One of its main uses is transoesophageal

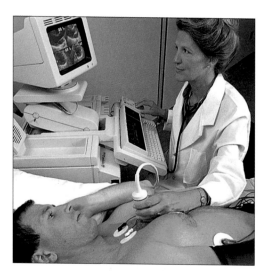

ECHOCARDIOGRAPHY
Ultrasound is used to create an image of the heart through a computer. It can show the shape and size of the heart muscle as well as valve disorders and congenital heart disease.

echocardiography, which enables pictures of the heart to be taken from the oesophagus (the tube that runs from the throat to the stomach). Because the oesophagus lies directly behind the heart a more detailed view can be seen.

The ultrasound transducer is attached to a tube which is passed down the oesophagus. A short-acting sedative is given to the person in order to relax the muscles and minimise any discomfort.

RADIONUCLIDE TESTS

These tests are more specialised than the ones discussed so far. A small and harmless amount of a radioactive substance (an isotope), such as thallium or technetium, is injected into the bloodstream and carried around the circulatory system into the heart. There it is detected by a gamma camera, which picks up any emitted radioactive rays. The isotope decays rapidly so that the dose of radioactivity someone receives is very small – about the same as that received when undergoing a chest x-ray.

During radionuclide tests, pictures are generated through a computer showing the heart's chambers as they empty and fill with blood. Images of the blood flow to the heart muscle can also be obtained. This test may be done either while the person is stationary or exercising on a treadmill, as with the exercise ECG.

Types of scanning

Two types of radionuclide scanning are used to look at the heart: thallium scanning and technetium scanning. Thallium is used to study the blood flow to the heart muscle; and technetium is used to test the size and pumping activities of the heart chambers to assess how well the heart is ejecting blood, helping to establish the efficiency of the heartbeat.

The risk of damage to the patient from the tiny amount of radioactive material used is extremely slight. But nuclear scanning is usually not used with women who are pregnant or breastfeeding.

Radionuclide scanning is time consuming, expensive and requires more specialist equipment and staff compared to ECG and echocardiography. It may sometimes be necessary, however, to get much more detailed information than is supplied by other tests on the blood and oxygen supply to the heart.

POSITRON EMISSION TOMOGRAPHY (PET) SCANNING

This is a very specialised procedure that is particularly useful for predicting whether someone will recover after a heart attack or benefit from a coronary artery bypass. It is also used to check impaired blood flow. PET scanning gives much better resolution than radionuclide scanning.

First, a mild sedative is taken, then a substance (usually carbon, nitrogen or oxygen) is radioactively tagged and injected into a vein from where it travels to the heart and is taken up by the muscle cells. Positively charged particles, positrons, are emitted by the radioactive gas, causing the release of tiny amounts of gamma rays. An image is created from these through a computer, which can reveal the degree of activity going on in different parts of the heart muscle (showing how the muscle uses energy).

RAPID COMPUTED TOMOGRAPHY (CT) SCANNING

This gives pictures of the heart muscle when x-rays are passed through the body at different angles. A computer-generated image gives a much more detailed picture of the heart than a conventional x-ray, as it can show where the heart muscle is failing during the pumping cycle.

The patient lies on a table which slides inside a large x-ray machine. The machine directs x-rays in cross sections through the person's body. Occasionally a contrast material may be injected into a vein to make the image clearer. There is very little risk in this procedure.

MAGNETIC RESONANCE IMAGING (MRI)

This is a new technique that gives a high-quality image of the heart and major blood vessels, and uses no radiation. It is very useful for diagnosing congenital heart defects.

The patient lies on a table which slides inside a large magnetic machine, and radio waves are passed through the chest. The machine detects energy signals given off by atoms of body tissues which are constructed into an image. MRI pictures are similar to x-rays but show more detail.

There are no risks associated with MRI, but people who have pacemakers or other internal metallic objects which may cause interference cannot undergo the procedure.

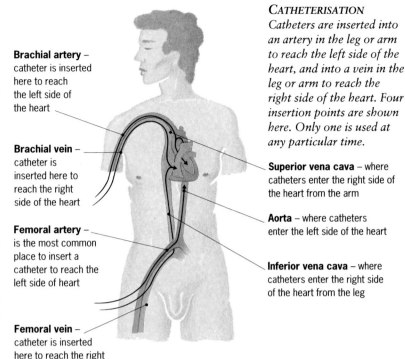

Brachial artery – catheter is inserted here to reach the left side of the heart

Brachial vein – catheter is inserted here to reach the right side of the heart

Femoral artery – is the most common place to insert a catheter to reach the left side of heart

Femoral vein – catheter is inserted here to reach the right side of the heart

CATHETERISATION
Catheters are inserted into an artery in the leg or arm to reach the left side of the heart, and into a vein in the leg or arm to reach the right side of the heart. Four insertion points are shown here. Only one is used at any particular time.

Superior vena cava – where catheters enter the right side of the heart from the arm

Aorta – where catheters enter the left side of the heart

Inferior vena cava – where catheters enter the right side of the heart from the leg

CARDIAC CATHETERISATION

This procedure is used to investigate the heart's pumping ability, valve efficiency, and any coronary artery blockages. A long flexible tube, called a catheter is used. It may be fitted with a minute measuring device or dyes may be injected through it into the heart.

Under a local anaesthetic, a catheter is inserted either into the groin or the arm and is passed along a vein or artery up into the heart. X-ray screening is used to make sure the catheter is placed in the heart correctly.

After the catheter is properly inserted, an electrocardiograph monitors the heart continuously for about 45 minutes. You do not actually feel the catheter in the heart. When the test is over, the catheter is removed. Occasionally a few stitches are needed where it was first inserted. The test is performed on an empty stomach and some medication may be given beforehand. The whole procedure takes about an hour.

Variations

The catheter may have a specialised device on the end to measure oxygen levels in the blood, blood pressure in arteries or heart chambers (balloon flotation catheters), or electrical impulses in different areas of the heart (electrode catheters).

continued on page 98

Balloon flotation catheter

This special kind of catheter is often used to measure pressures in the ventricles of the heart and the pulmonary artery, and blood flow. A catheter with a small balloon on the tip is inserted into the veins or arteries until it reaches the heart. The air-filled balloon enables the catheter to move through the heart, as it is propelled by the blood flow, and a device monitors blood pressure. The catheter is often left for a few days in order to monitor heart function continuously.

Home Tests

You can assess your health with do-it-yourself cholesterol and blood pressure measuring kits, a heart rate monitor to measure your response to exercise, and simple tests for checking whether your weight is within healthy limits.

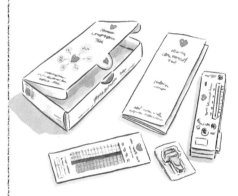

CHOLESTEROL SELF-TESTING KITS
Results from these kits may not always be accurate; check with your doctor if you are concerned. A blood cholesterol level greater than 5.2 millimoles per litre (mmol/l) is the upper limit of normal cholesterol levels. A cholesterol level above 6.5 mmol/l is far too high, putting you at high risk for heart disease. Prompt action should be taken to reduce it.

CHOLESTEROL KITS

Many self-testing kits are able to give a cholesterol reading in minutes from a finger-prick sample of blood. A high blood cholesterol reading, however, is only one risk factor of heart disease. High blood pressure, smoking and a lack of exercise must also be taken into consideration.

When performing a cholesterol test, be sure to read and follow the instructions carefully and bear in mind that blood cholesterol levels vary from day to day. They can also be affected by general state of health, the time of day or even the time of year (possibly being higher in winter). If your levels are too high, it is important to have a second test to confirm this result and possibly even a third test.

Kits usually give only total cholesterol levels, whereas a test done by your doctor will give LDL and HDL levels (see page 38). If you have suffered a minor illness such as

Blood pressure and cholesterol self-testing kits can be bought in many pharmacies and health food stores. For most adults, a blood pressure reading that is less than 140/90 indicates there is nothing to worry about. For this reason, purchasing a kit is an unnecessary expense; it is enough to have it checked once a year by a doctor. But self-testing kits which you can use at home may be useful for someone who has had high blood pressure diagnosed and wishes to monitor it carefully.

a cold or the flu, you should delay testing for about three weeks. If you have suffered a major illness, delay testing by about three months, until you are fully recovered. Consult your doctor if you are concerned.

With some home blood pressure monitors, all you have to do is place a finger on a sensor which displays a blood pressure reading.

Other more complex but cheaper types involve wrapping a cuff around your arm and automatically or manually inflating it, and reading the pressure on a gauge.

Bear in mind that blood pressure fluctuates with stress, emotional upset and illness, so if your reading is high, make a note of it and take it again in a few days.

If your levels are confirmed to be high by your doctor, then you will need to try to lower them. Follow a low-fat, high-fibre diet and eat lots of fruit and vegetables, which are high in antioxidant vitamins (A, C and E).

Prick finger
with needle
supplied

1 *Prick your finger with the needle provided. Bear in mind, if you squeeze your finger too hard more plasma – the clear part of blood – will come out and you will get an inaccurate reading.*

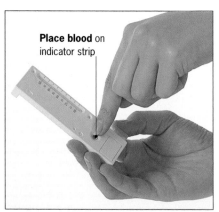

Place blood on
indicator strip

2 *Place your finger on the indicator strip provided and put blood on the spot indicated in the instructions. Wait for a few minutes (as specified) and then compare your reading with the key.*

MEASURING YOUR PULSE

During exercise it is important to monitor your pulse rate. You can achieve a rough guide by counting the pulse in the neck or in the wrist. Stop exercising while measuring your pulse. Count the beats of your pulse for 15 seconds, then multiply by 4 to determine your pulse rate per minute. (Do not press so hard as to block the flow of blood as you will not feel a pulse.) The average pulse rate at rest is 70 beats per minute. A simple heart rate monitor, however, will give you a far more accurate reading than this.

NECK PULSE (CAROTID ARTERY)
'Draw' a straight line from the base of your ear to the top of your breast bone. At the mid-point along the line, gently press two fingers against your neck until you feel a pulse.

Press pulse lightly

WRIST PULSE (RADIAL ARTERY)
Place two fingers (index and middle) between the bone and the tendon just under the ball of the thumb and press gently until you feel the pulsing of the blood in the artery.

Do not push too hard

ARE YOU OVERWEIGHT?

The chart below gives the ranges of normal weights for men and women at different heights. Check whether you are in the normal weight range. Bear in mind that your age and build will also determine which end of the range you are on. If you are at all concerned about being either underweight or overweight, consult your doctor or a nutritionist for advice on changing your diet. See page 62 for the healthy heart diet.

Also, you may wish to embark on a more regular exercise programme, as this will help burn up those extra calories. See page 142 for the approximate number of calories you need per day to maintain your weight. You should not eat more calories than you burn.

HEART RATE MONITORS

To exercise in your target heart rate zone (see page 70), use a heart rate monitor for accurate heart rate readings. If you have a diagnosed heart problem, discuss your target heart rate zone with your doctor. A heart rate monitor consists of eletrodes mounted on an electronic transmitter, and attached to your chest with an elastic belt. It will pick up electrical impulses from the heart and send them to a wrist monitor (which looks like a watch). Both the chest band and the wrist monitor are light and comfortable.

HEART RATE MONITOR
Read instructions carefully before using your monitor.

IDEAL WEIGHT CHART

Check your weight against your height. The figures for women's heights include 5.0 cm (2 in) heels, men's include 2.5 cm (1 in) heels.

HEIGHT	MEN (acceptable weight)	WOMEN (acceptable weight)
1.57 m (5 ft 2 in)		46–59 kg (102–131 lb)
1.60 m (5 ft 3 in)		48–61 kg (105–134 lb)
1.63 m (5 ft 4 in)	54–67 kg (118–148 lb)	49–63 kg (108–138 lb)
1.65 m (5 ft 5 in)	55–69 kg (121–152 lb)	50–64 kg (111–142 lb)
1.68 m (5 ft 6 in)	56–71 kg (124–156 lb)	52–66 kg (114–146 lb)
1.70 m (5 ft 7 in)	58–73 kg (128–161 lb)	54–68 kg (118–150 lb)
1.73 m (5 ft 8 in)	60–75 kg (132–166 lb)	55–70 kg (122–154 lb)
1.75 m (5 ft 9 in)	62–77 kg (136–170 lb)	57–72 kg (126–158 lb)
1.78 m (5 ft 10 in)	64–79 kg (140–174 lb)	59–74 kg (130–163 lb)
1.80 m (5 ft 11 in)	65–81 kg (144–179 lb)	61–76 kg (134–168 lb)
1.83 m (6 ft)	67–83 kg (148–184 lb)	63–78 kg (138–173 lb)
1.85 m (6 ft 1 in)	69–86 kg (152–189 lb)	
1.88 m (6 ft 2 in)	71–88 kg (156–194 lb)	

SEEKING A SECOND OPINION

After you have been diagnosed by your doctor, you may wish to seek a second opinion if:

▶ *The diagnosis is very serious.*

▶ *The proposed treatment is extensive, risky or experimental.*

▶ *Surgery is suggested.*

▶ *There is a choice of treatments and you are unsure which one is best for you.*

▶ *You do not feel happy with the information your doctor has supplied.*

▶ *You do not have confidence in your doctor for any reason.*

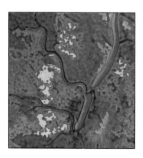

CORONARY ANGIOGRAM
This is used to assess arterial disease due to atherosclerosis, and is also used to see blood clots. Dye is injected via a catheter and an x-ray of the heart is taken. Here, a blockage is seen in one of the coronary arteries where the red dye is broken.

Catheters are also used for other treatment procedures, such as angioplasty which helps to clear blocked arteries (see page 111) and valvuloplasty which opens narrowed valves (see page 117).

Serious complications of catheterisation are very rare, but there may be bruising in the groin or a weakened pulse in the arm.

ANGIOGRAPHY AND VENOGRAPHY

These are procedures that are used with catheterisation to make the investigation of blood vessels clearer and to show blockages and clots in vessels. In angiography, a dye is injected through a catheter into an artery. X-ray pictures are then taken of the dye's flow through the artery. Venography is based on the same principle, only the dye is injected through a vein to show any blockage.

In coronary angiography, opaque dyes are injected into the chambers of the heart or coronary arteries via a catheter. These structures can then be seen more clearly on a monitor. This is the most common way to examine the extent of atherosclerosis.

In left ventriculography, a dye is injected into the left ventricle of the heart to show its pumping efficiency or any leakage.

With these procedures a small number of people experience nausea or vomiting after an injection of dye or, even more rarely, an allergic reaction to the dye itself.

MAKING A DECISION

Diagnostic tests can be exhausting and stressful, and the outcome may be rather frightening, presenting you with a decision to make about treatment and changes in your daily habits. It is important to bear in mind, however, that no diagnostic test is 100 per cent accurate, no matter how carefully it is done. One test is not expected to give the right answer but each test should supply information that should lead the doctor to the correct diagnosis when all the factors are taken into consideration.

If you have been diagnosed as having a heart problem, you need to make sure you understand exactly what the disorder is, how it was caused and what the prescribed treatment is, in order to make the correct decision to improve your health.

If you want a second opinion, ask your GP for another referral and inform the first specialist that you have decided to go for a second opinion.

A NATURAL APPROACH

You may have decided with your doctor about the medical options for treatment, yet you still feel that something is missing. There are a number of natural therapists who take a different approach to the diagnosis and treatment of illness. They will pay attention to you as a whole person, including body, mind, emotions and spirit, unlike conventional doctors who may concentrate more on the physical symptoms.

A naturopath, homeopath, traditional Chinese medicine practitioner, an aromatherapist or herbalist may give you some insight into the causes of your illness and suggest treatment methods that you can use in addition to your medical treatment to aid your return to health. All the alternative therapists will ask detailed questions about every aspect of your life. They will also ask similar questions to your doctor, including your symptoms; information on previous illnesses, accidents and hospitalisations; chronic illnesses and allergies; illnesses that run in the family; results of any previous medical diagnostic tests; and lifestyle habits, such as smoking.

Depending on the diagnosis and which therapist you have consulted, you will be prescribed various treatments. The naturopath, for instance, will advise dietary changes and exercise, herbal remedies and relaxation techniques. The homeopath uses very dilute but potent extracts from natural remedies. The aromatherapist may suggest the use of various oils for relaxation and stress relief. A traditional Chinese doctor may use acupuncture (see page 101) to relax you, lower your blood pressure and relieve pain, and herbal remedies to dilate the arteries, stimulate the heart's contractions and the circulatory system in general. There are many herbs with medicinal properties that a trained herbalist can administer with great effect to relieve your symptoms.

No matter what the diagnosis or what treatment course you take with your doctor or surgeon, it is important to see your body as inseparable from your lifestyle and to make any necessary changes in your habits to improve your health.

Conventional and alternative medicine can be used in combination to achieve maximum benefit, as long as the doctors and therapists involved are informed of all the treatments you are undergoing.

Natural treatment options

You can accelerate your recovery with a variety of natural therapies, ranging from acupuncture to herbal medicine to those designed to relieve anxiety, such as yoga and meditation.

Many doctors who practise strictly conventional medicine recommend 'natural remedies' to their patients with heart and circulatory diseases. Voicing feelings, avoiding stress, sleeping well, exercising more and eating healthily are very natural and they form a major part of every heart disease recovery plan.

HYDROTHERAPY

Any therapy based on the use of water is called hydrotherapy. Hydrotherapy can improve circulation, ease joint and muscle pain and aid relaxation. It is often prescribed by naturopaths.
Warm baths
To calm the body generally and lower blood pressure, a warm bath with lavender oil is recommended.
Cold showers
To stimulate heart and circulatory function, take a cold shower for just a few seconds daily. This treatment, however, should not be undertaken by elderly or sick people.

Circulation in the legs can be improved by pouring cold water on them, particularly below the knees, every morning.
Swimming
Swimming regularly provides an excellent cardiovascular workout and can help prevent some heart disorders. It is also a therapeutic exercise for recovering heart and stroke patients. Caution: Hydrotherapy should always be practised under the supervision of a trained therapist.

But natural therapies (also called alternative or complementary therapies) also embrace many other types of treatments that can be useful in fighting heart disease. Some treatments, like yoga and meditation, ease the mind, helping to relieve stress; others, such as acupuncture, act directly on the body tissues; and others, such as the Feldenkrais Method (see page 144), may help you to relate more closely to your body's needs.

Natural therapies have been used by people around the world for centuries. Some are simple and can be done at home, while others require the aid of a trained therapist. Most doctors would not object to treatments that offer physical or psychological benefits with few, if any, risks attached.

FINDING A BALANCE

Before using natural therapies, it is important to discuss your plans with your doctor. Herbal medicines, for example, might cause a bad reaction when taken together with the medication your doctor is prescribing. You should also talk to your doctor before you take up a movement-based therapy, such as yoga or t'ai chi.

Similarly, you should give your natural therapist complete details of your medical history, symptoms and habits. This will influence the type of treatment you require.

With the cooperation of your doctor, it is possible to combine conventional and natural medicines. For example, if you are told to give up smoking you might want to use acupuncture to help you stop. Herbal teas might help you get the sleep you need without taking drugs. Relaxation exercises and meditation can also be useful in getting to sleep or in reducing your stress level. More unusual therapies like laughter therapy or

The success of natural therapies
Some people believe that an important reason for the effectiveness of these therapies is the amount of attention paid to the patient by the practitioner. Being allowed to talk about your feelings to a sympathetic listener is, after all, good therapy and will almost certainly make you feel better.

THE KNEE JET
Spraying cold water on the legs to improve the circulation has been a popular hydrotherapy treatment since the 1800s.

HOW TO FIND A THERAPIST

Below are some ways you may find a therapist. Once you have done so, check the therapist's professional qualifications. Ask how long the person has been practising. Above all, heed your instincts. A natural therapist should be someone you like, trust and can confide in.

▶ *Ask the therapy's national body for a list of local practitioners.*

▶ *Ask a practitioner of another therapy for a recommendation – they often know one another.*

▶ *Ask your doctor.*

▶ *Check the yellow pages for listings of therapists or of natural health centres.*

▶ *Get recommendations from friends.*

▶ *Check notices at your local health food shop.*

crystal healing have made some people feel better and certainly do no harm, as long as a conventional diagnosis is sought first.

In fact, most natural therapies pose no danger to health, as long as you use them with your doctor's knowledge and approval. It is, however, particularly important not to stop taking any medication without first discussing the possible consequences with your doctor.

HEALING THE BODY

Some therapies aim to treat specific physical symptoms and generally improve physical health. Some of these also have the added benefit of healing the mind.

Naturopathy

In the 19th century, some physicians recommended a cure whereby the body was inspired to heal itself. Known as the Nature Cure, the only 'prescription' was healthy food, exercise, clean air and water. Today, naturopaths follow this tradition, although most are not as restrictive and believe that

the body often needs help in the form of orthodox, herbal or homeopathic medicines in order to heal itself. Naturopathy (see page 122) is multi-disciplinary, focusing on diet, exercise, hydrotherapy (see page 99), relaxation exercises and herbal remedies. Some naturopaths also practise therapies such as massage and osteopathy.

Aromatherapy

This is the practice of using essential oils (pure oils extracted from plants) to treat specific disorders. It is based on the idea that individual aromas, or mixtures of them, have different therapeutic effects. For instance, lavender is often used to calm anxiety and relieve stress. Aromatherapy is beneficial in aiding relaxation and thereby lowering blood pressure. Massage with essential oils can improve the circulation. Consult an aromatherapist for the most appropriate oil.

Oils can be used in different ways. Only a tiny amount of oil should be used: add a teaspoon to the running water of a warm bath.

MASSAGE FOR HEALTH

Massaging the body, particularly when you are using aromatherapy oils, is very conducive to relaxation, and can thereby help to reduce high blood pressure. Back and face massages are particularly good for relieving stress.

Massage can give great relief from leg cramps (see page 88), which may occur as a result of arterial disease.

Fluid retention, which can result from congestive heart failure and some valve disease, may be relieved by a vigorous body massage, but you should always check with your doctor first that you are well enough for it. Massage is good stimulation for the circulatory system for everyone and can help prevent disorders such as varicose veins.

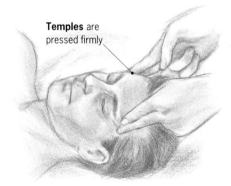

Temples are pressed firmly

FACE MASSAGE
The masseur may use long, stroking movements on the face or put pressure on various pressure points, particularly around the eyes where many people hold tension.

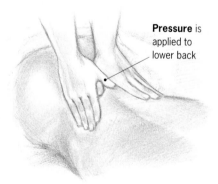

Pressure is applied to lower back

BACK MASSAGE
The masseur will use long, firm strokes to warm the muscles, then firmer pressure on tense spots, followed by cupping and 'chopping' to stimulate the circulation.

To make an inhalation: add a few drops of your chosen oil to a basin of boiling water, place a towel over your head and put your face over the basin. Then breathe deeply for 2 minutes. For an aromatherapy massage oil, add 1 drop of essential oil per tablespoon of base massage oil. Base massage oils include almond, wheatgerm or sunflower, which are available in health food shops and supermarkets.

Traditional Chinese medicine

Practitioners of traditional Chinese medicine treat symptoms and diseases using a highly specialised and individualised combination of acupuncture and herbal remedies.

Acupuncture and acupressure

Based on an ancient Chinese system of stimulating certain energy points in the body, acupuncture and acupressure aid recovery from illness and restore the body's natural energy balance. Acupuncture uses needles to stimulate these points, while acupressure uses finger or hand pressure.

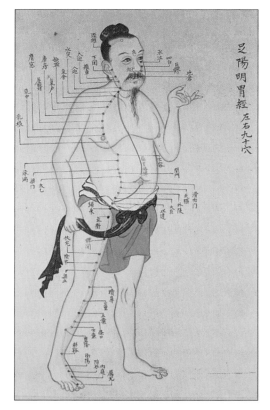

ACUPUNCTURE MERIDIANS
This ancient Chinese diagram shows some of the critical points for treatment with acupuncture. These points lie on meridian lines along which chi – the life force – flows.

According to theories of Chinese medicine, acupuncture works by regulating the life force known as chi. Too little chi causes weakness, while blockages preventing its flow around the body can cause illness. Chi is believed to flow along 12 invisible lines known as meridians: these connect the body's internal organs where the chi is stored. The acupuncturist increases or unblocks the flow of chi by using very fine stainless steel needles inserted along the meridians at particular points, thereby relieving your symptoms. There are over 1000 of these points in the body, each of which is thought to have a different effect.

In the treatment of heart disease, both acupuncture and acupressure are used to stimulate the circulation, providing relief from high blood pressure, angina and varicose veins. While conventional doctors may not agree with the method of treatment for these illnesses, it is generally accepted that both acupuncture and acupressure are successful in the relief of pain, relaxation, stress reduction and overcoming addiction. Doctors explain these effects as being due to the stimulation of points which release endorphins, which are the body's natural pain-killing hormones.

Acupuncture can only be carried out by a qualified therapist but you can perform acupressure as a self-help remedy. It is best to ask a practitioner to advise you on the pressure points relevant to your illness (some points are illustrated in Chapter 6). To be of lasting benefit, acupressure needs to be done at least three times a week for about an hour each time. You should be in a relaxed, comfortable position before you start. Use your finger and press firmly but not too hard. This pressure should then be maintained on the relevant point for several minutes at a time. If you practise on someone else, note the following: be gentle with older people or anyone who is ill or very upset. Avoid doing acupressure on someone who is intoxicated or has just eaten.

Herbal medicine

Like modern medications, herbs – the precursors of today's drugs – can be dangerous if they are used incorrectly. One of the most widely used and well known heart drugs, digitalis, which has been used for over 200 years to treat heart failure, comes from the leaves of the foxglove plant. The leaves

Moxibustion
Some acupuncturists use moxibustion, either instead of needles or in combination with them, to treat high blood pressure. In this procedure the downy covering of the leaves of a herb called *Artemesia moxa* are gently burned above an acupuncture needle, or needles may not be used at all. The moxa may be rolled into a stick and held, lighted end down, just above the skin over the relevant acupuncture point.

MOXA STICKS
Made from the herb, Artemesia moxa, *burning moxa sticks may be used to relax tense back muscles, relieve stress or pain, and lower blood pressure.*

HERBS AND YOUR HEART

A wide range of herbs can help the heart and circulatory system. A herbalist may prescribe some of these. You may take them in teas, in lotions or compresses, or simply use them in cooking. Caution: herbal medicines are powerful substances and should only be taken under the supervision of a qualified practitioner.

HERB	FUNCTION
Alfalfa (*Medicago sativa*)	Breaks down plaques in arteries
Balm (*Melissa officinalis*)	Relaxes blood vessels in arms and legs; aids relaxation
Bromelain (pineapple) (*Ananas comosus*)	Relieves symptoms of angina; prevents clots; diuretic
Buckwheat (*Fagopyrum esculentum*)	Repairs arteriole walls
Bugleweed (*Ajuga reptans*)	Strengthens the heart; makes it beat more slowly
Camomile (*Chamaemelum nobile*)	Relieves stress and anxiety
Cayenne (*Capsicum frutescens*)	Stimulates the circulation to arms and legs
Dandelion (*Taraxacum officinale*)	Diuretic
Knotted figwort (*Scrofularia nodosa*)	Stimulates the heart and circulatory system; diuretic
Garlic (*Allium sativum*)	Antioxidant; dissolves clots
Ginger (*Zingiber officinalis*)	Lowers cholesterol level; makes platelets less sticky; stimulates circulation
Gingko (*Gingko biloba*)	Strengthens blood vessels; reduces clotting
Hawthorn (*Crataegus oxycantha*)	Improves coronary circulation; reduces high blood pressure by dilating arteries; strengthens heart muscle; slows heart down; breaks down plaques in arteries
Lily-of-the-valley (*Convallaria majalis*)	Unclogs arteries; relaxes the heart; helps arrhythmias; diuretic
Mistletoe (*Viscum album*)	Slows heart rate; reduces blood pressure; breaks down plaques in arteries; strengthens capillary walls. Toxic in large quantities
Motherwort (*Leonurus cardiaca*)	Prevents palpitations; relaxes, strengthens the heart; regulates blood pressure; reduces blood cholesterol levels
Onion	Reduces cholesterol in the blood; anticoagulant
Skullcap (*Scutellaria lateriflora*)	Lowers blood pressure; relieves stress by strengthening nerves
St John's wort (*Hyperium perforatum*)	Relieves stress and anxiety; aids relaxation
Valerian (*Valerian officinalis*)	Relieves stress and anxiety
Yarrow (*Achillea millefolium*)	Dilates arteries and reduces blood pressure; diuretic

themselves, however, are poisonous; just because a substance is natural does not mean it is safe. You can buy many dried herbs and herbal preparations in health food shops, but when you are treating a serious illness it is always best to consult a qualified medical herbalist, preferably with the knowledge and support of your own doctor.

Herbalism can offer a wide variety of benefits to an ailing heart. Proponents claim that certain herbs, taken in the right dosages and combinations, act as natural diuretics, lower cholesterol, improve circulation, and even dissolve blood clots. Some plants used in herbal remedies, such as garlic, ginger and onion, are foods as well as herbs and therefore pose no health risks. Many studies have shown that all three are instrumental in lowering cholesterol levels and blood fats, as well as reducing high blood pressure.

There are different herbal preparations for drinking, including teas, infusions and decoctions, as well as those applied to the skin, such as poultices and ointments. Herbalists often recommend heart tea (see opposite) for calming down a fast heartbeat. People who react to stressful situations and get palpitations from stress may find it calms them and soothes their nerves, but anyone with diagnosed arrhythmias (see page 114) should consult their doctor before taking it. Hawthorn berry tea is also recommended daily as a preventative against heart problems. Although useful to healthy living, it should be noted that a lifestyle of damaging habits cannot be overcome by using herbs.

Homeopathy

By treating sick people with tiny doses of substances that would cause exactly the same symptoms of a disease in a healthy person, homeopaths claim to be able to cure many illnesses. This theory, and the principle behind it of treating like with like, has been advocated since the time of the ancient Greeks. It was turned into the formal system of medicine known as homeopathy by a German doctor named Samuel Christian Hahnemann (1755–1843).

Homeopaths believe that the more diluted the medication is, the stronger its action. Hahnemann wrote: 'The power to heal is released so that even a totally inert substance can come to influence the vital force.'

Scientists, on the other hand, assert that the doses found in homeopathic remedies are so small that they are worthless in a therapeutic sense. Most doctors have no objection to their patients taking homeopathic remedies, so long as they are informed and their patients continue with conventional medical treatment. Although homeopathic remedies can be bought in many health food shops and pharmacies, treatment of any serious condition such as heart disease should be undertaken by a qualified homeopath since the remedies prescribed will not have the same effects on everyone. However, some over-the-counter remedies may give relief to symptoms. *Arnica*, for example, is used for shock and may help your body get over the trauma of a heart attack, bypass surgery or an angina attack.

HEALING THE MIND

A large part of the process of recovering from a heart attack or major surgery is in the mind. A positive mental outlook is a

Heart tea

Mix two parts mistletoe, two parts motherwort, four parts balm leaves, four parts St John's wort and eight parts hawthorn leaves and blossoms in a teapot. Pour boiling water onto herbs, leave to steep for 5 to 10 minutes, then drink two to three cups, as needed.

HERBAL PREPARATIONS

Your herbalist will advise you on which herbal preparation you need.

Herbal teas are available in health food shops as loose leaves or in teabags. Infusions can be made from any part of the herb or using the whole plant. Pour 450 ml (16 fl oz) boiling water onto 70 g (2½ oz) of chopped fresh herbs or 30 g

HAWTHORN BERRY INFUSION
This infusion may improve your circulation and help clear out arteries. Drink a cup three times daily. To sweeten the infusion, add a little honey.

(1 oz) of chopped dried herbs, and cover. Leave for 10 to 15 minutes and strain.

Decoctions can be made from the root or bark of the herb. Add 60 g (2 oz) of chopped fresh herb 30 g (1 oz) of crushed dried herb to 750 ml (1¼ pints) cold water, bring to the boil and simmer until liquid reduces to 570 ml (1 pt). Cool; strain through a nylon sieve. Drink a cup three times daily.

For a poultice, crush or pound herb and mix with a little hot water to make a paste. Spread liberally on a strip of thin cloth and apply to the skin.

Add dried hawthorn berries to an infusion pot

Pour boiling water onto berries in infusion pot

Steep infusion for at least 10 minutes before drinking

BREATHING MEDITATION

This is a very relaxing and soothing meditation, often taught to beginners. Sit in a comfortable position in a quiet place, in soft light (candles create a pleasant atmosphere).

▶ *One: count each in-breath, until you reach 10. Start again, and keep repeating for about 3 minutes.*

▶ *Two: count each out-breath to 10; repeat for about 3 minutes.*

▶ *Three: 'watch' each breath – become conscious of the breath moving in, through your lungs, then out again. Do this for about 3 minutes.*

▶ *Four: concentrate on the point at which breath first enters your body – the edge of your nostrils. As it goes in, feel 'life and energy' entering your body. Repeat for about 3 minutes.*

▶ *Five: sit quietly to absorb the relaxing effect of this meditation.*

good aid to recovery. Therapies that work on the mind can also help the body by aiding relaxation and reducing tension.

Meditation

One of the most ancient techniques for achieving control over the mind is meditation. This takes a variety of forms which may include silent contemplation on a word, phrase (mantra) or image; chanting; or simply counting your breaths. To obtain the best results, you should meditate for 10 or 15 minutes both morning and evening. (See page 36 for 'humming meditation' or this page for 'breathing meditation'.) Meditation may also include visualisation (see page 83). Many people suffering from high blood pressure have found that practising meditation has greatly reduced, even eliminated, their need for prescription drugs.

Yoga

A series of slow stretches and breathing exercises designed to deeply relax the mind and body, yoga is an excellent form of meditation. Yoga also improves flexibility, mobility and circulation. It is an effective form of pain relief, but it is vital that you know which posture to do for a specific source of pain – you should always consult a qualified instructor. An important aspect of yoga for the heart patient is its emphasis on deep breathing. Yoga has been proven very effective in lowering high blood pressure and reducing stress, which makes it a good choice because it is suitable for people

MEDITATION
Cultures and religions around the world, such as Buddhism, have long used meditation as part of a way of life. Buddhists believe that you should meditate at least once daily for a healthy mind.

YOGIC BREATHING FOR HIGH BLOOD PRESSURE

Lie down on the floor: place one hand on your stomach and the other on your chest. Inhale slowly, making sure your stomach bulges out, then slowly exhale, feeling your stomach deflate. Pay attention to the hand on your chest: there should be very little movement there. Repeat the procedure for several minutes. This deep breathing exercise teaches you to breathe from your abdomen, essential for stress management. It uses minimum effort for a maximum intake of oxygen.

of any age or level of fitness. Bear in mind that the advanced postures require great flexibility and should not be attempted by beginners or the unfit.

In the mid-1980s, Dr Dean Ornish, an American cardiologist, used yoga for relaxation and blood pressure reduction as a component of his programme for treating heart patients. His patients were also advised to follow a vegetarian low-fat diet, and to walk for 30 minutes every day. Eighty-two per cent of his patients showed some degree of reversal of arterial disease in their follow-up angiograms. Yoga was thought to play a major role in achieving this effect.

Biofeedback

Very effective in helping to control blood pressure, biofeedback allows individuals to gain control over functions such as brain waves and blood pressure (see page 141) by teaching them the power of concentration and relaxation with the help of machines that are sensitive to body patterns.

Hypnotherapy

Both physical and psychological complaints can be treated with hypnotherapy. The hypnotist will aim to induce a state of deep relaxation in the patient in order to make suggestions such as to give up smoking, or simply to let go of stress. If the patient is receptive, hypnosis can be very effective for changing habits, learning to cope with stress, giving up addictions and relieving pain. It is also possible to learn to hypnotise yourself. Autogenic training (see page 42) is a popular form of self-hypnosis.

CHAPTER 6

HEART AND CIRCULATORY DISORDERS

---

*The heart and circulation can be afflicted by many
different disorders, with a wide variety of causes,
sometimes unavoidable, most often linked to lifestyle.
Each requires specialist diagnosis and treatment.
Conventional medicine is almost always the primary
method of treatment, but natural therapies can
play a part in relieving symptoms and
helping your recovery.*

HEART DISORDERS

A healthy lifestyle can go a long way towards warding off many types of heart disease. However, congenital heart disease, infections or other illnesses are sometimes unavoidable.

There are a number of heart disorders with different causes, symptoms and treatments. In some cases, natural therapies can be used in conjunction with conventional treatment and may help to minimise symptoms or aid in recovery. Because many heart disorders can be serious or indeed life-threatening, always check with your doctor before embarking on any course of natural therapy to ensure that it does not conflict with your medication.

CONGENITAL HEART DISORDERS

About one per cent of babies are born with a congenital heart disorder – that is, one that is present from birth. The heart is one of the first organs to develop, starting as a single, pulsating tube with arteries at one end and veins at the other. Between the sixth and twelfth week of gestation, often before the mother realises that she is pregnant, this tiny tube folds back on itself to develop the basic structures of the mature heart. During these crucial weeks in the heart's development, it is particularly vulnerable to damage.

If the mother contracts a viral infection, such as rubella (German measles), in these early weeks there is an increased chance that her baby's heart will develop abnormally. Alcoholism in pregnant women may cause a heart murmur in the foetus. Most congenital heart disorders, however, have no known cause and cannot be avoided. Congenital heart disorders are not hereditary, although some defects are slightly more common in twins.

There are many types of congenital heart defects but they can all be divided into two main types: those which cause too much blood to flow through the lungs and not enough around the body, and those that result in too little blood reaching the lungs, and therefore too little oxygen in blood flowing around the body.

Hole in the heart

One of the most common problems is a structural abnormality called 'hole in the heart'. The name refers to a hole in the septum (partition) between the chambers of the heart. This may be a hole between the ventricles (ventricular septal defect) or the atria (atrial septal defect). Together these defects account for 50 per cent of all congenital heart diseases. Both result in too much blood flowing to the lungs, which leads to breathlessness and exhaustion. Surgery is often necessary to correct it.

Patent ductus arteriosus

This is the second most common congenital heart disease, accounting for about five to ten per cent of congenital heart conditions. It occurs when the passage (ductus arteriosus) between the foetus' pulmonary artery (the artery to the lungs) and the aorta does not close after birth. This results in excess blood flowing to the baby's lungs, causing breathlessness and possible infection of the heart lining. Surgery is performed in infancy to close the passage, with a good outlook for the baby.

Transposition of arteries

The two most important blood vessels of the heart, the pulmonary artery and aorta, may be transposed, with the pulmonary artery growing from the left ventricle instead of the right and the aorta from the right

Congenital heart disorders

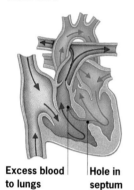

Excess blood to lungs | Hole in septum

HOLE IN THE HEART
A hole in the septum between the ventricles results in too much blood flowing to the lungs.

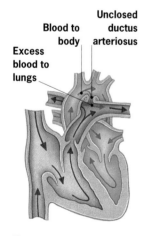

Unclosed ductus arteriosus
Blood to body
Excess blood to lungs

PATENT DUCTUS ARTERIOSUS
Oxygenated blood is pumped from the aorta back into the lungs instead of to the body.

DID YOU KNOW?
Although folic acid (a B vitamin) is essential for the development of the foetus' nervous system, excessive quantities can cause an abnormally slow foetal heart rate. Pregnant women should therefore take care not to take too many supplements.

TETRALOGY OF FALLOT

This is a complex disorder which results from the combination of four different abnormalities. It occurs in one out of every 2000 births and accounts for 10 per cent of all congenital heart diseases. The valve in the pulmonary artery is narrowed; there is a hole in the wall between the two pumping chambers of the heart (a ventricular septal defect); the aorta is abnormally large and in the wrong place; and the muscular wall of the right ventricle is abnormally thick and inflexible. The result is that much of the blood circulates to the body without being oxygenated in the lungs, causing a 'blue baby'. Corrective heart surgery is vital and may even be performed on babies, in severe cases. Almost 90 per cent of those operated on will survive for at least 25 years after the operation.

instead of left ventricle, so oxygenated blood goes to the lungs and deoxygenated blood to the body. This results in a 'blue baby' where the skin, lips and nails have a bluish pallor. Immediate surgery is required for this disorder. A further operation is usually necessary during the child's first 18 months.

Atria and ventricles

Abnormalities can occur in any of these chambers. They may not develop properly or even at all. They may be too small to pump sufficient blood or they may be connected up the wrong way so that some blood bypasses the lungs and circulates in the body or only circulates through the lungs, missing out the body.

Pulmonary and aortic valves

These one-way valves at the entrance to the pulmonary artery and the aorta respectively may be too narrow, forcing the heart to pump too hard as it tries to push blood through. Surgery is sometimes necessary.

Narrowing or leaking of a heart valve or a major artery is another common problem (see page 115 for valve disorders). When a valve is narrowed, it limits blood flow, which causes a variety of problems including congestive heart failure and heart rhythm disorders.

A valve that does not close properly will leak, and the blood will flow back in the wrong direction.

Diagnosis

Some abnormalities can be detected before birth when the mother is given an ultrasound scan. This safe and painless technique uses high frequency sound waves to build up a picture of the baby's development in the uterus.

If serious abnormalities are detected, then specialist medical staff can be on hand at the birth to provide immediate, and often lifesaving, care (see page 108). But some disorders only become apparent after birth when a baby may become blue, have laboured breathing or collapse suddenly.

Sometimes congenital heart disorders only become apparent towards the end of the child's first year of life or even remain undetected until pre-school or school medical check-ups when strange heart sounds or an unusual pulse rate alert the doctor.

Several different procedures, either singly or in combination, can then confirm the diagnosis. These include x-ray examination and an electrocardiogram or ECG (see page 91), cardiac catheterisation (see page 95) and echocardiography (see page 94).

Treatment

If a defect is minor then an operation might not be carried out, but severe abnormalities can only be corrected by surgery. However, many congenital disorders actually heal themselves in time. Half of all 'holes in the heart' close up by themselves during infancy and only about one-third of children born with heart defects actually need surgery.

FATIGUE
A child with a heart problem is often tired and irritable and needs a lot of rest.

Years ago breastfeeding was discouraged for babies with congenital heart disease because it was believed that it would tire them out too much. It is now thought, however, that babies actually use less energy and breathe more efficiently during breast-feeding than during bottle-feeding. Also, breast milk protects the baby from infections because of the mother's antibodies it contains. Small, frequent feedings are recommended.

LIFESTYLE AND ATHEROSCLEROSIS

As with any heart or circulatory disorder, there are a number of lifestyle changes that are essential to prevent further damage from atherosclerosis. These include:

▶ *Lose weight if overweight and reduce cholesterol levels by eating a low-fat diet, and lots of fresh fruit and vegetables.*

▶ *Quit smoking (see page 36), and minimise alcohol and caffeine intake.*

▶ *Exercise regularly.*

▶ *Learn and practise relaxation and stress management techniques (see page 150).*

▶ *Follow blood pressure lowering advice (see page 43).*

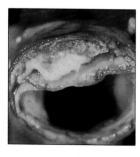

*ATHEROMA
This cross-section through an artery shows a thick deposit of fat and calcium which causes atherosclerosis.*

TREATMENT IN THE UTERUS

Doctors are now attempting to cure some life-threatening congenital heart disorders before a baby is born. At Guy's Hospital in London, a procedure called balloon angioplasty is being tried to widen narrowed aortic valves and is meeting with some success. The aortic valve is the one-way valve situated at the exit of the left ventricle in the aorta. If it does not open properly the ventricle is unable to pump enough oxygenated blood around the body.

The procedure involves inserting a catheter into the heart of the foetus, through the abdomen and uterus of the mother using ultrasound for guidance. The catheter, which is only one millimetre wide, has a tiny balloon at one end which is carefully positioned in the narrowed aortic valve and gently inflated, pushing the valve open.

When surgery is needed, doctors prefer to correct the whole problem at one time to minimise disruption to the child's life. But it is sometimes necessary for a child to have two operations, an early one to remedy the worst of the defect and to prevent further damage occurring, and another later on when he or she is older, and hopefully stronger, to complete the repair. In a very few cases, where defects cannot be totally corrected, treatment will consist of minimising symptoms and helping the person live as long and comfortable a life as possible.

Outlook

This will vary depending upon the type of disorder, the age of discovery, the degree of damage, and the date and success of treatment. Many children go on to lead normal and healthy lives, but even after surgery problems can still surface – including an irregular heart rhythm and endocarditis (infection of the valves or endocardium, see page 117), both of which require regular medical observation.

Extra care needs to be taken to avoid all infections. The child needs to be given antibiotics before any dental or medical procedure, and should also avoid other children with infections. Also, the child needs to have a healthy diet and plenty of rest.

Natural therapies

There are no natural therapies that can be recommended for congenital heart disease, as the defect needs to be corrected.

ATHEROSCLEROSIS

Atherosclerosis ('hardening of the arteries') is caused by the build-up of fatty deposits. These first appear as fatty streaks, often where arteries branch off. As the streaks get bigger, the artery walls are damaged and calcium deposits form – these are then called atheromas or plaques. Platelets, red blood cells, blood fats and fibrin (a protein involved in clotting) accumulate on plaques, making them bigger. With exertion or high blood pressure, plaques may crack and cause the artery wall to bleed. A blood clot forms which reduces blood flow, causing angina or intermittent claudication (see page 129); or the blood flow may be obstructed, causing a stroke or heart attack. Atherosclerosis reduces the diameter of arteries and makes artery walls less flexible, further increasing blood pressure.

Atherosclerosis usually occurs in middle-aged and elderly people, as arteries thicken and stiffen with age. It is most common in men in their forties, but after menopause women are just as susceptible. Causes of atherosclerosis include high blood pressure, high blood cholesterol levels, smoking, a sedentary lifestyle, family history of heart disease, diabetes or obesity. Stress is also a major factor as the stress hormones, cortisol and adrenaline, increase the production of triglycerides (a fat in body tissue) and cholesterol, as well as the stickiness of platelets.

Symptoms and diagnosis

The symptoms and therefore diagnosis will depend on the cause and location of the diseased arteries. Atherosclerosis will cause angina if it occurs in the coronary arteries (see page 110), stroke if in the brain arteries (see page 127) and intermittent claudication if in the leg arteries (see page 129).

Treatment

The most important step is to quit smoking. It is also essential to reduce blood cholesterol by following a low-fat, high-fibre diet and increasing intake of fresh fruit and vegetables. Blood pressure also needs to be lowered (see page 23). Medication to lower cholesterol or blood pressure may be given.

A Hole in the Heart

The causes of congenital heart disease are not usually known, although infection in the mother and environmental factors may play a part. Surgery may sometimes be necessary, but most children with congenital heart disease recover and lead healthy lives, and it is very unusual for a family to have more than one affected child.

Karen and Mark were delighted when Louise was born. She seemed healthy at birth but in her check-up at six weeks old, a doctor found that Louise had a heart murmur so she had to have a chest x-ray, ECG and echocardiogram. Louise had to be sedated for the echocardiogram to stop her wriggling. She was diagnosed as having a primum atrial septal defect (a hole in the bottom part of the septum) and a leaky mitral valve. She had the hole patched up when she was eight weeks old, but Karen and Mark were told she would need an operation at age four to repair the mitral valve. Louise is now four and is small for her age. She is not able to play with her friends for long periods as she tires easily.

WHAT SHOULD MARK AND KAREN DO?

Mark and Karen need to prepare Louise and themselves for the operation. They talk to Louise about going to hospital and try to explain what will happen with pictures and games. They also tell her she will be able to play with her friends when she gets better. They need to make sure she does not tire herself out before the operation. Karen and Mark should get counselling to make sure they understand the whole procedure and how to deal with it. They need to overcome their understandable but unjustified feelings of guilt that they caused Louise's defect in some way, in order to give her the love and support she needs to recover.

EMOTIONS
Having your newborn baby diagnosed with heart disease is traumatic and often causes feelings of grief, anger and guilt.

HEALTH
A child with a congenital heart defect may suffer breathlessness, fatigue and poor weight gain.

LIFESTYLE
A baby with a heart defect has a good chance of survival, but take care to prevent infection.

Action Plan

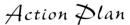

EMOTIONS
Join support group at the hospital to talk about grief and fear. Get as much information as possible.

HEALTH
Watch Louise closely for fatigue or breathlessness. Make sure she does not get overtired or catch a cold, and that she has a healthy, balanced diet.

LIFESTYLE
Take care to prevent infection and consult the doctor immediately so that antibiotic treatments can be started. Tell Louise's dentist, school and friends' parents about her medical condition.

HOW THINGS TURNED OUT FOR LOUISE

Karen and Mark joined a parent support group run by the cardiac centre. Louise was admitted to hospital and had a four-hour operation. She was allowed to go home after ten days. For the first few weeks she was tired and irritable, but soon regained her energy. After about six months Louise started taking part in normal activities. She will need to take antibiotics before any medical procedures to prevent any chance of infection.

DISEASED CORONARY ARTERIES

Several physical conditions can affect the health of the coronary arteries and result in angina, heart muscle damage or even a heart attack. Stress, too, can lead to coronary spasm, which may temporarily cut off blood flow to the heart.

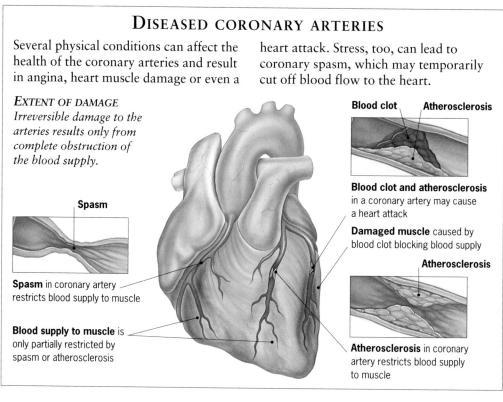

EXTENT OF DAMAGE
Irreversible damage to the arteries results only from complete obstruction of the blood supply.

Spasm

Spasm in coronary artery restricts blood supply to muscle

Blood supply to muscle is only partially restricted by spasm or atherosclerosis

Blood clot   **Atherosclerosis**

Blood clot and atherosclerosis in a coronary artery may cause a heart attack

Damaged muscle caused by blood clot blocking blood supply

Atherosclerosis

Atherosclerosis in coronary artery restricts blood supply to muscle

---

HAWTHORN
The flowers, leaves and berries of this shrub (Craegus spp.) have been used by herbalists for over a hundred years to treat heart disorders. A hawthorn berry infusion is recommended for clearing out arteries and improving circulation (see page 103).

If the atherosclerosis is well advanced, then surgical procedures may be performed such as balloon angioplasty (see page 111). This pushes the plaque apart and widens the artery. This procedure often needs to be repeated within a couple of years. Laser catheters may also be used (see page 111).

Natural therapies

Therapies may help limit the damage caused by atherosclerosis and some may actually reverse it. Naturopaths recommend taking supplements of the antioxidant vitamins A, C and E (see page 59) to prevent the oxidation of 'bad' LDL-cholesterol which causes fatty deposits in arteries. Important catalysts for the actions of these vitamins include zinc (found in liver, fish and eggs), manganese (in nuts, cereals and egg yolks), selenium (in fish and shellfish) and vitamin B_6 (in cereals and meat).

Some fats are important for preventing atherosclerosis, including the oils found in fish, omega-3 and omega-6. Other sources of omega-3 include sunflower, linseed and safflower oils, and for omega-6, evening primrose oil, blackcurrant seeds and borage.

Herbalists recommend eating bromelain (pineapple), which breaks down fibrin (protein in clots), and garlic, onion and ginger, which help reduce blood cholesterol. Also,

herbs can be taken as teas or infusions; these include bamboo, hawthorn berry, lime blossom and mistletoe to break down plaques, and lily-of-the-valley and motherwort to dilate the arteries.

Aromatherapy oils, such as juniper, lavender, lemon and rosemary, can be used in massage or baths to purify the blood and break down plaques.

Because stress hormones increase the production of cholesterol, stress reduction is essential for lowering cholesterol levels. Learn relaxation or visualisation exercises (see page 83), meditation (see pages 36, 104), or autogenic training (see page 42).

ANGINA AND CORONARY HEART DISEASE

When the coronary arteries are damaged due to atherosclerosis, blood clots or spasm of the artery walls, the blood supply to the heart is restricted and angina results. Angina (see page 86) is chest pain that occurs as a symptom of coronary heart disease (also called coronary artery disease). If the coronary arteries become totally obstructed, then a heart attack (myocardial infarction) may occur (see page 112).

Angina occurs whenever the heart's workload exceeds the ability of the coronary arteries to supply it with blood. This blood starvation of muscle is called 'ischaemia'. Angina nearly always disappears quickly with rest because the demands on the heart are lessened, and the coronary arteries can again meet the heart's demand for blood. The pattern of angina tends to be predictable, although trigger factors vary between individuals. If the pattern changes for the worse, however, and attacks become more frequent and/or more severe for over three months, a heart attack will occur in one-third of cases unless action is taken.

Specialist medical advice should always be sought if angina is suspected, and if a diagnosis is made, then individuals will have to make changes in habits, diet and causes of stress. Natural remedies may also be helpful to relieve some of the symptoms.

Diagnosis

Doctors use several procedures to investigate angina and coronary heart disease, including standard and stress ECG (see page 91), echocardiography (see page 94) and nuclear scanning techniques (see page 94).

If such tests indicate that there are problems with the supply of blood to the heart, a more sensitive procedure is needed to discover exactly what is going on in the heart and where troublesome narrowing of the arteries has occurred. Doctors may then use coronary angiography (see page 98).

ANGINA TRIGGER Strenuous work such as gardening and lifting heavy objects may bring on an angina attack.

Treatment

If the coronary arteries are not seriously impaired, then treatment will aim to help the sufferer adopt a healthier lifestyle to lower blood pressure and heart rate.

In more severe cases, however, drugs may be used to reduce the heart muscle's workload. Drugs are also used for pain relief.

Drugs

Beta-blockers are used to slow the heart rate, reduce the heart muscle's contractions and lower blood pressure, reducing the workload on the heart.

Nitrates lower blood pressure by dilating the blood vessels. Most nitrates are used to relieve the symptoms of an angina attack once it has started or to prevent one occurring in an 'at risk' situation. These are taken as oral sprays or tablets placed under the tongue, and offer relief within 5 minutes. People who get angina even when they are not exercising are often helped by longer lasting forms of nitrate preparations which are either taken as tablets or absorbed slowly from a skin patch. Skin patches should be removed for 8 hours before replacing to prevent the build-up of tolerance to the drug.

Calcium antagonists also dilate the coronary arteries, and reduce blood pressure by dilating blood vessels throughout the body and by slowing the heart rate.

Surgery

For people whose angina is not sufficiently relieved by drugs or whose coronary arteries have been narrowed by atherosclerosis to such an extent that there is a high risk of a heart attack, a more direct approach is needed. There are two surgical alternatives which either attempt to clear the blocked artery or bypass it.

Coronary angioplasty

In a procedure known as coronary angioplasty, a catheter with a small balloon at the tip is inserted into an artery in the arm or groin and threaded into the blocked coronary artery. When the catheter reaches the narrowed area, the balloon is then inflated for up to 2 minutes, pushing the walls of the artery apart. Catheters can also be fitted with lasers which vapourise blockages, or with tiny cutters to shave off the atheroma from the artery walls. The fatty bits are then removed with a vacuum device.

Clearing out arteries

There are a number of different procedures using catheters to open arteries narrowed from plaques.

The balloon catheter is inserted into the artery then inflated to push it open

A catheter with a 'shaving' device is used to shear plaque off the artery walls

A laser beam may be emitted from the end of the catheter to vapourise the plaque

Acupressure for angina
Apply pressure to these points during and after an angina attack.

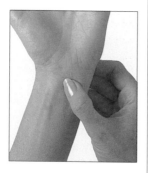

PRESSURE POINT H 7
This point is on the front of the wrist crease on the little finger end, just inside the small bone.

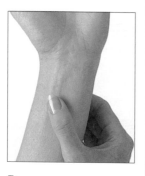

PRESSURE POINT P 6
This point is on the front of the wrist, two fingers away from the wrist crease between the two tendons.

CORONARY ARTERY BYPASS SURGERY
This may be done when attempts to clear blocked arteries have failed. Here two of the coronary arteries have been bypassed.

Coronary angioplasty and the new catheter techniques are generally simpler and safer procedures than coronary artery bypass grafting, but about a third of arteries cleared in this way become clogged up again within a year, hence the necessity for making lifestyle changes to avoid this.

Coronary artery bypass graft

If blockages recur or if they are difficult to reach by catheter, your doctor may recommend surgery to bypass the affected area. In a coronary artery bypass graft, a small length of vein, usually from the leg, is removed and grafted from the aorta to the coronary artery beyond the blockage to allow blood to flow to the heart muscle. Internal mammary and other arteries are often used. Usually two or three arteries are by-passed, but it can be as many as five.

During this operation, the heart is stopped and its functions, and those of the lungs, are temporarily taken over by a sophisticated piece of equipment called a cardiopulmonary bypass machine, commonly known as a 'heart-lung machine'. Forty per cent of those who have had this operation will have to have it again in ten years time.

Natural therapies

There are a range of natural therapies that may be used with your doctor's supervision to help treat angina. Treatments focus on reducing atherosclerosis (see page 108) and blood pressure (see page 124).

Acupuncture (see page 101) is widely used for angina in China. Acupressure, where hand or finger pressure is used instead of needles, can be just as effective. The symptoms of angina can be relieved by applying deep thumb pressure to H 7 and P 6 (see left) for at least a minute. Consult a practitioner of Chinese medicine and ask to be shown how you can perform acupressure on yourself at home.

Angina can be reduced in severity by learning to relax and lower blood pressure. This can be achieved by autogenic training (see page 42) or biofeedback (see page 141) as well as meditation (see page 36, 104). Hypnosis can relieve the pain of angina and aid relaxation.

HEART ATTACK (MYOCARDIAL INFARCTION)

When one or more coronary arteries becomes completely blocked, a heart attack (myocardial infarction) may result. During a heart attack, an area of heart muscle dies from lack of blood and oxygen. The amount of damage to the heart depends on where the blockage occurs and how big an area of heart muscle dies.

A blockage can happen in two ways. Most commonly a blood clot or 'thrombus' (see page 125) suddenly obstructs the already narrowed artery, but occasionally atherosclerosis (see page 108) can be so severe that the artery simply clogs up completely.

Symptoms

The vast majority of heart attack victims suffer pain that is similar to angina but it is more severe and longer lasting and does not cease with rest. In almost 70 per cent of cases the pain radiates through the jaw and neck and down the left arm. Breathing can be difficult and laboured and made worse by lying down. Nausea, dizziness, sweating and belching up air are also common.

Once a heart attack victim has survived the early crisis, the chances of survival become increasingly better. Those who show no signs of heart failure (see page 120) 48 hours after the onset of an attack, whose pulse is reasonably normal and who do not have any damage to the electrical pathways of the heart have a good chance of recovery.

Diagnosis

The principal tool doctors use to confirm a heart attack is the ECG (see page 91). However, changes to the heartbeat pattern

Veins are joined to aorta to restore blood flow

Vein from leg used to bypass artery

Vein from leg used to bypass artery

Blockage in coronary artery

Blockage in coronary artery

often do not appear until several hours after a heart attack starts and sometimes do not appear at all. Therefore doctors generally rely on the patient's description of his or her symptoms, and work on the assumption that a heart attack is taking place. The diagnosis can then be confirmed later.

Doctors can also monitor the patient's blood for enzymes which are released by damaged heart muscle cells. Among the easiest to measure is the enzyme creatine kinase (CK). CK levels typically peak between 24 and 48 hours after a heart attack and remain raised for up to five days.

Treatment

Heart muscle can only survive for a few hours after its blood supply is cut off, so speed is vital in the treatment of someone who is suffering a heart attack. In this situation doctors have three priorities: to relieve pain, control any abnormal heartbeat rhythms that develop, and prevent further damage to the heart muscle.

Intravenous injection of drugs from the opiate family, such as morphine in most countries, and diamorphine (better known as heroin) in the UK, are frequently used to relieve pain. Such drugs work extremely quickly and are very effective.

Many heart attack sufferers develop dangerous abnormalities in their heart rhythm (see page 114) and these must be corrected quickly or they can prove fatal. Half of all heart attack sufferers die from the most serious of these, a condition known as ventricular fibrillation. Here the ventricles beat in such a fast and chaotic manner that hardly any blood is pumped around the body. The sufferer becomes unconscious, breathing stops and death follows within minutes.

Drugs, such as lignocaine, can be used to prevent this rhythm disturbance after a heart attack, while the use of a large electric shock jolts the heart back into a normal

rhythm (defibrillation) and restores order. Clot-dissolving (thrombolytic) enzymes are given as soon as a heart attack is diagnosed – often on arrival in a casualty ward. Other treatment includes giving oxygen, if there is unstable angina, and nitroglycerine. Aspirin may also be used as an antiplatelet as well as a painkiller (see page 114).

Depending on the patient's condition, he or she may be given beta-blockers (to reduce pain and make the heart beat more slowly); diuretics (if congestive heart failure occurs); and vasopressors (to raise blood pressure, or if shock occurs).

It is unlikely that one coronary artery will be completely blocked without the others also being clogged up to some extent. Either coronary angioplasty or coronary artery bypass grafting (see page 112) is sometimes needed to prevent another heart attack, but first the patient needs to be stabilised before invasive examinations and surgery are done.

Natural therapies

Recovering from a heart attack may involve medical procedures to unclog arteries, but you can adopt a number of measures which will go a long way towards preventing a heart attack and improving your chances of survival if you have already had one. Chapter 7 deals with recovery from a heart attack in more detail.

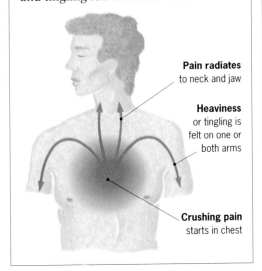

DURING A HEART ATTACK

The most obvious symptom of a heart attack is crushing chest pain which lasts at least 20 minutes, and the heaviness and tingling felt down the arms.

Pain radiates
to neck and jaw

Heaviness
or tingling is felt on one or both arms

Crushing pain
starts in chest

Caution with drugs

As with all prescription drugs, caution must always be taken with heart drugs, many of which are dangerous if administered incorrectly. Make sure you understand all the instructions on the label or given by your doctor, and if you are unsure of anything, ask your doctor or pharmacist. Be sure to follow instructions exactly.

Discuss side-effects with your doctor and contact him or her immediately if side-effects become very severe. Tell your doctor if symptoms persist because it may be possible or necessary to change your drug.

Always inform your doctor of any other medication you are taking, including the contraceptive pill and any herbal remedies; of any chronic illnesses; and if you are pregnant or trying to conceive. Keep drugs in a cool, dry place, well out of reach of children.

Herbal history

Many modern drugs have been extracted from natural herbs, such as aspirin, which comes from the bark of the white willow, and digitalis, which comes from foxglove. Digitalis acts as a diuretic, strengthens the heart's contractions and reduces blood pressure. These properties were discovered by William Withering, an English physician in 1775, and since then digitalis has been widely prescribed for congestive heart failure. Infusions or teas of foxglove leaves are commonly used in South America for heart tonics, but foxglove is highly poisonous and should only be taken on the advice of a qualified physician or herbalist.

Atherosclerosis is the most common cause of coronary heart disease leading to a heart attack and this needs to be treated (see page 108). Also, treatments for angina (see page 110) will prevent another heart attack; and the control of hypertension is essential (see page 124).

Some herbal remedies may strengthen your heart's contractions. These include: bugleweed, motherwort, knotted figwort and hawthorn berry (see page 102). Ask a qualified herbalist for advice, and consult your doctor before you take any herbs.

HEART RATE AND RHYTHM DISORDERS

The heart's pacemaker, the sinoatrial node, controls the rate and rhythm of the heart by directing its electrical system (see page 20). There are two types of abnormal heart rhythms, or 'arrhythmias': those in which the heart beats too quickly, called tachycardias, and those in which the heart beats too slowly, known as bradycardias.

The most common cause of arrhythmias is coronary heart disease (see page 110). Inadequate blood supply to the heart disrupts the transmission of electrical signals around the heart. Arrhythmias also occur during and after heart attacks (see page 112) when the heart's electrical pathways can be damaged; from congenital heart disorders (see page 106); or from disorders of the thyroid gland (which produces hormones that stimulate the heart).

Symptoms

Both types of arrhythmias, tachycardia and bradycardia, can cause palpitations, dizziness, sudden fainting and breathlessness as the heart beats less efficiently, so less blood reaches the brain and the lungs.

If the rhythm disturbance is severe, the person quickly becomes unconscious and normal rhythm needs to be restored immediately. Death follows in a few minutes if the person is not resuscitated.

Treatment

There are two main emergency methods of treating dangerous arrhythmias: jolting the heart back into a normal rhythm using a large electric shock, a procedure known as defibrillation, and/or the use of specialised anti-arrhythmic drugs such as lignocaine (see page 113).

Patients who have mild symptoms do not require treatment. But for an arrhythmia

---

ASPIRIN – THE WONDER DRUG?

Aspirin is often recommended by doctors for people thought to be at risk of a heart attack as well as those recovering from one. They are normally advised to take 75 mg of aspirin a day. This is because as well as its properties of reducing fever, as a painkiller and as an anti-inflammatory, it also acts as an antiplatelet, reducing the chances of a blood clot by stopping platelets sticking together. It is often prescribed for people who have had a coronary bypass operation.

Only low doses are required to produce an effect which is why 'mini aspirin' is often recommended for heart disease sufferers. The US Doctors Aspirin Trial, which began in 1988, has shown a 44 per cent decrease in the risk of heart attacks in aspirin takers over five years.

Although aspirin reduces the chances of stroke caused by clots, at higher doses it increases the chance of stroke caused by bleeding (brain haemorrhage). However, at the low doses prescribed for heart disease there is no significant risk.

It can also cause severe stomach irritation and stomach bleeding in some cases. People with a clotting disorder and a tendency to bleed, a stomach ulcer, an intolerance to aspirin, or asthma may be advised not to take it. Some people may be given special coated pills for safety.

While doctors regard daily doses of aspirin as invaluable in treating some patients with heart disease, among other problems, they do not recommend it in every case. Aspirin should only be taken regularly under medical supervision.

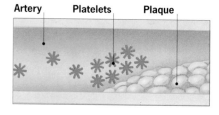

Artery · Platelets · Plaque

BEFORE TAKING ASPIRIN
A cracked plaque in a blood vessel bleeds and then platelets start to form clumps, leading to a clot.

Aspirin

AFTER TAKING ASPIRIN
Aspirin reduces the stickiness of the platelets so they clump together less easily and a clot is less likely to form.

which causes severe symptoms, various long-term drugs may be prescribed, or a pacemaker may be fitted.

Pacemakers

A pacemaker is a small, battery-powered device. The battery, which is inserted under a flap of skin in the chest or stomach, is wired to an electrode implanted in the heart. The electrode sends out timed electrical impulses to make the heart contract and keep it beating normally.

Pacemakers only operate when they sense the heart losing its rhythm. They are relatively easy to fit and their batteries last for five to ten years before they need to be replaced in a small operation, which is usually carried out under local anaesthetic.

People with pacemakers should avoid activities where there is a strong electromagnetic field, such as working on the engine of a car when it is running. Contact sports or shooting with a rifle will interfere with the positioning of a pacemaker. Airport monitoring devices will not harm pacemakers but they may set off metal detectors.

Defibrillator

Patients with repeated tachycardia may have an automatic cardiac defibrillator implanted, which can return a rapidly beating heart to a normal rate and rhythm. The device is a small electric generator with three wires. It is implanted in the muscle of the abdomen, with an electrode implanted under the skin and the wires attached to the heart. It responds to an increase in heart rate with an electric shock which stops the heart for a split second, giving the sinoatrial node a chance to regain control.

Natural therapies

Arrhythmias need to be treated medically but some natural therapies may assist in relieving symptoms.

Arrhythmias that result from a mineral deficiency may be treated with nutritional therapy. Magnesium is necessary for maintaining muscular contractions by balancing the effects of calcium (which makes muscles contract). Sources of magnesium include nuts, soya beans, beans and bran. Potassium, essential for slowing down the heart, is found in fruit and vegetables, with bananas the best source. Do not take mineral supplements without consulting your doctor.

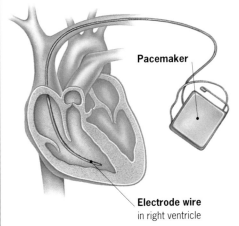

RESTORING RHYTHM

The fitting of a pacemaker is done under local anaesthetic. The pacemaker leads are threaded through a vein into the right ventricle, the right atrium or usually both.

Pacemaker

Electrode wire in right ventricle

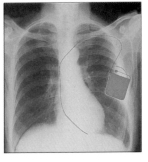

PACEMAKER IN PLACE
Once fitted, the pacemaker (red square) is scarcely noticeable.

There are some herbs recommended for irregularities in heart rhythm, including bugleweed, night blooming cereus, lily-of-the-valley, mistletoe and hawthorn berries. These are usually taken as teas. Always consult a herbalist for the appropriate remedy and do not start taking herbs or stop taking medication without consulting your doctor.

Acupuncture and acupressure may help relieve palpitations by inducing relaxation.

Stress management is essential for controlling arrhythmias. Meditation (see pages 36, 104), autogenic training (see page 42) and yoga (see page 104) can all be effective.

HEART VALVE DISORDERS

The four valves of the heart ensure that blood travels in the right direction. The heart's efficiency depends upon these valves working correctly (see page 20). There are two types of valve disorders: the valves narrow and fail to open wide enough to allow sufficient blood through (called 'stenotic'); or the valves fail to close properly, allowing blood to flow backwards (called 'leaky', 'regurgitant' or 'incompetent').

Stenosis is usually due to inflammation of the valve from bacteria, to an accumulation of calcium deposits which is caused by ageing, or to a valve abnormality which makes them more susceptible to calcium deposits. Leaky or regurgitant valves are normally caused by coronary heart disease, bacterial infection called endocarditis (see page 119),

ACUPRESSURE FOR ANXIETY: POINT H 3 Anxiety can often bring on palpitations. Pressing this point at the inner end of the elbow crease when the elbow is bent will help you to calm down.

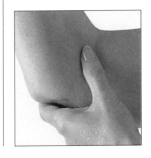

CARDIOPULMONARY RESUSCITATION (CPR)

CPR is an emergency first aid procedure, used when the heart stops beating for more than a few seconds, to keep up a temporary supply of blood to the brain, heart and other organs, allowing the patient to survive until medical help arrives. Carried out correctly, CPR can save lives but rescuers must be properly trained.

Broken ribs and internal bruising from poorly performed CPR will probably decrease the patient's chances of survival. Relatives or friends of anyone at high risk of a heart attack should learn CPR. The ABC formula forms the basis of CPR training. 'A' is for airway. 'B' is for breathing. 'C' is for compression.

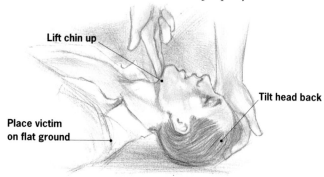

Lift chin up

Tilt head back

Place victim on flat ground

1 *If the victim is unconscious and has no pulse, call for help immediately. Place the victim on his or her back on a firm, flat surface. Kneel to the side of the victim. Clear the mouth of any objects such as food. To open the airways: put a hand on the victim's forehead and tilt it back. Place two fingers on the victim's lower jaw bone and lift it up to move the tongue away from the throat.*

Listen for victim's breathing

2 *Check if the victim is breathing by listening for any breathing sounds, feeling for air movement on your cheek and ear and watching for chest movement. If the victim is not breathing, start mouth-to-mouth resuscitation.*

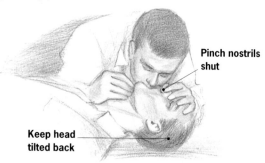

Pinch nostrils shut

Keep head tilted back

3 *Mouth-to-mouth: keep the forehead tilted back and pinch the victim's nostrils shut. Open your mouth, take a deep breath and make a tight seal around the victim's mouth. Breathe slow breaths into the mouth – one breath every five seconds. Refill your lungs after each breath. The victim's chest should rise with each breath.*

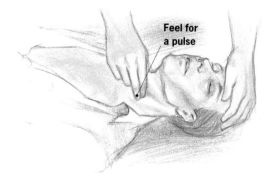

Feel for a pulse

4 *Feel for a pulse at the neck (carotid artery). If there is none, then compression is required.*

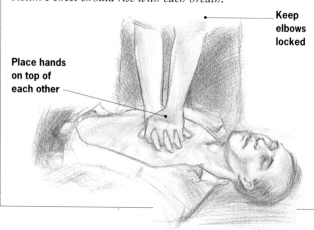

Keep elbows locked

Place hands on top of each other

5 *Compression: place the heel of your hand two fingers up from the bottom of the breastbone. Place your other hand on top of the first. Make sure your shoulders are directly over your hands and your elbows are straight and locked, in order to use your own body weight for compression. Compress the chest smoothly and evenly, using the heel of your hand. Keep fingers off the victim's ribs. Apply enough force to depress the breastbone 4 to 5 cm (1½ to 2 in) at a rate of 80 compressions per minute. Between compressions, let the chest return to the normal position, but keep your hands in place on the chest. Count aloud. After 15 compressions, breathe into the victim's mouth twice. After four cycles of 15 compressions and two breaths, check again for a pulse and breathing. If there is none, continue the procedure until help arrives.*

or rheumatic fever. Both types of valve disorder can also be congenital. The most common valve disorders involve the mitral and aortic valves on the left side of the heart.

Symptoms

The range of symptoms is very wide. If the mitral valve between the left atrium and left ventricle becomes narrowed (stenotic), blood builds up in the atrium and goes back to the lungs. Blood vessels in the lungs, squeezed between this congestion on one side and blood being pumped in by the right ventricle on the other, begin to leak. Fluid enters the lung tissue and the lungs are unable to expand fully and take in adequate oxygen. The result is breathlessness, fatigue and, in severe cases, congestive heart failure (see page 120). A further complication is that the left atrium can enlarge and arrhythmias (see page 114) may develop.

Mitral valve leakage (or regurgitation) is another common problem. Here the cusps of the valve do not close properly and blood leaks back into the atrium when the left ventricle contracts. This reduces the amount of blood being pumped forward by the left ventricle which has to work much harder to compensate. Symptoms may not appear for years, but if the problem is not remedied the left side of the heart will eventually be weakened and permanently damaged by the strain. This leads to symptoms similar to congestive heart failure, including shortness of breath, fatigue, weakness, swelling of the ankles and palpitations.

Diagnosis

Doctors can glean quite a lot of information about how the valves are working by simply listening to the heart with a stethoscope (see page 20). If the doctor suspects that one or more valves is not working properly, then several specialist procedures can be used to establish what is going wrong and where. The most useful is echocardiography (see page 94) but x-rays can also be used as can cardiac catheterisation (see page 95).

Treatment

Although treatment with drugs, such as diuretics which encourage the loss of fluid from the body, can ease some of the symptoms, the best long-term solution is surgery to repair or replace the problematic valve.

Catheterisation can be used to widen a narrowed valve in which there is limited blood flow. In a procedure known as

(see page 120)

Rheumatic fever

Rheumatic heart disease, caused by rheumatic fever, was once the most common cause of serious valve problems, although this disease is now quite rare because of modern antibiotics.

It usually affects children aged five to 15. It begins as a bacterial infection (streptococcus) which causes a sore throat (however, not everyone who gets streptococcus will develop rheumatic heart disease). Other symptoms include tender swollen glands, rapid heartbeat, chills, joint pain, rash and fatigue.

If it is not treated early with antibiotics the infection can develop into an acute fever that lasts ten to 14 days, and can attack the heart valves. The valves become scarred, leading to malfunction, which may not be immediately noticeable – indeed it may not show up for 30 years. Some people have no problems or only mild discomfort for much of their lives. But eventually damaged heart valves will cause serious problems as the heart becomes less efficient.

INFECTION OF THE VALVES

Valve infections are most commonly caused by the bacteria *streptococcus viridans*. The infection starts as a sore throat and travels to the heart in the blood. It is most likely to attack valves that are congenitally deformed or those damaged by other diseases. A damaged valve may need to be surgically repaired.

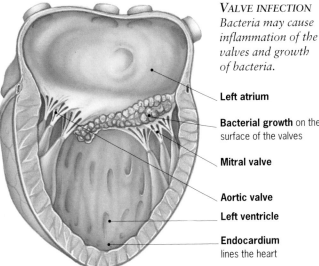

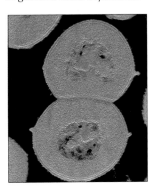

STREPTOCOCCUS VIRIDANS
This micrograph shows the bacteria in their typical paired formation. This bacteria may also be found in gut and tooth infections.

VALVE INFECTION
Bacteria may cause inflammation of the valves and growth of bacteria.

Left atrium

Bacterial growth on the surface of the valves

Mitral valve

Aortic valve

Left ventricle

Endocardium lines the heart

Take care with infection

Anyone with a heart valve problem should take extra care of their teeth and gums. Mouth infections can let bacteria into the bloodstream and cause further damage to the valves (a condition called infective endocarditis). Antibiotics should always be taken before dental treatment to prevent further risk of infection. Other serious infections, such as in the urinary tract or in the lungs, can also pose a risk, as can any kind of surgery.

DANDELION
The leaves and roots of the dandelion are effective diuretics and are used to lower high blood pressure and reduce swelling of the legs.

balloon valvuloplasty, a catheter fitted with a small balloon is inserted into an artery in the groin or arm and guided into the heart. Once inside the affected valve, the balloon is inflated, pushing the valve cusps apart. This procedure will need to be repeated if the cusps do not stay apart permanently.

Leaky or regurgitant valves can often be repaired, either by cutting out some sections of tissue to allow for a closer fit or by clinching in the surrounding tissue to push the valve cusps closer together. However, in many cases valves cannot be repaired and valve replacement is the only solution.

Replacement valves

There are two types of replacement valves: mechanical (made of metal and plastic) or biological (made from animal or donated human tissue, including pericardium from the patient's own heart or from someone who has died). Mechanical valves are tough and long-lasting but blood clots tend to form on their surfaces, and patients fitted with mechanical replacement valves must have life-long treatment with anticoagulant drugs. These reduce the blood's normal tendency to clot. Biological valves do not cause this problem to such an extent but they are less durable and up to 50 per cent of people need the valve replaced within ten years.

Natural therapies

Once valves are damaged, surgical repair or replacement is necessary; however the symptoms of valve disease can be relieved by some natural measures. The most noticeable symptom is breathlessness, resulting from fluid build-up in the lungs. Herbal teas such as dandelion and yarrow are effective diuretics and will reduce this fluid build-up, relieving breathlessness. Unlike diuretic drugs, they do not leach the body of potassium. Check with your doctor before using these teas along with diuretic medication.

People with metal or plastic valves need to take anticoagulants. Herbalists recommend garlic, ginger, onion and bromelain (from pineapple) as natural anticoagulants. Do not stop taking your anticoagulant medication without consulting your doctor.

HEART MUSCLE DISEASE

If the heart muscle becomes damaged, the heart loses its pumping power and, in severe cases, heart failure can follow. Disease of

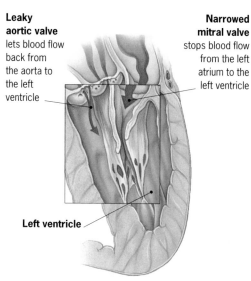

Leaky aortic valve lets blood flow back from the aorta to the left ventricle

Narrowed mitral valve stops blood flow from the left atrium to the left ventricle

Left ventricle

DISEASED VALVES
Valves may become narrowed or leaky, often as a result of infection. Some valves can be repaired while others need to be replaced.

the pericardium (the membrane surrounding the heart muscle), and the endocardium (the membrane lining the heart muscle) can also cause serious problems.

Disease of the heart muscle, called cardiomyopathy, has many causes. The muscle can be gradually weakened by a series of heart attacks; damaged by other diseases such as coronary heart disease, high blood pressure, valve disease, neurological disorders and blood disorders; or affected by alcoholism or a deficiency of nutrients such as thiamin (vitamin B_1).

Inflammation of the heart muscle, called myocarditis, can occur as a result of viral or bacterial infections, chemicals, drugs, radiation and immune system disorders. Most people will recover from myocarditis but some may suffer complications leading to heart failure and arrhythmia.

There are three types of cardiomyopathy. Dilated cardiomyopathy occurs when the walls of the ventricles become weak and cannot pump efficiently. This is often caused by alcohol or by a viral infection, high blood pressure or heart valve defects. Hypertrophic cardiomyopathy occurs when the muscles of the heart wall thicken, reducing the volume of the heart chambers and restricting the amount of blood pumped. Restrictive cardiomyopathy occurs when the heart's chambers do not fill properly so blood goes backwards into the veins. The causes are not well understood.

Alcohol and the heart

Excessive drinking can cause dilated cardiomyopathy. This occurs because alcoholics often do not eat properly, replacing food with alcohol, which results in deficiencies of nutrients including vitamin B_1, B_2, B_3, B_6, folic acid, calcium, magnesium and zinc. Also, chemical additives in alcohol and alcohol itself are toxic to the heart in large quantities.

If an alcoholic stops drinking before heart failure occurs, he or she may not suffer too much heart damage. However, heart muscle damage is irreversible, so if heart failure does occur, 50 per cent of patients will die within a year and more than 75 per cent of patients will die within five years.

Giving up an alcohol addiction is not easy. However, once you have made the decision to do it there is help available. You should contact your local Alcoholics Anonymous (AA) organisation which can provide support, encouragement and motivation, through their self-help groups.

Some natural therapies, such as acupuncture or hypnosis, may help in overcoming both the physical and psychological effects of withdrawal. Meditation can be used to strengthen your will-power and combat withdrawal symptoms (see page 36). Yoga (see page 104) will keep you tranquil when you begin to feel depressed, anxious or irritable during withdrawal. A naturopath (see page 122) or dietician can help with advice on a healthy diet to replace the nutrients lost through excessive alcohol intake.

Pericarditis

If the pericardium, the tough protective bag or sac surrounding the heart, becomes infected by viruses, or occasionally bacteria, an inflammation known as pericarditis can result. This causes pain which is worse with deep breathing or when the heart is beating rapidly. In some cases pericarditis causes the inner layer to produce too much lubricating fluid, which can compress the heart and reduce its ability to pump effectively. Rarely, the pericardium can become scarred and thicken, further restricting heart movement.

Endocarditis

Bacteria can also infect the lining of the heart chambers and valves causing inflammation, a condition known as endocarditis. A gum or tooth infection can cause this, which is why susceptible people must take antibiotics 1 hour before they embark on dental treatment and 6 hours after it.

Symptoms

Symptoms depend on the type of cardiomyopathy. Dilated cardiomyopathy causes palpitations, swollen ankles, breathlessness and chest pain; hypertrophic cardiomyopathy causes breathlessness, chest pain, fatigue and fainting; restrictive cardiomyopathy causes enlarged liver, swollen ankles, fluid retention in abdomen and lungs; myocarditis causes chest pain and shortness of breath; endocarditis produces the symptoms of valve disease (see page 117).

Treatment

Heart muscle infections caused by bacteria can often be cured by antibiotics if they are detected promptly. However, as there are often few specific symptoms until serious damage has occurred, early diagnosis is difficult. But when the heart muscle becomes seriously damaged, heart transplantation is the only option.

Heart transplant

To qualify for this operation, individuals must be younger than 60 years and they must have a life expectancy of only two or three years. Potential candidates undergo a

---

PERICARDITIS

Pericarditis occurs when the inner layer of the pericardium becomes inflamed and produces too much fluid. This compresses the heart, and interferes with its pumping action.

Labels: Right atrium, Right ventricle, Inner layer of pericardium, Outer layer of pericardium, Fluid build-up compresses heart, Left atrium, Left ventricle, Inner layer of pericardium, Outer layer of pericardium, Fluid layer, Myocardium

DR CHRISTIAAN BARNARD
The world's first successful heart transplant from one human to another was carried out in 1967 by the South African surgeon Christiaan Barnard.

variety of tests to see if a heart transplant is appropriate. Contraindications, such as pulmonary hypertension, infection, a serious disease, drug or alcohol abuse, extreme obesity, and inability to stick to the programme of medication, will rule them out. Tests will also be carried out to see if their immune system would reject the new heart.

If selected, they will be placed on a waiting list and from then until the time of being called, they must stay within 2 to 3 hours travel to the hospital (a donor heart can only survive for 4 to 6 hours before the transplantation is completed). The donor of the heart must have the same blood group and tissue type as the recipient and have no sign of infection. The donor's race and sex are of no account; the heart size does not have to be the same, but there cannot be too great a difference.

The transplant is a straightforward operation in skilled surgical hands. Patients are connected to the heart-lung machine and the old heart is removed by the surgeon who will make an incision in the atria, aorta, and pulmonary arteries and then connect the new heart to them.

After the transplant, patients need to stay in the hospital for one to three weeks. To control rejection of the heart by the immune system they will be given immunosuppressive drugs. These and other drugs will need to be continued throughout their life and will be adjusted to minimise side-effects. Biopsies will be performed every week for the first six weeks after surgery to test that the tissues are free from infection. This will continue fortnightly for six weeks, then monthly for three months, then quarterly and half-yearly. With a transplant, there is an 80 per cent one year survival rate, and 60 per cent after five years.

Natural therapies
Heart muscle damage cannot be reversed by any means, but some of the symptoms can be relieved. Natural diuretics, such as dandelion or yarrow tea, can be taken to reduce fluid retention, and other herbs – valerian, balm, motherwort, skullcap, St John's wort – can be used for relaxation.

CONGESTIVE HEART FAILURE
Congestive heart failure, or simply heart failure, occurs when the heart can no longer pump enough blood to meet the body's

demands. It is a gradual process, and can often take many years. Any damage to the pumping capacity of the heart caused by high blood pressure, coronary heart disease, heart attack, rhythm disorders or valve defects or disease can lead to heart failure.

Once heart failure has begun it gets progressively worse. The heart compensates for failing to meet the body's demands for blood by pumping faster and harder. The arteries contract, making the already struggling heart's task of pumping the blood around the body much more difficult. Also, pressure builds in the veins because the heart is not able to pump blood efficiently through the arteries. This makes the heart get progressively weaker.

Meanwhile, the poor circulation of blood to the kidneys means they cannot function properly or excrete enough sodium, or salt, in the urine. The levels of sodium rise causing water retention in the body, and a general build-up of fluid in the body tissues, which puts further pressure on the heart.

Symptoms
The symptoms of heart failure include shortness of breath even at rest – this gets worse when lying down because of a build-up of fluid in the lungs; fatigue during exercise; swelling of the legs, feet, hands and sometimes trunk of the body. Heart failure can be mild or severe, but it is often referred to as congestive because of the filling of the lungs and tissues with fluid.

Left or right heart failure
Doctors often refer to left heart failure or right heart failure, depending on which side of the heart is most affected. The job of the left atrium and ventricle is to take oxygenated blood from the lungs and pump it around the body. Therefore left heart failure results in fluid accumulating in the lungs. This means that breathlessness is the most important symptom.

DID YOU KNOW?
About one per cent of the Western world's population suffers from congestive heart failure and the likelihood of developing the condition increases with age – ten per cent of all those aged over 80 suffer from congestive heart failure.

The right atrium and ventricle's job is to collect deoxygenated blood returning from the body and pump it to the lungs. During right heart failure, the blood flow is also decreased, but in this case the fluid that accumulates produces swelling in the legs, stomach and liver.

Both left and right heart failure ultimately result in less blood being pumped to the body, causing general fatigue.

Diagnosis

Doctors establish a preliminary diagnosis of heart failure from a physical examination and from the patient's symptoms, and then confirm this using x-ray and echocardiography examinations (see page 94).

Treatment

Rest can play an important role in the treatment of heart failure. If the patient is very elderly or is content with an inactive lifestyle, there may be no point in further treatment as heart failure generally progresses slowly and the symptoms are greatly improved by rest.

There are several other ways to minimise the discomfort of heart failure. Lose weight if you are overweight (see page 51). Reduce the amount of salt in your diet (see page 51). Limit your fluid intake to 2 litres (3½ pints) a day, except in hot weather or hot climates or when you are suffering from sickness, diarrhoea or fever. Drink alcohol only in moderate amounts or not at all. Do not smoke at all. Try to do some regular mild exercise if at all possible, such as walking for 20 minutes daily, but take care not to overstrain yourself.

Drugs

The symptoms of heart failure can be relieved by long-term treatment with drugs such as digitalis, which strengthen and regulate the heart's pumping action; diuretics, which reduce the amount of fluid in your body; and vasodilators, such as ACE (angiotensin-converting enzyme) inhibitors, which widen the constricted blood vessels and so reduce the pressure against which the heart has to pump, easing its workload.

Sluggish blood circulation means that people suffering from heart failure are more at risk from the formation of blood clots (thrombus) which can block vital arteries. They are therefore often given anticoagulant therapy, which helps to prevent clotting. All grades of heart failure can usually be controlled by diuretics or ACE inhibitors and by reducing the amount of salt in the diet. As a result of these advances in drug therapy, the outlook for heart failure patients has been greatly improved. However, while the majority of cases can be treated with one or more of the drugs mentioned above, if heart failure becomes very severe, a heart transplant may be the only hope (see page 119).

Natural therapies

There are no therapies that will restore a failed heart; but there are some measures that will help to relieve symptoms. Herbal diuretics, made from dandelion and yarrow, can be taken as teas to reduce fluid retention. Check with your doctor first to see if they will conflict with a prescribed diuretic.

You can also increase your intake of onion, garlic and ginger, which are believed to be anticoagulants.

Acupressure, massage and hydrotherapy may help relieve swelling in the legs, and improve the circulation.

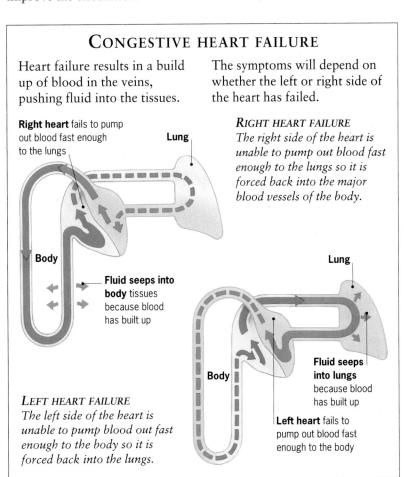

CONGESTIVE HEART FAILURE

Heart failure results in a build up of blood in the veins, pushing fluid into the tissues.

The symptoms will depend on whether the left or right side of the heart has failed.

Right heart fails to pump out blood fast enough to the lungs

Lung

Body

Fluid seeps into body tissues because blood has built up

LEFT HEART FAILURE
The left side of the heart is unable to pump blood out fast enough to the body so it is forced back into the lungs.

RIGHT HEART FAILURE
The right side of the heart is unable to pump out blood fast enough to the lungs so it is forced back into the major blood vessels of the body.

Lung

Body

Fluid seeps into lungs because blood has built up

Left heart fails to pump out blood fast enough to the body

The Naturopath

Dealing with heart disorders requires attention to rest, exercise and nutritional needs, plus physical therapy and stress management. A naturopath will prescribe a combination of these based on the individual's symptoms.

Origins

The idea of naturopathic medicine began with Hippocrates over two centuries ago. He believed that attention to diet, rest and exercise was the key to health. Modern naturopathy, which focused on hydrotherapy as well as dietary measures, was then developed in Europe in the 1800s by therapists such as Vincent Preissnitz.

A Bavarian monk, Father Sebastian Kneipp, originated the idea of health farms as we know them today. One of his followers, Benedictine Lust, then brought naturopathy to the US, where it became a very popular method of treatment.

WATER CURES
This variable pressure shower was popular as part of early hydrotherapy and was used to stimulate the circulation.

Naturopaths have the skills to advise and guide patients with heart disease towards a programme which will suit their individual needs, and help to rebuild their health so that they can have a longer, more fulfilling and active life.

What is naturopathy?

Naturopathic medicine is a system of health care which helps to mobilise and support the body's self-healing processes. A naturopath uses various natural approaches rather than any specific therapy. The emphasis is always on measures which are in harmony with nature, and are tailored to the individual's needs. The naturopath's objective is to help you to take more responsibility for your own health and develop your potential for better health.

What happens in the consultation?

At an initial consultation, the naturopath will question you about your health problems and how they are affected by the food you eat, your work, exercise, the weather and other aspects of your lifestyle.

Your previous illnesses and injuries may also have a bearing on the way your body deals with the present disorder, so these will be noted. Illnesses such as rheumatic fever in childhood, for example, may cause a weakness in the heart valves which doesn't become evident until much later on in life when your ability to compensate for it becomes weaker.

The naturopath will carry out a complete examination including measurement of your pulse rate and blood pressure, listening to your heart and lungs with a stethoscope, and inspection of your skin, eyes and other areas of your body. The naturopath will then discuss possible treatments with you, emphasising the measures you can carry out yourself.

What sort of treatments do naturopaths prescribe?

The naturopath will take into account your doctor's diagnosis and treatment of your heart problem, and will then decide what you can do in the way of diet, exercise and other measures to cope more effectively and improve the health of your heart.

The naturopath will also make recommendations on ways you can reduce physical and emotional stress on your heart and show you methods of strengthening and sustaining its function with herbal and nutritional support. The naturopath will give you guidelines for rest and relaxation and for appropriate exercise (see Chapter 4). The use of baths and compresses or other forms of hydrotherapy may be recommended to help to improve the circulation.

Most naturopaths recommend things that you can do in your own home, but there may also be physical therapies such as massage which the naturopath will do. These will improve the function of the self-healing processes in your body and will not conflict with the conventional medical treatment you may receive for your heart trouble.

How does the naturopath decide which treatments to give?

The naturopath's consultation and examination is intended to reach a diagnosis of your specific condition, as well as to make an assessment of how it relates to your overall health and vitality.

Some calculations using your blood pressure and pulse rate, for example, will give the practitioner a useful guide to the amount of tension in your circulatory system. If it is low it may indicate weakness and loss of vitality and a naturopath might suggest a warming and energy-producing diet. High tension suggests more pressure and congestion in the body, and in this situation you may be recommended to eat more raw fruit and salads.

The naturopath will also decide whether you need stress-relieving instruction, or whether acupuncture or massage may benefit you.

What sort of recommendations does a naturopath make for heart disease?

Your naturopath will first try to ensure that you have a good basic diet. A healthy diet helps to detoxify and to provide antioxidant nutrients (see page 58) which protect the cells

against damage. The essentials of a healthy diet for heart conditions are described in Chapter 3.

Naturopaths can also give advice on special diet programmes to help specific problems associated with heart trouble. To relieve fluid retention caused by circulatory problems, a naturopath might suggest following a strict diet for a few days, including cutting out salt and taking natural diuretics. Any diets should only be followed under the supervision of a naturopath and you should always check with your doctor before commencing them.

Do naturopaths prescribe nutritional supplements for heart patients?

While placing an emphasis on a balanced wholefood diet for recovery, most naturopaths recognise the need for extra antioxidant nutrients in sufferers from heart disease. Vitamin E, vitamin C and beta-carotene (vitamin A) may all be indicated in appropriate doses in addition to minerals, such as magnesium, for sufferers of angina and other disorders in which blood vessels are constricted. Appropriate forms and dosages of supplements need to be determined by a practitioner.

What sort of exercise will a naturopath suggest for the heart?

There are many forms of exercise which can be beneficial for the heart such as walking, swimming, gardening, yoga or t'ai chi. The naturopath will tailor activity to the individual's needs.

Will naturopathic treatment conflict with my doctor's advice?

Naturopathy is directed at improving the function of self-healing processes in your body and it will usually not conflict with the conventional medical treatment you may receive for your heart problem. Many doctors now recognise the important complementary role that naturopathy can play in total health care and will refer their patients to qualified practitioners. You do not need a medical referral to seek the advice of a naturopath, but if you are on any kind of medication you should consult your doctor before beginning a naturopathic treatment.

Where can I find a naturopath?

Contact the General Council and Register of Naturopaths for a list of registered naturopaths.

Most naturopaths work in private practice and some may hold posts in residential naturopathic clinics with spa baths and other facilities.

WHAT YOU CAN DO AT HOME

Good quality sleep is essential for your body to repair damaged tissues, particularly those affected by a heart attack. You can improve your sleep without resorting to any medication by simple hydrotherapy in your own bathroom.

Just before going to bed, sponge or spray your lower legs (below the knees) with cold water for 1 or 2 minutes. Dry them off and when you climb into bed your feet will be warm and sleep will generally follow easily. You can repeat the process if you are restless during the night.

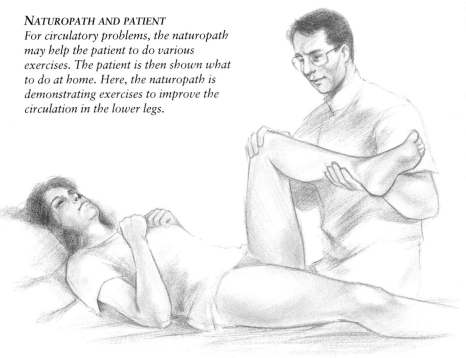

NATUROPATH AND PATIENT
For circulatory problems, the naturopath may help the patient to do various exercises. The patient is then shown what to do at home. Here, the naturopath is demonstrating exercises to improve the circulation in the lower legs.

CIRCULATORY DISORDERS

The health of your arteries and veins may be impaired by a variety of factors, and the resulting damage may lead to life-threatening conditions such as a stroke.

Blockages or degeneration may occur in any of the blood vessels in the body, with various effects.

HYPERTENSION

Each time the heart beats it creates a wave of pressure which pushes blood along the arteries and veins of the body. Hypertension is blood pressure that stays abnormally high over a prolonged period, even when resting.

Between five and ten per cent of all adults suffer from hypertension, although it is estimated that only half of these are aware of the fact and in turn only half of these are having proper treatment.

Like any pumping system, the body's circulation can only work efficiently within a certain range of pressure. If the pressure is too low, not enough blood reaches vital organs, including the brain. If it is high for a prolonged period, the extra pressure will damage the heart and the system of blood vessels. The increased pressure of the blood damages the inside walls of arteries, making atherosclerosis more likely. Hypertension also doubles the risk of heart attack and increases the risk of stroke by four times for both men and women.

Causes

Hypertension may have a specific cause. This can include obesity, coronary heart disease and other heart disorders, kidney problems, a disorder of the adrenal glands which produce hormones that help regulate blood pressure, thyroid problems and even the side-effects of some drugs such as oral contraceptives and those used for treating ulcers and arthritis. Blood pressure tends to rise as people get older and their arteries and other blood vessels become less flexible.

The middle-aged and elderly are therefore especially at risk and should have their blood pressure checked once a year.

In the majority of cases of hypertension, however, no specific cause can be found; doctors refer to these people as having 'essential' hypertension.

Symptoms

Hypertension rarely causes any symptoms and can therefore 'silently' undermine an individual's health over a number of years. Symptoms, such as dizziness, headache, blurred vision and tiredness, only arise if blood pressure is extremely high. Normally symptoms do not appear until the body has been damaged by hypertension.

Treatment

Many people with hypertension can lower their blood pressure into the healthy range through a few simple lifestyle changes: a low-fat diet, more exercise and less stress, as well as giving up smoking. Those who find this difficult, and whose condition is persistent, severe, and damaging to organs such as the heart and kidneys, will require medication, sometimes for life.

Drugs

Drugs commonly prescribed for persistent hypertension include beta-blockers, ACE inhibitors, diuretics (to eliminate excess fluid which increases blood pressure) and vasodilators. As with all drugs, antihypertensives, as they are known, have side effects and different drugs will suit different individuals. Generally, however, the side effects caused by antihypertensives tend to be mild and usually do not interfere with a normal, active life.

FOCUS ON

HYPERTENSION
The blood vessels in the eye are rapidly affected by high blood pressure, and blurred vision may result. Examination of the eyes is a useful way to diagnose hypertension as the doctor will notice burst blood vessels.

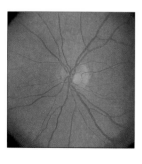

Natural therapies

Consult your doctor before undertaking natural therapies for hypertension.

Naturopaths often recommend a diet of mineral-rich foods for reducing high blood pressure. This includes calcium (dairy products, sesame seeds, spinach and broccoli), magnesium (nuts, beans, dark green leafy vegetables and seafood) and potassium (fish, bananas, potatoes, avocados, tomatoes, apricots and peaches).

Herbalists prescribe diuretics such as lily-of-the-valley, dandelion and yarrow to decrease blood pressure and swelling; and specific herbs that can be taken as infusions include lime blossom or camomile flowers in place of tea and coffee. Check with your doctor to be sure they will work well with blood pressure lowering medication.

Homeopathy can be successful in treating high blood pressure, but it is essential to consult a trained therapist.

Acupuncture and acupressure (see page 101) can help to reduce high blood pressure, but should not replace medication. Try pressure point LI 4 as shown (right).

Biofeedback (see page 141) has been proven in many studies to be effective in enabling the individual to reduce his or her own blood pressure by becoming aware of how the body reacts to various factors.

For the reduction of stress, aromatherapists suggest adding a few drops of lavender oil to a warm bath. An aromatherapy massage is also therapeutic and oils specific to your condition will be used.

Yoga (see page 104) has been proven to reduce stress and high blood pressure. A study of 3000 people reported by the Yoga Biomedical Trust in 1984 found that 84 per cent of those with hypertension improved.

THROMBOSIS AND EMBOLISM

Blood clotting is a natural safety mechanism of the body which prevents excessive bleeding, but sometimes the clots themselves can cause problems.

Thrombosis

A thrombus is a blood clot that forms inside a blood vessel. This may be caused by atherosclerosis (see page 108), as fatty deposits become hard, crack and bleed. Blood clots form and may grow large enough to block the blood vessel. If the vessel is a coronary artery, this can cause a heart attack, or if it is a blood vessel supplying the brain, the result can be a stroke.

A deep vein thrombosis is a blood clot in a deep vein of the leg or pelvis which causes inflammation. The thrombus results from an injury to the vein wall, or stagnation of

ACUPRESSURE POINT LI 4 FOR HYPERTENSION This point is at the bottom of the crease formed by pressing the thumb and index finger together. Apply firm pressure for a few minutes every day.

YOGA FOR HYPERTENSION

The following routine, called 'The Cat', is good for relaxing and relieving tension and is safe to do. It is advisable to join a class run by a qualified instructor who can teach you exercises specific to your health needs, which can then be done at home when they have become more familiar.

Drop lower back

Keep knees slightly apart

Arch back as high as possible

Keep stomach in

Relax hands by feet

1 Start on all fours, with knees slightly apart, palms facing forwards and directly under shoulders. Breathe in slowly, drop lower back and raise your head. Hold for 10 seconds.

2 Breathe out and arch your back as high as you can, dropping your head down between your arms. Hold for 10 seconds. Repeat steps one and two ten times.

3 Sink back on your heels, put your hands by your feet with palms facing upwards and forehead lightly touching the ground. Stay in this position for 3 minutes. Get up slowly and relax for at least 15 minutes.

Blood clots

Blood clots may form in either arteries or veins and block the blood supply to an organ. A blood clot may also travel from one place in the body to another.

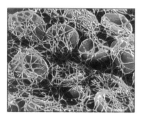

BLOOD CLOT
This thrombus, magnified 2200 times, is composed of red blood cells trapped in a net-work of fibrin strands (yellow). A thrombus usually forms when blood flow is blocked in an artery.

CORONARY
THROMBOSIS
This thrombus (the clump of red, lower centre) is seen protruding from an arterial entrance to a chamber of the heart. It is likely to cause a heart attack.

the blood flow while a person is confined to bed during a long illness or after surgery. For this reason hospital patients are encouraged to get out of bed as soon as possible or they are given a routine of leg exercises and physiotherapy sessions. Many also have to wear elastic stockings which temporarily increase the blood pressure in the legs and prevent clots forming. Sometimes anticoagulant drugs are also given.

Embolism

When a part or all of a thrombus in a blood vessel breaks off and is carried in the blood to other areas, it is called an embolus and it causes an embolism (blockage). Some other causes of blockage include atheromas, fat globules, cancer tumours, air bubbles, or amniotic fluid from the uterus in pregnancy – these may travel in the bloodstream until they lodge in and block a narrower vessel.

Pulmonary embolism occurs when a deep vein thrombus breaks off and is carried in the veins, through the heart, to the pulmonary artery which feeds the lungs. The embolus can block the vessel, cutting off some or all of the blood supply to the lungs often with fatal consequences.

Virtually any area of the body can be affected by an embolism. They commonly occur where arteries branch off and the embolus blocks one or both branches. For instance, cerebral embolism may lead to stroke, amniotic fluid can escape into the mother's blood and cause a pulmonary embolism, and an embolus blocking an artery in the leg can cause gangrene.

Symptoms

The symptoms of thrombosis and embolism depend on where and how severe the blockage is. Any obstruction to an artery reduces

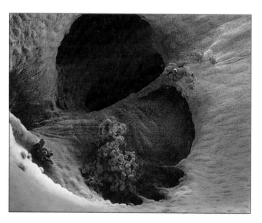

the amount of fresh oxygenated blood it can supply. If the blockage is serious enough, the organ or area of the body supplied will begin to die. If it is an area of heart muscle, a heart attack can ensue. If it is part of the brain, a stroke may be the result. These are sudden events and normally there is no warning. However, if the area affected is distant from the heart, such as an arm or leg or fingers or toes, the area may become cold, white and painful. In severe cases, skin and muscle may die, become gangrenous and may need to be amputated.

Diagnosis

When an artery becomes blocked, blood flow and therefore blood pressure downstream of the obstruction is reduced. This fact is often used by doctors to investigate suspected thrombosis or embolism. First, blood pressure is measured in the arm to gain information about the overall blood pressure. If someone is suspected of having a blockage in one of the legs, for example, blood pressure is then taken there and compared with that in the arm.

Blood pressure testing can also be used to test for blockages in the carotid arteries in the neck which supply the brain. Small branches of these arteries supply the eyes, and so measuring blood pressure there gives valuable information. This is done using tiny devices which sit on the front of the eyes like contact lenses.

Often these simple tests can give doctors enough information to locate and treat the blockage, but sometimes more detailed investigation is needed such as angiography (see page 98), to see the blood flow and the exact position of the blockage.

Treatment

Thrombosis and embolism can be treated with specialised clot-dissolving (thrombolytic) drugs. These are given directly to the affected area using a catheter. People who have had a thrombus or embolism may be prescribed anticoagulant drugs long-term to prevent a recurrence.

However, if these drugs do not work, an operation known as an embolectomy may be needed. A catheter is inserted into the artery and then pushed gently through the blockage. A tiny balloon at the end of the catheter is inflated. The catheter and balloon are carefully withdrawn, bringing the

EXERCISE FOR THROMBOSIS

Blood clots may occur as a result of atherosclerosis. It is also common in bedridden patients due to lack of activity.

The following exercises can be done by inactive people to improve circulation in the legs to prevent clots forming.

ANKLE FLEXING
Sit on a chair with shoes off. Bend ankle forward and backwards and circle it round. Repeat with other ankle.

Relax upper body

Flex ankle in all directions

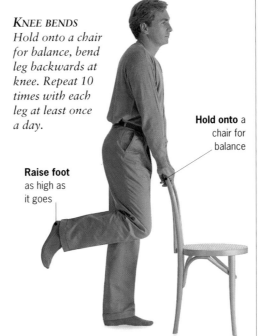

KNEE BENDS
Hold onto a chair for balance, bend leg backwards at knee. Repeat 10 times with each leg at least once a day.

Hold onto a chair for balance

Raise foot as high as it goes

Keep moving
The more you sit in one place, the more you increase your chances of developing a blood clot. This is particularly true on long-haul travel by airplane. To avoid this, wear loose clothing and roomy shoes. Take a walk around the plane once an hour and stretch your legs periodically when seated.

blood clot, or whatever has caused the obstruction, with it. In severe cases it is sometimes necessary to bypass the blocked artery (see page 112). This is done by removing a vein from elsewhere in the body and grafting it to the artery on either side of the blockage to bypass the obstruction.

Natural therapies

Natural therapies can help decrease the chance of blood clots forming. Naturopaths advise using onion, garlic, ginger and bromelain (pineapple) for preventing clots. Lecithin, a type of fat, decreases the stickiness of blood platelets, therefore reducing the risk of clotting. Some natural therapists advise lecithin supplements, but dietary sources, such as soya beans, are adequate.

The antioxidant vitamins A, C and E (see page 59) are recommended. Some therapists suggest taking supplements, but eating five servings a day of fruit and vegetables should give you sufficient quantities.

The pain of blood clots can often be relieved by the use of herbal lotions, compresses and poultices. Arnica and comfrey are commonly used for these.

STROKE

A stroke is a brain injury that results from an interruption in the blood supply. This occurs when an artery becomes blocked by a thrombus or an embolism or because a blood vessel in the brain ruptures. The affected area of brain tissue dies.

Strokes that are caused by thrombosis or embolism are more common in the middle-aged or elderly whose arteries may have become clogged by atherosclerosis over the years. Strokes caused by the sudden rupture of blood vessels in the brain (cerebral haemorrhage) also affect the young.

Symptoms

A stroke caused by an embolism is a sudden event and there is no warning. If, however, the problem is due to clotting in the main artery which supplies the brain and runs up the neck, known as the carotid artery, there may be some warning signs, including bouts of weakness, confusion and difficulties with speech, and tingling or clumsiness in a limb. If the stroke is caused by the rupture of a blood vessel, there will be a severe headache preceding it.

The effects of a stroke will vary depending on the location of the blockage as well as its extent. In a cerebral thrombosis, a blood clot will form within the walls of a cerebral blood vessel, causing an obstruction to blood flow. Permanent brain damage will result if the blood supply is completely stopped or if it is reduced to less than a quarter of its normal level.

In a cerebral embolism, a blood clot or other matter (see page 126) that has travelled to the brain from another part of the body (such as an artery in the neck) can obstruct a cerebral artery. These clots usually lodge in the left middle cerebral artery; this will cause weakness or paralysis in the right side of the body, and will also affect speech, memory and personality.

If the stroke occurs in the right side of the brain the left side of the body will then be affected and, in addition to paralysis, there may be speech, calculation and sensation difficulties, and a loss of the ability to recognise pictures, objects and colours. There may also be unsteadiness, dizziness and nausea.

Mild strokes last from a few minutes to less than a day and cause minor symptoms – dizziness, speech difficulties, vision problems and nausea. These are usually warning signs that a more serious stroke is imminent, prompt treatment may ensure that permanent damage does not occur. More serious strokes have more critical consequences, with paralysis, loss of speech and vision, loss of control over bodily functions and mental confusion.

Diagnosis

Techniques used to confirm the diagnosis of a stroke include angiography and computed tomography, also known as a CAT or CT scan (see page 95), which uses x-rays linked to a computer to build-up a cross-sectional image of the head and brain, and magnetic resonance imaging, or MRI (see page 95), which does much the same thing using magnetic fields and radio waves.

Treatment

Anticoagulant drugs are often given to prevent another stroke, and some ruptures, blood clots and embolisms can be dealt with by surgery. (Anticoagulants are not given in haemorrhagic strokes.) But generally the treatment centres on rehabilitation.

STROKE REHABILITATION
This patient had a stroke in the left side of her brain and so she can no longer write with her right hand. Here, she is being taught to write with her left hand.

Rehabilitation

Nursing care and intensive physiotherapy aim to restore as much of an affected person's former abilities as possible. Rehabilitation needs to start immediately after a stroke to ensure maximum recovery.

First, the patient is taught good posture and balance, which is affected by a stroke. Then, gentle supervised exercise begins, with walking practice. It may take one to six months for the patient to learn to walk unaided. Swimming with the assistance of a trained therapist is invaluable for improving mobility and strength (which is often impaired after a stroke).

Therapy is often needed for speech and vision which may be partially or sometimes fully recovered if rehabilitation treatment starts early with qualified professionals.

Natural therapies

Natural therapies may help in the recovery from an embolic stroke, but they should only be undertaken with your doctor's advice. A healthy diet, including anticoagulant foods (onion, garlic, and ginger) can aid recovery and help to prevent another stroke. Naturopaths suggest stroke patients take supplements of vitamins E and C, evening primrose oil, lecithin and fish oils.

A herbal treatment recommended for stroke patients to improve circulation is a yarrow infusion: pour a cup of boiling water on 2 teaspoons of dried yarrow and leave to infuse for 15 minutes. Drink hot three times a day.

BRAIN HAEMORRHAGE
This CT scan of the brain of a stroke patient shows a haemorrhage (the orange oval shape on the left) caused by the rupture of blood vessels due to hypertension.

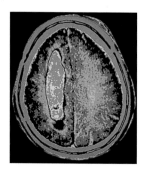

Homeopaths (see page 103) often prescribe *Arnica 200c* to be taken as soon as possible after a stroke. To dissolve clots, *Arnica 6c* and *Kali mur 6x* should be taken twice a day for one month.

Acupuncture (see page 101) can help to stimulate circulation as well as to promote relaxation, both of which are important for the prevention of another stroke.

Massage (see page 100) helps to stimulate the circulation and to prepare a stroke patient for exercise sessions. Aromatherapy oils can be chosen specifically for this.

ANEURYSM

An aneurysm is a ballooning of an artery wall, usually resulting from damage to the wall caused by atherosclerosis or hypertension. It may also be congenital.

Small aneurysms called berry aneurysms are commonly found in the brain arteries. Warning signs of these include a drooping eyelid, dilated pupil and double vision. A ruptured brain aneurysm will cause serious bleeding, usually felt as a severe headache, and will cause a stroke. Aneurysms may exist for years and be symptom free.

Aneurysms are also found in the aorta. The swelling may eventually split the wall of the aorta and will be felt as a large lump in the abdomen. Aneurysms can cause many problems by bursting, pressing on organs, nerves or blood vessels, or forming a clot.

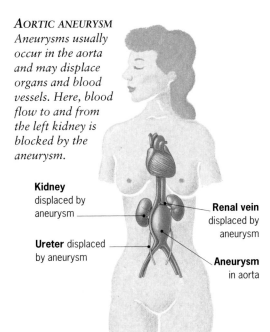

AORTIC ANEURYSM
Aneurysms usually occur in the aorta and may displace organs and blood vessels. Here, blood flow to and from the left kidney is blocked by the aneurysm.

Kidney displaced by aneurysm

Ureter displaced by aneurysm

Renal vein displaced by aneurysm

Aneurysm in aorta

Diagnosis

Brain aneurysms are usually diagnosed with a CT scan (see page 95). Aneurysms elsewhere can be seen on x-rays and ultrasound scans (see page 94).

Treatment

Aneurysms cannot be reversed but they can sometimes be prevented from getting bigger by a reduction in blood pressure. Usually aneurysms, particularly aortic aneurysms, need to be removed by surgery before they rupture to avoid serious damage. Often part of the wall of the aorta needs to be replaced with some artificial tubing.

Natural therapies

Once an aneurysm is formed there is no alternative to surgery for treating it. However, a healthy cholesterol and blood pressure level will go a long way towards preventing aneurysms (see atherosclerosis, page 108 and hypertension, page 124).

INTERMITTENT CLAUDICATION

This is not a disease but a pain that usually occurs during walking or other exercise, in the thigh and calf muscles, buttocks or arch of the foot. It is caused by a restriction in the blood supply to the leg, usually due to atherosclerosis (a build-up of fatty deposits) in the leg arteries. It is particularly common in people who smoke. Exercise increases the muscles' demand for glucose and oxygen which cannot be met because of the blockage in the blood supply, hence the cramps.

Intermittent claudication may occur in just one or both legs. If left untreated blood clots may form and cut off the blood supply to the muscles. Gangrene will result and amputation is necessary.

Treatment

The most important action is to stop smoking. Regular exercise will improve the blood supply to the legs. Pain felt during exercise will stop during rest.

Drugs may be given to dilate the arteries and to reduce blood clotting. These will not stop progression of the disease, however, without changes in smoking habits, diet and exercise. Dietary changes include reducing saturated fats in the diet.

In severe cases, bypass surgery (see page 112) or balloon angioplasty (see page 111) may be performed to clear blocked arteries.

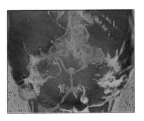

BRAIN ANEURYSM
This coloured x-ray angiogram shows an aneurysm in an artery in the brain (the orange 'berry' in the centre where the artery branches), probably caused by high blood pressure. If it ruptures it will cause a stroke.

Which kind of cramp?
Everyone is bound to suffer leg cramps at some point, so it is important to know which are simply due to overworked or unfit muscles, and which are due to arterial disease. Those caused by the former are constant, usually go away with stretching or massage and do not recur on a regular basis. Cramps caused by arterial disease are intermittent, usually occur with any exercise, even just walking, and stop when you rest. If you experience leg cramps even when doing mild exercise, seek the advice of your doctor.

SELF-HELP FOR VARICOSE VEINS

To prevent varicose veins, keep your weight within limits, avoid standing for long periods of time, take regular exercise and wear flat shoes. If you already have varicose veins, try these measures to relieve them.

▶ *Wear support stockings.*

▶ *Start an exercise programme – walking or swimming are best.*

▶ *When sitting or lying down, elevate your legs above hip level.*

▶ *If a vein bursts and bleeds, bandage it tightly and keep the leg raised until the bleeding stops. Consult your doctor as soon as possible.*

Natural therapies

As intermittent claudication is usually caused by atherosclerosis, the treatment is directed at this (see page 108). Naturopaths recommend walking for one hour daily and taking vitamin E supplements (consult a naturopath for quantities). Also, eat foods rich in magnesium such as nuts, beans and peas, and wholegrain breads.

The homeopathic remedy is to take *Baryta muriatica 6c* three times a day for three weeks, and *Proteus 30c* during attacks.

Herbalists recommend an infusion made from hawthorn berry to improve the circulatory system. Pour one cup of boiling water onto 1 tablespoon of berries; steep for 20 minutes. Drink two to three times a day.

VARICOSE VEINS

Blood returning from the feet and legs to the heart has a long, hard climb against the pull of gravity. To help it on its way and to prevent too much pressure being placed on the walls of the vessels at the bottom of the system, the veins are divided into short sections by one-way valves which only allow the blood to move upwards.

If the valves in the deep veins of the legs begin to fail, blood is forced back into the surface veins which swell, twist and stretch under the pressure, causing varicose veins.

Varicose veins are more common in women than men. They affect about half of all women and a quarter of all men over the age of 40. Pregnancy, being overweight, and work which involves standing for extended periods of time all tend to increase the risk of developing the condition.

Symptoms

Some people with varicose veins experience aching, swollen and tired legs and, in severe cases, skin rashes and ulcers can develop. But for many there is no discomfort or pain

– the principle concern is the appearance of their legs as the affected veins become blue, twisted and prominent.

Treatment

In mild cases of varicose veins, using support stockings and, if possible, less standing still and more walking can be enough to relieve the symptoms. Lying down and raising the legs may relieve swelling.

A procedure known as sclerotherapy can also be performed. Here, a blood clot is artificially created in the vein by the injection of a chemical solution. The clot blocks the varicose vein causing blood to be diverted through unaffected veins.

In severe cases surgery is the only long-term answer. This is done in one of two ways. A long wire can be threaded through the vein from the groin to the ankle, the vein is tied to it and then pulled out, a procedure called stripping. Alternatively, the small veins connecting the affected superficial veins to the deep veins can be cut and tied off.

Natural therapies

Naturopaths recommend vitamin E and C supplements for their antioxidant properties. Also, increase your intake of citrus fruits, apricots, blackberries, cherries, rosehips and buckwheat, all of which contain rutin, which improves the elasticity of veins.

Herbal remedies relieve discomfort and pain. Make a soothing poultice from coltsfoot leaves, or a herbal tea from valerian; herbal tablets, such as gotu kola or ginkgo biloba, can be bought in health food stores. The use of ginger, cayenne, raw beetroot and hawthorn berries is also recommended.

Homeopathic remedies, *Pulsatilla*, *Carbo veg* or *Lycopodium*, may help improve the circulation. Consult a homeopath.

Yoga is also useful for improving the circulation (see page 104). Adopt this posture to relieve pressure on your legs: lie at right angles to a wall and place your feet up against the wall so that your legs are at a comfortable angle. Stay in this position for 3 minutes every day.

Or use hydrotherapy to stimulate the circulation. Fill one basin with hot water and another with cold water and ice cubes. Soak a towel in each basin; wring out before using. Place the hot towel on the vein for a minute, then the cold one for 30 seconds. Repeat three times; end with the cold one.

SWIMMING
The ideal exercise for someone whose varicose veins make walking painful, swimming will improve your general circulation and strengthen your heart.

CHAPTER 7

THE ROAD TO RECOVERY

The pain and shock of a heart attack or of having heart surgery can help you to change your life for the better. Coming close to death provides motivation enough to adopt a healthier lifestyle. The process of rehabilitation, with the guidance of health professionals, involves adopting a healthier diet, following a supervised exercise programme and learning stress and anger management techniques.

SPEEDING YOUR RECOVERY

Many heart patients claim that they feel better after recovering from their heart attack or surgery than they have for many years, because of a new lifestyle and a readjustment of priorities.

RISKY BUSINESS

After a heart attack, you can do almost everything that you could do before. But there are a few activities that you should avoid.

▶ *Do not run for buses. Regular exercise is good for you, but sudden exertion is not.*

▶ *Avoid heavy digging in the garden.*

▶ *Rest for half an hour after eating or having a hot bath, and do not have the two within two hours of each other. Take showers instead of baths, where possible.*

▶ *Do not carry heavy objects, such as luggage, even for short distances.*

▶ *Do not push yourself beyond your limit – know when to stop.*

Full recovery from a heart attack or bypass surgery takes two to three months. During this time, as you resume your life, your emotions and your physical capability will go through several changes. Once your hospitalisation is over, you will begin to recuperate at home, gradually resuming your former life, but with changes that should ensure future health.

The speed and extent of recovery from a heart attack depends on the amount of physical damage suffered. Heart muscle that has died does not regrow so any damage is permanent.

The location of the damage is also an important factor. A small area of dead muscle in a vital position, for instance at the base of a heart valve or in an area vital to the heart's internal electrical system, can cause greater disability than a larger amount of dead muscle in a less important position. If part of your heart is damaged, it is essential to ensure that further damage

does not occur and to minimise the strain on your heart. Similarly, if you have had bypass surgery, you need to take action to recover your health and prevent further damage to your arteries.

THE NEED FOR SLEEP

Sleep is a vital part of the process of healing your heart. At first you may find yourself sleeping 10 to 12 hours each night as well as taking a nap of 2 hours or more every afternoon. This is not unusual – often people need more sleep for about a year after a heart attack. But since you will almost certainly feel worried and anxious, sleep may not come easily or be completely restful.

If you have trouble getting to sleep, try taking a warm (not hot) bath before bedtime, drinking a herbal tea with a sedative effect such as camomile or valerian or doing relaxation exercises (see page 82). Many people find that they sleep better after a massage. Ask your partner to massage your shoulders or rub your back with some lavender-scented oil to help you to drop off.

ACTIVITY IS IMPORTANT

Paradoxically, as well as needing more rest, your body also needs to remain active. Many people are surprised by how soon the hospital staff encourage them to get out of bed. Bed rest actually weakens the muscles. After only three weeks in bed, even a healthy person loses one-third of his or her strength and regaining that strength will take three weeks. Also, lung infections are common in those confined to bed for long periods. Cardiologists therefore recommend getting up and sitting in a chair or even walking with the aid of a nurse in the day or two after a heart attack. A week later you

RELAX AND REST
If you have trouble sleeping, ask your partner to give you a shoulder rub. It is an effective way to relieve tension and anxiety.

may be climbing stairs or taking a shower alone, depending upon the severity of your heart attack and the advice of your doctor.

But all activity, and exercise in particular, must begin gradually. After a heart attack, the damaged heart muscle must form a scar. This takes about six weeks. During that time you must not exert yourself any more than your doctor allows, and do everything that your doctor recommends. You will have to walk this fine line between doing too much and not doing enough during the entire period of your recovery. Your best guides are your doctor's or cardiac rehabilitation manager's advice and the advice that your own body is giving to you. Listen to your body. If you feel tired, stop what you are doing and rest.

UNDERSTANDING YOUR EMOTIONS

Heart trouble often leads to a troubled heart. You may feel that a part of you died in the heart attack. A heart attack causes psychological damage to a degree not seen with many other forms of illness. The heart is more than a mere biological pump. It has an especially important position in people's perceptions of themselves, a significance reflected in all human language and culture, particularly as the centre of love.

Many patients find themselves asking, Why me? Others lash out at their partners and families, blaming them for their heart disease. Although this anger is very common, it is also very damaging, since anger and stress raise both blood pressure and cholesterol levels. It is important to learn to control anger (see page 152).

Many people feel let down by their bodies. Depression is a common reaction, as well as insomnia and a general lethargy and lack of interest in life. If these symptoms are severe or persist for more than a week or two after you get out of the hospital, you should talk to your doctor about getting counselling. Also, stress management techniques should be learned (see page 150).

Overcoming depression

To overcome the mild depression that is most common after a heart attack or heart surgery, you need to become optimistic about your recovery, recognising that most people who survive a heart attack go on to lead normal lives. People with optimistic attitudes take control of their lives and begin taking the steps that will lead them back to health.

Your first step in the healing process is to acknowledge that you have heart disease. (Surprisingly, many people refuse to face this fact.) Next, you need to recognise that although you will never be cured of heart disease, you can learn to control it through diet, exercise and stress management.

CHANGE YOUR DIET

The dietary advice for heart patients is the same as it is for everyone else. You should eat more fruit, vegetables, bread and pasta and less fatty foods such as meat, oil, butter and full-fat dairy products. But since most heart disease is caused by clogged arteries, you have added incentive to change bad eating habits to prevent another heart attack. If you are overweight, you will also need to lose weight. Eating a low-fat diet will help you do this and maintain your new lower weight. See Chapter 3 for more information on eating for a healthy heart.

Caffeine and alcohol

Both alcohol and caffeine should be consumed only in moderation. Taken in excess, alcohol can raise your blood pressure and caffeine can cause palpitations.

continued on page 136

Diet for depression

There is some evidence that the amino acid tryptophan relieves depression, as it is used by the body to make serotonin, a chemical that is essential for various processes in the brain involving moods.

Tryptophan is found in milk, fish, peanut butter, nuts, soya beans, and cooked dried beans and peas. Eating any of these foods together with carbohydrates, such as bread, pasta and potatoes, facilitates the uptake of tryptophan in the brain.

SELF HELP FOR DEPRESSION

Survivors of heart attacks often feel depressed and at a loss as to how to piece their lives back together. Acupressure and aromatherapy may help you overcome depression.

AROMATHERAPY
Put three drops of clary sage essential oil into a basin of steaming water. Cover your head with a towel and inhale. Or put 6 drops of oil onto a handkerchief and inhale.

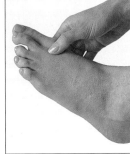

ACUPRESSURE
Point Liv 3: two finger widths towards the ankle from the junction of the big and second toes.

A Recovering Cardiac Case

Having a coronary artery bypass graft is often the turning point in a person's life and the start on a path to recovery. With modern knowledge about the factors which cause coronary heart disease and advanced surgical techniques, thousands of patients have become living testimonials to the fact that heart disease can have a happy ending.

Tom is a 51-year-old freelance computer consultant who set up his own business six years ago after being made redundant from a large multinational company. His wife, Alison, is a primary school teacher, and they have two children. Sarah has just left university and is looking for a job in marketing, while Nick is still at university studying for his engineering degree.

Following Tom's redundancy, the family income dropped dramatically. It became necessary to remortgage their house; the children's university expenses have severely stretched

their income, causing Tom and Alison many sleepless nights.

Tom was diagnosed with angina at age 43, and he was so frightened that he gave up smoking and went on a weight-loss and exercise program. Although he lost 4.5 kg (10 lb) quite quickly Tom finds it difficult to maintain his motivation. A fortnight after the diagnosis, he had balloon angioplasty (see page 111) to clear a severely blocked coronary artery, and has been on anti-angina medication since then.

Tom and Alison are still very concerned about his health as his

father died of a heart attack at the age of 67. Their relationship has become very strained as they see no solution to their financial problems – Tom's freelance earnings are not enough to get them out of trouble. They are also worried about Tom's increasing angina attacks.

Tom had a coronary angiogram which showed extensive narrowing in three of his coronary arteries. One month later, on the cardiac surgeon's recommendation, he had coronary artery bypass graft surgery (see page 112). He had to stay in hospital for a week after the operation.

FAMILY
Marital relations suffer when a member's health problems become exacerbated by financial considerations. Professional guidance is often needed to work through the problems.

EXERCISE
The cardiac patient needs to begin exercise as soon as possible in order to improve cardiovascular efficiency.

DIET
Keeping to a low-fat, high-fibre diet is essential for preventing fatty deposits in any more arteries.

WORK
Self-employment can be even more stressful if financial security is at stake, and it may make it difficult to take time out after a cardiac operation.

HEALTH
To avoid further heart problems, it is essential to make appropriate lifestyle changes that include a healthier diet, no smoking, a reduction in alcohol, regular exercise and stress management.

WHAT SHOULD TOM DO?

Tom has now been discharged from the hospital and he needs to follow the doctor's instructions carefully. He is told to rest often in the early days after surgery, but to resume gentle activity as soon as he is able. However, he should not go out on cold or windy days.

Tom is also not allowed to drive for at least four weeks and if he travels as a passenger, he should pad the seat belt, but definitely wear it! He should not lift anything heavy and avoid all strenuous activity.

Tom is told that he should follow the recommendations of his cardiac rehabilitation manager who gives him a daily activity sheet. Tom should keep to his rehabilitation course which involves a team of cardiologists, specialist nurses, physiotherapists, occupational therapists, psychologists, pharmacist, dietician and physicians. Tom should follow the low-fat diet prescribed by the dietician and should practise relaxation exercises.

He is advised to discuss all stresses and worries with the psychologist. These not only relate to his health, but also to family, finance and business worries. He and Alison also need to find solutions to their financial situation in order to reduce the stresses on them both. They should discuss this with their children and ask them to help out.

Action Plan

DIET
Eat low-fat meals, and plenty of fresh fruit and vegetables. Avoid sugary foods. Eat small amounts at a time. Avoid alcohol. Follow all instructions given by the dietician.

EXERCISE
Do leg and breathing exercises at home as instructed. Walk daily but don't overdo it. Dress comfortably and don't get cold. Visit the physiotherapist weekly.

FAMILY
Talk to Alison about any concerns, including feelings of depression. Ask the children to assist with household tasks to minimise stress on Alison. Go to counselling with Alison to discuss worries and anxiety. Ask for advice about resuming sexual relations.

HEALTH
Make sure diet and exercise programmes are followed precisely and monitor progress. Do relaxation exercises daily to relieve stress.

WORK
Initially, only take on small contracts. Don't agree to any deadlines that will prove difficult to meet and cause stress. Get assistance if necessary. Talk to the bank about the mortgage again. Tell Nick to look for a part-time job and jobs during the holiday period.

HOW THINGS TURNED OUT FOR TOM

Tom experienced chest discomfort, and some pain for weeks after the operation. His doctor prescribed painkillers. On the day after getting home from hospital, Tom was able to sit in a chair and the following day he moved around the house a little. By the second week he started walking daily, gradually increasing his distance over the next few weeks. He rested every afternoon and did not have too many visitors.

He followed a low-fat diet, with plenty of fresh fruit and vegetables. Tom discussed his feelings of depression with the rehabilitation psychologist and practised relaxation exercises at home. The physiotherapist assisted Tom with breathing exercises to prevent mucus build-up in the lungs, and leg exercises to improve his circulation. Alison attended parts of the rehabilitation course with him so she could give him support.

After a few weeks he began to return to normal daily activities. His angina disappeared and his recovered health restored their relationship. They resumed sexual relations after six weeks.

After two months Tom began to take small freelance assignments, making sure he did not agree to anything with tight deadlines. Alison continued to work and Sarah and Nick found jobs, easing the financial strain a little.

Driving a car

Many people worry about driving safely following a heart attack. Doctors recommend that people who have been hospitalised should not drive for at least four weeks after discharge, depending on the severity of the disorder and the side-effects of medication. This is because your condition may not be stable enough to enable you to drive safely, your medication may affect your alertness and driving may cause you too much stress. Discuss the risks with your doctor. You must also inform your insurance company before returning to driving.

Limit caffeine drinks (coffee, tea, and cola) to two per day. If you are a heavy coffee drinker, you could try changing to decaffeinated. Coffee substitutes (made from chicory and dandelion root) and caffeine-free herbal teas, however, are far more healthful and some teas, such as camomile, are particularly relaxing.

Although some studies have shown that alcohol may have a protective effect on the heart (see page 64), more than two drinks a day is harmful in other ways (see page 119). Too much alcohol will also damage your weight-loss programme. If you are on medication for your heart or blood pressure, it is important to ask your doctor if alcohol should be avoided altogether.

BUILDING UP FITNESS

Generally, you will be advised to begin with gentle walking and to avoid walking either up or down hill. You are allowed to exercise out of doors but you should avoid extreme weather conditions. Along with eating a low-fat diet, regular exercise is probably the most important thing you can do to keep your arteries clear.

Many hospitals now run cardiac rehabilitation programmes. If your hospital does not have one, ask if there is one in your area that you can join. These programmes provide a structured setting in which you can build up your physical strength, find out how to make the necessary changes in your diet and learn to control stress. They are beneficial for people of all ages.

Cardiac rehabilitation programmes are usually organised in four phases. Phase I is when you are in hospital recovering from a cardiac event. Phase II sees you recovering at home. This can take between two to six weeks. During Phase III, you attend the rehabilitation centre for regular exercise and education sessions until your optimal physical condition is achieved. This often takes from 6 to 12 weeks. Phase IV is when you are no longer a patient but are back in the community attending a support group, or joining a fitness club, although you may still be in touch with your cardiac rehabilitation manager (see page 138).

Whether you join a cardiac rehabilitation group or not, you should exercise regularly, gradually increasing the time and effort. You should discuss the appropriate amount and type of exercise with your doctor. You may feel breathless when you begin exercising, possibly because you were out of shape before your heart attack or surgery, or because you still have some heart problems. It is important to tell your doctor about any episodes of breathlessness.

One of the best forms of exercise for heart patients is simply taking a 20-minute walk

CARDIAC REHABILITATION EXERCISES

Phase I of a cardiac rehabilitation programme is when you are still in hospital following a heart attack or heart surgery. During this time, care must be taken to avoid strain or exertion, and the doctor's instructions must be followed. The following exercises are advised in Phase I, when it is important to start moving a little but you should be very careful not to overexert yourself. These exercises are usually followed by walking increasing distances around the hospital building and then up and down stairs.

ARM LIFTS
When sitting down, lift your arms up one at a time. If you feel up to it, you should do it while standing.

DEEP BREATHING
Take in deep, relaxed breaths, making sure that your abdomen rises and falls with each one.

KNEE BENDS
Do alternate knee bends while you are holding onto the bed. Walk around the bed if you are up to it.

ANKLE STRETCH
When sitting down, move your ankles side to side and in circles to stimulate circulation in the legs.

HEALING YOUR HEART WITH VISUALISATION

You can use your mind and your imagination to help your heart heal. Creative visualisation is often used by cancer patients to imagine their bodies fighting off the cancer cells. Heart patients can use the same technique. Simply set aside some time where you can sit quietly without being disturbed. Then, close your eyes and relax. Imagine your heart. Try to visualise the problem – perhaps the blockage in the arteries or the scars from your surgery. Think about the kind of healing your heart needs. Are the arteries full of plaque that needs to be washed away? You might imagine an army of tiny cleaners scrubbing away the debris. Spend some time thinking about the image in detail. After a few minutes, open your eyes and take a few deep breaths. By doing this healing exercise for 10 minutes every day you will feel more in control of your recovery.

every day. Make sure you warm up and stretch before any exercise (see Chapter 4), including walking.

It is essential to go for regular check-ups with your doctor to assess whether your physical fitness is improving satisfactorily.

It is also a good idea to record your progress by keeping an exercise journal, writing down what you did every day and how you felt. Then, on days when you become discouraged, you can look back and see how far you have come.

RESUMING SEXUAL RELATIONS

Many people want to know when they can begin sexual activity again, but are too shy to ask their doctors. And many doctors, particularly when talking to older people, neglect to give advice on this issue.

Cause for anxiety

Most people's sex lives resume as before following a heart attack or surgery. For some patients, however, anxiety about triggering a heart attack, or their medications, can make sex difficult. Talking to your doctor can help. He or she can determine whether or not your medication is causing

problems (such as failure to become aroused). Your doctor will also be able to reassure you that very few people die during lovemaking. This is because making love is actually not a particularly strenuous form of physical exertion.

Proceed with caution

When resuming sexual relations after a heart attack or surgery, proceed slowly and gently. Do not make love after eating a heavy meal or having an alcoholic drink – both will make your heart beat faster and any exertion will put it under more strain. Instead, try making love in the morning when you are well rested or in the afternoon, after a nap. Begin by gently touching and caressing one another. If you want to proceed to intercourse, find a position that feels comfortable – the missionary, or man on top position, can put too much stress on the man's upper body and on the woman's chest. Instead, try sex side by side, from the rear, or with the woman on top. Many experts recommend simply touching, hugging and kissing. This provides physical closeness without the anxiety that heart patients sometimes feel during sex.

If you find, despite these recommendations, that your sex life does not return to normal or that you continue to have problems with arousal, you may need a change in your existing medication. A sex therapist may be able to help if problems persist.

Contact your doctor if you experience any of the following warning signs: breathlessness or rapid heartbeat for more than 15 minutes after sex; feeling exceptionally tired immediately after sex or on the following day; chest pain or discomfort during sex; heartbeat irregularities during or after sex; and insomnia during the night after sex.

Smokers must quit

Smokers have only half as much chance of surviving both short-term and long-term after a heart attack as non-smokers. Yet half of the smokers who have heart attacks continue to smoke. Of those who quit after bypass surgery, between 40 and 75 per cent start smoking again.

Quitting smoking is always difficult, but in the aftermath of a heart attack it can be doubly so. You are anxious, irritable and depressed and may feel that you need cigarettes more than ever. Also, you are struggling with making changes in so many areas of your life that quitting smoking may seem impossible. But it is vital to your survival. See page 36 for ways to quit smoking.

BEING AFFECTIONATE
Recovering from a heart attack or surgery takes a lot out of you. Instead of rushing into sex, there are numerous other ways of being intimate until you feel ready for it.

Rehabilitation Manager

The aim of cardiac rehabilitation is to restore cardiac patients to reasonable physical health and quality of life and to promote changes in lifestyle to reduce the risks of further heart problems. The cardiac rehabilitation manager supervises this approach.

A NEW DIET
Changing your eating habits is essential for cardiac rehabilitation. The cardiac rehabilitation manager, together with a dietician or nutritionist, will ensure that you know the best way to cut out fat and eat healthy, nutritious food.

CARDIAC REHABILITATION
Exercise is a vital part of all the rehabilitation phases (see page 136) but should always be supervised. Phase I is when you are recovering in hospital. In Phase II you are at home. Phase III involves regular visits to the rehabilitation centre until you are fit, and in Phase IV you are no longer a patient, but may attend a support group.

The rehabilitation programme involves four phases from the time in hospital to returning to normal life. The initial focus is on physical exercises to restore health, and to develop the ability of the damaged heart to function as effectively as possible. But other risk factors, such as a high-cholesterol diet, smoking, heavy drinking and especially stress, must be addressed, as well as psychological and sexual problems.

What does a cardiac rehabilitation manager do?
The manager assesses each patient's needs and, together with the patient's doctor, devises a suitable programme for him or her from the courses and specialists available. The manager monitors progress and makes adjustments and referrals as required.

Who is involved in rehabilitation?
The core team is made up of nurses, and physiotherapists or occupational therapists, with supervision from consultant cardiologists, physicians or general practitioners. The team may be extended by a dietician, stress management counsellor, pharmacist, psychologist and exercise specialist.

The rehabilitation manager may also refer a patient to a sex therapist, vocational counsellor, social worker or other specialist.

What training does a manager have?
The rehabilitation manager is often a cardiac nurse or physiotherapist who is familiar with all the disciplines involved in the cardiac programme and is fully trained in advanced cardiopulmonary resuscitation.

Who benefits from rehabilitation?
Research shows that most people who have suffered a cardiac event will benefit from rehabilitation. The term 'cardiac event' covers heart attacks, heart failure and all cardiac surgery, including heart transplants. Patients suffering from less severe heart disease can also benefit. Approximately three-quarters of the patients who have been through a cardiac rehabilitation programme stay well and active for five or more years after their cardiac event, as opposed to only half of those who have not been in a programme.

What is in the exercise component?

The rehabilitation doctor gives you exercise tests at each phase to assess how well your heart is functioning and to evaluate the effects of your training. Until the heart muscle has healed, the patient is not able to exercise strenuously. So during Phase II, a programme of incremental brisk walking (where the distance covered is gradually increased) is usually the only exercise advised.

Phase III usually consists of several group exercise sessions per week under medical supervision, with equivalent sessions at home on the other days of the week. The sequence includes aerobic exercises to get the cardiovascular system working as well as possible, strength exercises to develop the major muscle groups so that you can live a normal life, and flexibility exercises to help prevent other problems developing, such as in the back and joints.

Ex-cardiac patients are encouraged in Phase IV to join support groups which meet regularly to take part in exercise classes and discussion groups. The rehabilitation manager may keep in touch through the group, and is available for further advice or referral if required.

What does education include?

During Phase I, the rehabilitation manager visits you to explain the rehabilitation process, talk about your work and home situation, and find out about particular problems you may have. You may be given booklets or attend seminars in the hospital which explain cardiac anatomy and disease and give advice about medication. The seminars allow you to ask questions and discuss fears and problems. Former cardiac patients may also take part to give the benefit of their experience.

During Phase III, various education sessions are given on the cardiac risk factors, especially diet, stress management, and giving up smoking. These are likely to take the form of structured discussion groups lead by an appropriate specialist.

Can my family be involved?

It is vital for close family or friends to be involved in your rehabilitation and to have a full understanding of the phases, to relieve their own anxiety about your illness, as well as to aid your recovery. They can help you to eat and exercise sensibly, support you in giving up smoking, and help you during a low patch. If you are having vocational, emotional or sexual problems, your partner or carer may be asked to join you in some counselling or therapy sessions.

During Phase III, partners or other close family are encouraged to attend the education sessions. When you graduate to Phase IV, it is helpful for your partner to join the support groups too and to share exercise activities. Apart from being fun to do together, this helps you to keep up good exercise and eating habits, and may also benefit your partner's health and well-being.

Is stress management important?

Learning about stress management is a vital part of cardiac rehabilitation. Stress management enables you to relieve stress before it causes further cardiac damage, by teaching you relaxation and creative activities.

Does cardiac rehabilitation help with psychological problems?

Talking to your rehabilitation manager or team, former patients, and other patients on your programme can help immensely. Simply finding out that other people have the same problems can be reassuring. For example, it is very common to feel far more emotional than usual during Phase I and II. If you are suffering from depression or excessive anger, your manager can refer you to a psychologist. The regular weekly sessions are individual and confidential.

What about sexual problems?

Difficulties with resuming sexual activities are common, especially after cardiac surgery (see page 137). The rehabilitation manager may refer you to a sex therapist who will then determine the nature of your sexual problem and help you solve it.

What about work problems?

The rehabilitation team can teach you exercises specifically designed to get you back to work. The manager can inform your employer when you are ready to return to work. If you have lost your job due to your illness, the rehabilitation manager may be able to get you reinstated.

If your condition prevents you from continuing in your previous work, the manager can refer you for vocational counselling, so that you can explore other options and also investigate any opportunities for further training.

If you support dependent family members, you can also be referred to a social worker, who can advise you on benefits you are entitled to and arrange extra help in the home.

WHAT YOU CAN DO AT HOME

Here are some pointers to help you during the first couple of weeks after coming out of hospital (Phase II):

▶ *Keep a daily diary of your physical and mental progress.*

▶ *Listen to your body and do not push yourself if you are having a low day.*

▶ *Use a relaxation tape as part of your daily routine.*

RELAXATION
When you feel stressed or negative, listen to some soothing music.

KEEPING CONTROL OF BLOOD PRESSURE

Following a diagnosis of heart disease or any kind of heart surgery it is essential to reduce high blood pressure with lifestyle changes and, if necessary, with medication.

CALM YOUR BLOOD PRESSURE DOWN

Try some of the following to help you lower your blood pressure in less formal ways:

▶ *Smile more.*

▶ *Laugh a lot.*

▶ *Chat with a friend.*

▶ *Pet an animal.*

▶ *Buy yourself a present.*

▶ *Read a book or magazine.*

▶ *Have a scented bath.*

▶ *Think positive thoughts.*

▶ *Chase negative thoughts away.*

*PET THERAPY
Research has shown that interacting with a pet lowers blood pressure, as it is relaxing and comforting.*

High blood pressure greatly increases the risk of developing heart disease as it increases atheroma formation. As arteries become narrower from fatty deposits and plaques (see page 108), high blood pressure may cause the plaques to break. The damaged wall will then bleed and a clot will form. The clot may become big enough to obstruct the artery completely.

High blood pressure also increases the severity of aneurysms (see page 129) and causes strokes (see page 127).

After a heart attack or heart surgery, or a diagnosis of a heart or circulatory disorder, if your blood pressure is dangerously high or you are at a very high risk of another heart attack, your doctor may prescribe medication.

Although medication may offer lifesaving benefits, these drugs can also have unpleasant side effects such as impotence, fatigue and depression. Some doctors estimate that as many as 90 per cent of their patients do not take the medication, perhaps because they are discouraged by the side effects.

MAKING CHANGES

In addition to drug therapy, doctors encourage their patients to make adjustments in their way of life – changing what they eat, the amount they exercise and the way they deal with stress.

As with all heart problems, a very low-fat diet and moderate aerobic exercise are recommended to reduce blood pressure, as is quitting smoking (see page 34). If you are overweight it is essential to lose weight. Stress management is also essential. All of these changes, followed rigorously, can lower blood pressure, enabling the patient to cut back or come off the medication.

THE STRESS CONNECTION

Blood pressure is linked closely to the emotions as evidenced by a phenomenon known as 'white coat hypertension' which results in higher than expected blood pressure measurements at the doctor's surgery. If just a simple visit to the doctor can raise your blood pressure, think how much more it is raised by all the hassles of daily life: family disputes, traffic jams and pressure at work. Reducing anxiety by avoiding stressful situations and changing how you react to unavoidable stress can therefore be helpful in keeping your blood pressure from rising.

Stress reduction

Learning how to relax can help to lower your blood pressure by a few points. You can either use a progressive relaxation method (see page 82) or take up yoga or meditation (see page 104). These methods not only lower your blood pressure while you are using them, but they also result in lower blood pressure throughout the day and carry lasting benefits.

Massage can be a great aid to relaxation. When used in combination with aromatherapy (see page 100), it can be particularly beneficial in lowering blood pressure. A trained aromatherapist will add certain essential oils (such as marjoram and ylang-ylang) to give you a massage designed to lower blood pressure.

Biofeedback has shown dramatic results in lowering blood pressure. A study done at St Luke's Hospital in New York (1989) examined the effect of biofeedback on 30 patients who had had hypertension for at least two years. After learning biofeedback techniques, their blood pressure fell to within the normal range.

In the *British Medical Journal* in 1981, results of a research study showed that a group of 200 workers with high blood pressure were able to bring their blood pressure down dramatically with the use of relaxation and biofeedback alone, and that eight months later they were still benefiting from the training. Many scientific studies support the use of biofeedback for stress relief and relaxation techniques.

THE DIET CONNECTION

There are foods you will be told to steer clear of to lower your blood pressure, such as those high in fat. Most doctors also recommend eating less salt, for instance by not using salt in cooking or on food, and avoiding processed foods that are loaded with salt (see page 51). But there are other foods that have been shown to lower blood pressure, which you may be advised to eat.

Mineral magic

Potassium, which is found in bananas, oranges and potatoes as well as other foods, may be able to help lower blood pressure since potassium deficiencies have been implicated as one of the causes of high blood pressure.

Calcium, too, may protect against high blood pressure. This mineral is found in dairy products (choose low-fat ones), leafy green vegetables, almonds and tinned fish, such as sardines, anchovies and salmon, which you should eat bones and all.

In one study, women who took 800 mg of calcium per day in supplements had a 23 per cent decrease in their blood pressure. The recommended daily amount for an adult is 700 mg per day – however, supplements are usually unnecessary. You can be sure you are getting that amount if you have three glasses of skimmed milk or 375 grams (12 ounces) of yogurt or 80 grams (3 ounces) of Cheddar cheese a day. (Always remember to use the low-fat dairy products in order to minimise intake of saturated fats.)

Although mineral supplements may be of help in some cases, you should not begin a course without first consulting your doctor. This is especially true if you are already taking diuretics.

Walking your blood pressure down
Exercise is one of the most effective ways of reducing blood pressure without medication. A study reported in *Harvard Health Letter* in February 1995 found that moderate walking (20 to 30 minutes three times per week) lowers blood pressure. Older people or those with a medical condition should consult their doctor before beginning a walking programme.

LOWERING BLOOD PRESSURE WITH BIOFEEDBACK

Biofeedback is a way of measuring physiological changes that indicate a changed mental state. By monitoring blood pressure, muscle tension and brain wave patterns, you can learn to control stress and tension, high blood pressure and pain.

A biofeedback machine measures muscle activity, brain waves or galvanic skin response (GSR shows the activity of sweat glands, which is related to stress levels) and can be used to learn to alter these where they indicate tension. In a standard machine, a hand-held monitor indicates the GSR or stress level of the person by a sound through an earpiece or visually on a screen. Sitting or lying in a comfortable position, the person is connected to the machine and receives feedback on their tension level. In order to produce a positive change you need to access the creative part of the brain, using relaxation techniques.

The machine can produce useful feedback so that the patient can learn from experience how to apply the relaxation methods to achieve the desired result.

Relaxation training may involve a combination of deep breathing, progressive muscular relaxation, autohypnotic suggestion, creative visualisation and meditation. There will also be a specific component: hypertensive patients will learn to lower their blood pressure. Each of these functions would not normally be under conscious control, but once the results of the patient's efforts are fed back, they can quickly learn to effect a change.

A further use for the biofeedback machine is in the treatment of muscular wasting, where the use of a muscle has been lost, for instance after a stroke. The patient can then learn to re-establish a whole range of activities.

MONITORING YOURSELF
Using biofeedback, you can monitor your muscle tension, fluctuations in skin temperature and changes in blood pressure. With relaxation exercises you can then influence these physiological factors.

CHANGING YOUR EATING HABITS

Dietary changes are essential for anyone with a heart or circulatory problem. The right diet can prevent further damage to your arteries and it may reverse existing damage.

Energy requirements
To lose weight it is necessary to burn more calories than you eat. The chart below provides a guide to the daily calories required by varying levels of activity. Note that these are estimates – if you are ill, pregnant or breastfeeding, your doctor will make different recommendations.

It is important for anyone with heart problems to be in the normal weight range for their height (see page 97). Being overweight is linked to increased blood pressure, raised blood cholesterol levels and adult onset diabetes. All of these lead to heart disease and are much easier to control if some weight is lost. Many people worry that they don't have the will-power to change their eating habits, but once you realise how much better you feel when you are following a healthy diet, then will-power is no longer a problem.

HEART PATIENTS AND WEIGHT GAIN

As well as overweight people developing heart problems, a common occurrence is for heart patients to gain weight. There are two reasons for this. The first is that they have stopped smoking. Unfortunately one of the common consequences of this is weight gain. However, the health benefits of giving up far outweigh the health risks of a modest weight gain. Battling with stopping smoking and losing weight at the same time may be difficult, so concentrate first on quitting

DAILY ENERGY REQUIREMENTS

Calculate your daily energy requirements, using this chart. First decide which activity category you fit into. Then multiply your weight by the figure given to give your daily calorie limit. The figures given are calories per kilogram of your body weight per day.

ACTIVITY	MEN (calories per kg body weight)	WOMEN (calories per kg body weight)
VERY LIGHT		
Office work, cooking, sewing, playing musical instruments	31	30
LIGHT		
Strolling, cleaning, shopping, golf	38	35
MODERATE		
Fast walking, gardening, cycling, skiing, tennis, dancing	41	37
HEAVY		
Manual labour, climbing, team sports	50	44
EXTRA HEAVY		
Athletes	58	51

EATING AWAY FROM HOME

Having a heart problem does not mean it is impossible to eat away from home. You just need to be careful. No matter what situation you find yourself in, you don't have an excuse to abandon your healthy diet.

Avoid, if possible, going to fast food restaurants that serve mainly high-fat burgers, fried foods and French fries. Milk shakes and creamy desserts are absolutely loaded with fat. If there is no alternative, try to pick a salad without any dressing.

Avoid fried foods. Instead, order stir-fried, steamed, grilled or baked dishes. And avoid creamy soups and sauces. Get into the habit of asking the waiter questions. Ask for vegetarian or low-fat alternatives.

If you are travelling by air, request a vegetarian, vegan, fat-free, diabetic or low-salt meal. Make sure you order it when you book your ticket.

When you are invited to friends, always tell them about your special diet and offer to bring something with you. This saves you from refusing their food or from indulging and feeling guilty.

and maintaining an even weight. Go on a weight-loss programme once you are more comfortable with giving up smoking.

The second reason heart patients may gain weight is because they may be much less active than formerly (and so have lower calorie requirements), and have more free time to eat. It is especially important, therefore, to follow a healthy diet plan and to exercise as advised by your doctor.

WEIGHT CONTROL

Weight-reducing plans need to combine diet and exercise. The recommended exercise for heart patients will vary depending on their medical condition. Cardiac rehabilitation programmes for patients following a heart attack or surgery will usually recommend a daily walk – gradually increasing the time and pace. Check what is suitable for you with your doctor.

Your doctor may also be able to advise you on where to get help. Sometimes dietitians or community nurses run weight-loss programmes for a fixed period of time, which may be enough to get you started. Be sure to ask what is available locally. Otherwise think about joining a commercial self-help group for weight control, but make sure that they are aware of your medical history. Be careful about joining a group that promises amazing results or sells 'nutritional supplements' for weight loss – most of these do not work and some may not be suitable for you to take along with any medication.

LOWERING CHOLESTEROL

Anyone with a heart or circulatory problem may need to reduce his or her cholesterol levels, as high cholesterol is a major factor in heart disease, and also contributes to the development of blood clots (see page 125) as well as arterial diseases such as intermittent claudication (see page 129).

Most people can reduce their cholesterol by dietary measures but others may need cholesterol-lowering medication, particularly those who have a family history of high cholesterol (see page 32). The dietary advice for heart disease is much the same as that which is prescribed for the prevention of heart disease (see Chapter 3). Changing your diet will help to prevent further damage to your arteries.

A cholesterol-lowering diet should be combined with an exercise programme. Regular exercise helps increase blood levels of 'good' high-density lipoprotein cholesterol (see page 38). Again, check with your doctor about the level of activity.

LOWERING TRIGLYCERIDES

Triglycerides are another type of fat found in the blood (see page 53), and a high triglyceride level is associated with heart disease. If your blood test has shown a high level, you will need to reduce it.

To lower your triglyceride levels, you should lose weight; avoid saturated fats, alcohol, sugar and refined starches (such as white flour); and restrict fruit juices and dried fruits (which are high in sugar).

ANTI-STROKE DIET

People who have suffered from a stroke need to follow many of the same measures as a heart patient – lowering blood pressure, cholesterol and triglycerides – to minimise the risk of another stroke.

CHANGING HABITS

The following tips may help with the change in your eating habits.

▶ *If you slip and overindulge, forgive yourself!*

▶ *The longer you stick to a healthier diet, the less likely you are to give in to cravings.*

▶ *If you are craving a snack, eat something healthy (see page 49).*

▶ *Clean your cupboard and fridge out – get rid of all temptation.*

▶ *Enlist the support of your family and friends. If they're eating tempting foods in front of you, it won't make your life any easier.*

WATCH YOUR WEIGHT Monitoring your weight and keeping it at a healthy level is of the utmost importance when you are recovering from a heart attack or surgery.

Feldenkrais Method

Living with heart disease often makes people fearful of exercise or even of moving around. By helping you to learn to move with 'a minimum of effort and a maximum of efficiency', the Feldenkrais Method can relieve this fear and give other benefits.

Origins

Born in Russia, Moshe Feldenkrais (1904–84), a physicist, settled in Israel in the 1950s. He developed his method of movement after suffering a severe sports injury to his knee. Instead of having surgery, as recommended by his doctor, he resolved to cure himself and was eventually able to walk without pain. He then taught his method to friends and family and was able to relieve their aches and pains. He set up the Feldenkrais Institute in Tel Aviv.

Among his most famous students were Israel's first prime minister, David Ben-Gurion, and the violinist Yehudi Menuhin. His book, *Awareness Through Movement* (1972), made his teaching available throughout the world.

AWARENESS THROUGH MOVEMENT *Moshe Feldenkrais developed a method of gentle movement that is practised all over the world.*

A method of awareness through movement consisting of a series of gentle movements explored under the guidance of a teacher, the Feldenkrais Method enables you to correct harmful patterns of movement developed in childhood. You are encouraged to become aware of how your muscles and joints feel, so that you can learn how to move in ways that create less stress.

How can the Feldenkrais Method help me after a heart attack?
The gentle movements performed in a lesson will help you to feel at ease with your body. Heart patients have often lost this feeling through fear of pain – either from an angina attack or from triggering another heart attack. If they have had surgery, they will also have suffered pain after the operation. In Feldenkrais lessons you learn how to organise all your movements in relation to gravity so that they become easier and more graceful. The movements taught in the lessons are pleasurable and easy since Feldenkrais teachers believe that the maximum learning occurs with minimum effort.

Can the movements be dangerous for someone with heart disease?
Any physical exertion can be harmful if it is done incorrectly or too strenuously. Feldenkrais teachers, however, are careful to ensure that their students work within their own limits. The movements, which teachers do not refer to as exercises, should never cause discomfort. You

should tell the teacher of your medical condition before the class begins. And, as with all activity for heart patients, you must consult your doctor before you begin classes.

Can the Feldenkrais Method help with pain relief?
The Feldenkrais Method does not offer direct pain relief, however it can make the movements you perform every day less painful by showing you how to move more harmoniously.

Particularly in one-to-one sessions called Functional Integration, the Feldenkrais teacher will gently lead you into positions that you may have associated with pain or fear. For example, someone whose chest is painful after heart surgery could learn to move their upper body more freely by making greater use of the range of subtle movements that are possible in the neck, shoulder, spine and ribs.

Can the Feldenkrais Method change mental attitudes?
The lessons often have a profound effect on how people feel and even behave. By learning to relax tense muscles, you will feel more at ease. Your breathing is likely to improve.

The lessons may have effects on an emotional level. Some people find that strong feelings arise during the lesson and are released when the teacher leads their body through particular movements. Although this is a fairly common effect, it is not the main focus of the Method.

Can the Feldenkrais Method improve circulation?

By releasing tension and showing you how to make your muscles work with one another, the method will improve your circulation. The movements in the lesson are too slow and gentle to be a form of aerobic exercise. But they can help to prepare you to perform more vigorous exercise, such as walking, jogging or swimming, by teaching you to move so that you do not put your body under unnecessary stress.

How long will it take before I notice an improvement?

Many people feel much better and more at ease after the first lesson. To change a lifetime of bad habits takes longer. A course of six to 12 lessons is average, although some people take occasional lessons for years to keep from sliding back into bad habits. Feldenkrais himself suggested one lesson for every year you have lived.

What happens during a lesson?

There are two types of lessons – one-to-one sessions and group lessons. The group lesson, Awareness through Movement, lasts 45 to 60 minutes. Classes are usually small, although Feldenkrais on occasion taught 100 students at a time.

Most lessons start with students in a resting position. The teacher then guides you through a sequence of movements and talks you through various positions. You are asked to pay attention to how movements feel by actively listening to your body. Both beginners and experienced students can attend the same class.

In the one-to-one lessons, known as Functional Integration, the teacher will guide you with gentle touch through a series of movements. You may be asked to lie on a low padded table, to sit on a chair or even to stand in a comfortable position. The teacher will then explore various patterns of movements with you asking occasional questions designed to stimulate your awareness.

Which type of lesson should I take?

One-to-one lessons are best for heart patients as the teacher can help you to overcome specific problems that you face. These lessons, however, are more expensive. Group lessons are also beneficial (but tell your teacher about your condition first).

FUNCTIONAL INTEGRATION
This involves gentle manipulation of the student by the teacher. Here the teacher is demonstrating how the student can move her shoulder and arm more freely and relieve muscle tension.

Some students prefer group lessons as they can initiate their own movements, but ideally you would do both kinds of lessons as they complement each other.

How are Feldenkrais teachers trained?

Teachers belong to the Feldenkrais Guild UK (affiliated worldwide) and study the method for 32 weeks over a four-year period before becoming members of the Guild. You can find a teacher by contacting the Guild. If there is no Feldenkrais teacher in your area, the Guild can inform you where to buy audio tapes which will guide you through the lessons.

WHAT YOU CAN DO AT HOME

This sequence of movements will help you to explore how you feel as you move. The point is not to do it right, but to pay attention to how you feel.

1. Sit on the edge of a chair upright, with feet flat on the floor. Turn your head to the right, as far as feels natural. Repeat four or five times. Notice how far to the right you were able to look.

2. Place your hands on either side of your neck so that they form a collar, fingertips on the back of your neck, wrists meeting under your chin. Now turn your head to the right again, repeating four or five times. On the last turn, hold the pose.

3. Gently take your hands off your neck. See if you can now look a bit further than you could before, again without straining.

4. Place hands on your neck again. Turn head to the right; hold. Return your gaze to the front, and again to the right several times (only the eyes move); return to face the front.

5. Remove your hands and rest. Feel how easily you are breathing.

6. Now turn your head to the right again. Compare how far you can look to the right now with how far you could in Step 1. Repeat the process, this time looking to the left.

Managing Stress

Stress is one of the leading causes of heart trouble and heart patients need to manage it. But you can learn to keep stress under control instead of letting it control you.

Much of the current research into the causes of heart disease points the finger at stress. It not only raises blood pressure, but it also raises cholesterol levels. For example, accountants at the end of the tax year and students at exam time have both been found to have raised cholesterol levels. Getting stress under control is therefore a vital part of your recovery programme.

Stress occurs when the situation a person is faced with is more than he or she can cope with. It happens dozens of times a day and can be brought on by little annoyances like the phone ringing while you are in the bath or a major life crisis such as heart disease.

PHYSICAL EFFECTS OF STRESS

Stress causes physical responses which are known as the fight-or-flight response. When you are faced with a stressful situation, your body prepares for action – your heart beats faster, your coronary arteries constrict, and your body's energy supply system, blood, moves into overdrive, flowing away from non-essential organs like the stomach to the muscles. Your body also prepares itself for possible injury, hence your blood clots more quickly. Although these changes are essential for running away from or facing up to danger, none of them is at all desirable in a person with heart disease. If stress and the reactions to it occurred only once in a while, there would be no problem; your body could simply go back to normal. But often stress occurs many times every day, keeping individuals in chronic anxiety states.

The risks to your heart

If you have had heart disease, you are at greater risk of your body being damaged by stress. This happens because narrowed and damaged coronary arteries are hyper-responsive to stress hormones, which make them constrict and even go into spasm, causing higher blood pressure and increased clotting which make the existing problems even worse.

Even though stress hits heart patients harder, you should not stop working or take to your bed in an attempt to avoid it – boredom can also be stressful – but you do need to learn to handle stressful situations more effectively. Ideally you should respond to challenges or difficult situations fast and efficiently and then relax.

STRESS AND YOUR HEART

When you become stressed the production of the hormones adrenaline and cortisol increases to prepare your body to cope with the anticipated threat even if it is only a psychological rather than a physical one. These hormones speed up the heart and increase the stickiness of blood platelets, making the blood clot more easily, and they increase the production of cholesterol and other fats such as triglycerides.

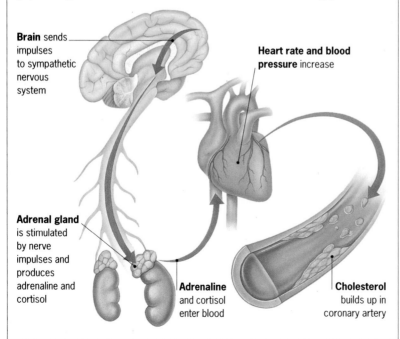

Brain sends impulses to sympathetic nervous system

Heart rate and blood pressure increase

Adrenal gland is stimulated by nerve impulses and produces adrenaline and cortisol

Adrenaline and cortisol enter blood

Cholesterol builds up in coronary artery

Pathway to health

Many therapies can make you more in touch with your inner feelings and emotions and will help you to respond to life's challenges. Counselling and support groups can be especially valuable. Ask your doctor to recommend. One-to-one counselling can provide you with a safe place to discuss your worries about returning to work or coping with the stresses of life. A support group can show you that you are not alone in your battle to recover. The members of the group can help each other stick to their low-fat, heart healthy way of eating. They can also provide emotional support. Many cardiac rehabilitation centres also have support groups in their programmes.

Art, dance and music therapy can all help you understand yourself. Under the supervision of a trained therapist, you will paint or draw, dance or play music as a way of expressing how you feel about your body, your life and your heart.

COPING WITH STRESS

Some people seem to be able to handle stress a lot better than others – they just never get bothered by traffic jams, queues, noisy neighbours or distressing news stories.

What protects people from stress may simply be a question of personality – some people are more laid-back than others.

People who are laid-back and rarely get angry also have a high sense of self-esteem, according to many studies. Hostile people have lower self-esteem. Improving your self-esteem does seem to be a means of making you more relaxed and improving your health. The more you think you are worth, the more likely you are to do things which preserve your health such as eating sensibly, exercising regularly, and keeping your stress levels as low as possible.

A new way of living and working

After a heart attack or major heart surgery, many people, feeling that they have had a brush with death, find themselves looking back at their lives. Some of the things that used to seem so important – meeting a sales target or keeping up with the neighbours – suddenly become unimportant. Reassessing your priorities is one of the things that makes stress management easier to learn. When you realise that keeping healthy and enjoying life are your main priorities, it is easier to put everything else into perspective.

The benefits of support

One factor that may help protect against the negative effects of stress is having a good social network. This doesn't mean knowing influential people or having dozens of acquaintances. It does mean that you feel connected with your family, friends and community. A study of over 13 000 people in Finland, as reported in the *American Journal of Epidemiology* in 1988, found that people who were socially isolated were two or three times more likely to die of heart disease and all other causes. Even just being a member of a club or religious organisation decreased the risk of early death.

Social isolation is believed to be as significant a factor in death rates as smoking, high blood pressure, high cholesterol, obesity and lack of physical exercise. Being a part of your community and becoming more involved with friends and family may also help you to regain your health.

A study at Yale University Medical School of 1192 healthy people aged between 50 and 79 showed that those with partners and strong family ties had lowered levels of the hormones noradrenaline and cortisol. Both are believed to influence blood pressure and the heart's response to stress, confirming that emotional support helps your heart.

MANAGING STRESSFUL SITUATIONS

The best way to deal with stressful situations is either not to be in them in the first place or not to let them bother you. With planning, you can arrange your life so that you face as little stress as possible. If you find seeing a particular friend or relative makes you tense, either stop seeing him or her, or if that is not possible, choose to see the person less often or for a limited amount of time. If you find certain chores burdensome, reward yourself with a swim, a massage, a walk in the park or a funny video when you have completed them. If someone is doing something that annoys you, either

Learn to laugh

Whenever you laugh, your body releases chemicals called endorphins which have an action similar to morphine – they make you feel good. Be sure you laugh every day so you will feel more able to cope with life's challenges.

A good way to unwind in the evening is to watch something funny on television. You can either videotape comedy programmes and save them up to watch later, or rent funny films. Humorous books and cartoons and cassette tapes of old comedy radio programmes are other good ways to lighten your life with laughter.

SOCIALISING FOR YOUR HEART
Getting together with friends and feeling connected with people in your community can reduce your risk of dying from heart disease.

decide that it's not worth being annoyed about or let the person know how you feel by telling him or her calmly what bothers you about such behaviour.

If you can't change a situation, then learn not to let it get on top of you. Remember, you are in control of how you feel. You can choose to let things make you angry, or not to let them bother you. Try changing the channels in your mind and thinking about something else – plan a holiday in the sun or think other pleasant thoughts.

Meditating, deep breathing to induce relaxation, progressive muscle relaxation, yoga and exercise can make stress easier to handle. They decrease your physical reactions to stress and help your body get back to normal faster after the fight-or-flight reaction has kicked into action. Deep breathing can be particularly useful because you can do it anywhere – standing in the supermarket queue, waiting for a red light to change to green, or at work.

Having a massage once a week, either from a friend or a professional massage therapist, is another way to relieve stress. It provides deep relaxation. If you have a massage with scented oils, a form of aromatherapy, you can achieve additional benefits. The massage therapist can choose oils to lift your mood and give you extra energy or to relax you and help you sleep.

LEARNING TO MANAGE TIME

A lot of stress comes from not having enough time to do everything that needs to be done. You can't make the day longer, but you can make better use of the time you have. When you are not in a hurry, you will feel more relaxed and in control of your life. Leave early for work and other appointments so that unexpected delays won't make you late. Carry a book with you so that you have something to do while waiting in line at the bank – that way you won't feel that you are wasting time.

RELAXING AT THE OFFICE

The workplace is often a major source of physical tension. Your neck may feel stiff, your shoulders knotty and painful and your back may ache from sitting for too long, bad posture, stressful meetings and long hours. These stretches can be done at your desk, and only take a few minutes but can provide great relief.

Put fingertips on shoulders

Twist at the waist in both directions

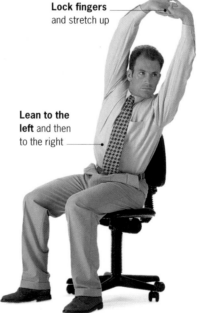

Lock fingers and stretch up

Lean to the left and then to the right

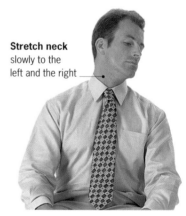

Stretch neck slowly to the left and the right

UPPER BACK
Place hands on your shoulders then twist at the waist until you feel a stretch across your upper back. Repeat in the other direction.

SIDE STRETCH
Shrug shoulders up and down until they are relaxed. Lock fingers with palms facing upwards. Stretch up as high as you can, then lean over to each side.

NECK
Sit up straight but keep your body relaxed. Slowly drop your neck to the left then to the right, and then to your chest. Then roll your head all the way to the left, then back to the centre and, finally, all the way to the right. Do not roll your head backwards as this puts pressure on your neck.

Returning to work

Most people can go back to the jobs they were doing before their heart attack or bypass surgery. In fact, working can help you maintain your self-esteem and make you feel part of society. But working can also be a source of stress. You will need to go back to your job equipped with a new attitude, since stress at work may have contributed to your illness in the first place.

Use time management skills to make sure that you give yourself enough time to get everything done. Get up a little early so that you don't need to start off in a hurry. Arrive at the office a few minutes early and sit down to organise your day. By planning what you are going to do, you can save time and avoid last-minute panics.

Timing helps

One method of seeing how well you are managing your time is to keep a diary – jot down everything you do in a day for a week or so. Then look at it and see if there are any tasks you can cut down, cut out or combine. Budget and allocate your time to specific tasks. Break big tasks into stages. Instead of finding them overwhelming and impossible, you will find that you are able to tackle them step-by-step.

Take it easy

You should also decide that you are going to take things a little easier at work. This does not mean becoming known as the lazy one. It does mean not over committing yourself. Refuse to be a perfectionist – learn to do a good enough job. To keep your workload at a manageable level, never volunteer to do extra tasks for which you do not have ample time available and delegate as many tasks as you can. At first you may find it hard to delegate. You may feel that you are the only person who can get things done properly, but if you make yourself ill you won't get it done at all.

When faced with an unpleasant or difficult task, take a few minutes to prepare yourself. Breathe deeply, shut your eyes for a moment, or stretch at your desk. Most importantly, don't simply put it off or 'forget' to do it. The problem probably won't go away and when it comes up again, it will have become more urgent or more out of hand, making your life even more stressful than if you had taken prompt action.

ART FOR YOUR HEART

Art therapy has now been introduced in many hospitals as an adjunct to counselling, to deal with the psychological effects of illness. After heart surgery, many patients find painting very relaxing, at the same time as expressing hidden feelings. Patients are encouraged to 'draw their feelings', often enabling them to express fears and anxieties that they could not verbalise. Art therapy has proved to be very valuable to heart patients, who often experience strong

feelings of depression after cardiac surgery. Drawings are sometimes literal, showing the person feeling depressed, or perhaps angry at the doctor, but are very often symbolic, expressing thoughts that were pushed away because they were too painful to deal with. A trained art therapist will analyse a patient's drawings, interpreting the colour, choice of subject and placement of objects in the picture (pictures may often depict recurrent dreams, which also give a key to feelings). The therapist may then make recommendations for subsequent drawings, to draw out other feelings.

ART THERAPY
This painting was done by a heart surgery patient who felt that he was excluded from joining in with his friends' activity. The blindfold represents his feeling of isolation from those around him.

Leave work at work

When the working day ends, you really must stop working. You should not only leave your work behind you physically, but mentally as well. If at all possible, do not take work home with you and make a concerted effort not to worry about work while you are at home.

It is especially important for individuals suffering from heart disease to unwind at the end of the day. Before you get home, take a walk round the block or in a park. When you get home, to reinforce the demarcation between your work life and your home life, change out of your work clothes into an at-home outfit, so that you feel more relaxed.

Join a health club and, after your doctor has given you the go-ahead, go for a workout or a swim after work, or just drop in to relax in the spa bath. Exercise is a proven method of releasing tension and is especially beneficial if it is done regularly. It is also good for your heart.

Stress Reduction

It is vital for survivors of heart attacks or heart surgery, and anyone with a diagnosed heart problem or hypertension, to reduce their stress levels. Dancing is a fun and effective way to release negative feelings and yoga routines are calming.

DANCING
Through the ages, various forms of dancing have been used as a means of relaxation and stress relief, and also as a way of expressing feelings, as in this 1911 painting of a masked ball.

Stress has many causes and it is often hard to imagine how the cause can be removed: for instance, what can you do about irritating colleagues or friends who are always late for appointments?

Stress responses are often learned when very young and by adulthood your habitual response to stress is likely to be ingrained. But even impatient, competitive people can change their response to stressful situations with dance therapy and yoga. Regular practice of stress reduction techniques can have long-lasting benefits to the health of your body and mind, and are particularly applicable to the task of attaining a healthier heart. Check with your doctor before doing these.

DANCING OUT YOUR NEGATIVITY

Dance is a universal expression of human emotions and 30 minutes of directed dancing can bring peace and relief from tension. Try the following formula for releasing a specific negative emotion.

Shake out arms

Shake out legs

Shake fists for feelings of frustration

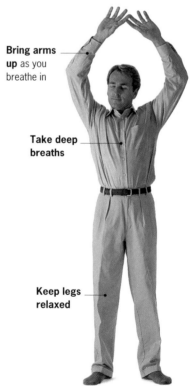

Bring arms up as you breathe in

Take deep breaths

Keep legs relaxed

1 *In a quiet room, start playing a tape of soft music to relax and get into the mood. Swing your body freely with floppy arms and legs, shaking them out.*

2 *Change the music to suit your mood, then just express yourself physically, depending on your feelings. Stamp and shout, or move slowly.*

3 *At the end of your session, start to wind down and relax, letting go of your emotions with a few deep, slow breaths. Then sit down quietly.*

YOGA

Yoga is an ideal way to wind down from stress. Try the following two routines on a daily basis for a month and notice how relaxed you feel.

Drop head to chest

Relax shoulders

Contract the abdomen as you breathe in

Keep palms facing upwards

Reach up as high as possible

Let your chest expand as you inhale

1 Exhale deeply, relaxing your shoulders and chest and contracting your abdomen. At the same time let your body go limp with your head and arms hanging and your palms facing downwards.

2 Standing with your feet slightly apart, inhale slowly, expanding your abdomen and raising your arms to shoulder height with the palms facing upward.

3 As you inhale, bring your hands together overhead. At the same time, rise up on tiptoe. Hold for the count of five. Repeat this sequence once more.

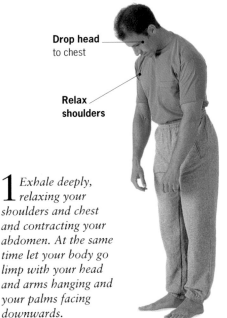

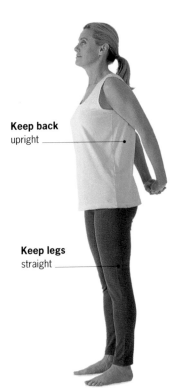

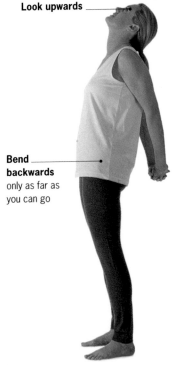

Keep palms facing outwards

Keep arms straight

Keep back upright

Keep legs straight

Look upwards

Bend backwards only as far as you can go

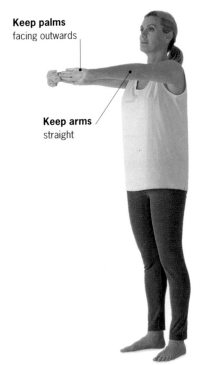

1 Stand straight; raise your hands to touch your chest with your palms facing outwards, fingers touching. Straighten your arms in front of you, feeling the elbows stretch.

2 Inhale slowly, and bring your arms behind you, then lower them until you can lace your fingers together, keeping your back straight and your head up.

3 Slowly bend backwards a few inches. Pull your arms upwards. Look to the sky. Hold for the count of five. Exhale, then relax. Repeat this sequence once more.

CONTROLLING ANGER
AND HOSTILITY

Anger and hostility can put you at great risk of developing heart disease. Learning to control these negative emotions will not only reduce the risk, but it will also help you to enjoy life more.

Personality types A and B were first described in the 1950s by the American cardiologists Meyer Friedman and Ray Rosenman (see page 32). Since then many studies have been carried out on the effect of personality on heart disease, and anger and hostility have been identified as major risk factors.

The Western Collaborative Group Study began in the 1970s, and followed 3154 healthy Californian men over nearly nine years to see which of them would develop heart disease. Each had filled in a question-naire designed to reveal personality type. The study found that of those patients who developed heart disease (336), all had one thing in common – they had answered seven questions which had been designed to eval-uate whether or not they were hostile in a way that indicated a high level of hostility. Subsequent studies also showed that the people who scored high on the anger and hostility sections of personality tests were more likely to develop heart disease. Thus, hostility seems to be an important link between personality and heart disease, along with how a person reacts to stress.

HOW ANGER HURTS YOUR HEART

Anger, hostility and aggression increase the risk of heart disease in several ways. They all cause blood pressure to rise. Several studies have also shown that the blood pres-sure of people who are often angry goes up faster and stays up longer.

Anger also makes the body produce more adrenaline and cortisol, which increase the amount of fat in the blood, and more noradrenaline, which makes the blood's platelets stickier. The increased fat is often deposited in the lining of the arteries where it forms plaques, while the sticky platelets tend to form clots more easily. When the clots attempt to get through the plaque-narrowed arteries, they get stuck, blocking them. When this happens in the heart, you have a heart attack; in the brain, a stroke.

People who are hostile may also be more likely to smoke, drink alcohol and overeat, possibly as a way of relieving the tension caused by their anger. All these habits increase the risk of heart disease. And some researchers also believe that angry people are more socially isolated – they don't trust others enough to make friends easily. Social isolation has been proven in study after study to impede recovery from illness, and contribute to death from heart disease.

Anger after heart disease

If being an angry person can damage your heart and lead to heart disease, it also has the potential to cause even more damage to a heart that is already weakened by disease. To make matters worse, now that you know how damaging anger is to your heart, you may find yourself getting even angrier because you are afraid to risk your health if you get angry. But you can learn to control your anger instead of letting it control you.

MANAGING ANGER

The key to protecting yourself from the harmful effects of hostility is learning to control it. Once people believed that the best thing to do with anger was to express it. Suppressing anger, it was thought, could be emotionally harmful, and perhaps even physically. Current research suggests that the best strategy for dealing with anger is neither to express it nor suppress it, but to

continued on page 155

ANGER-GENERATING SITUATIONS
A teenager playing loud music is only one of the situations that can make you feel angry without even realising it. It is important to recognise anger and then to deal with it appropriately. In this case, ask the teenager to turn the music down, or put in earplugs.

ARE YOU EASILY ANGERED?

If you spend your life feeling irritated, or have frequent bursts of aggression or anger then you are a likely candidate for high blood pressure, which will put you at risk of heart disease. At one time releasing anger was viewed as acceptable therapy for many emotional problems. Now the view is that it is best not to get angry, but rather to control yourself and express your feelings in a constructive way. Take this quiz and find out how angry you really get at everyday situations.

YOUR NEIGHBOURS REGULARLY PLAY MUSIC VERY LOUDLY. DO YOU:

a) Politely ask them to restrict the noise levels after certain hours?
b) Turn your own stereo or television up fully and hammer on the wall until they get the hint?

YOUR NORMAL ROUTE TO WORK IS DISRUPTED BECAUSE OF LOCAL ROADWORKS. DO YOU:

a) Reroute your journeys for the next few days?
b) Telephone the council from your car phone and shout at the receptionist about the situation?

YOU ARE STUCK IN RUSH HOUR TRAFFIC. DO YOU:

a) Spend the time preparing your thoughts for the day ahead or plans for the evening?
b) Pull up as close as possible to the car in front and rev your engine?

SOMEONE WRONGLY ACCUSES YOU OF A MINOR MISTAKE. DO YOU:

a) Calmly explain that there must be a misunderstanding?
b) Seethe about it for hours later and then verbally attack the accuser?

THE SUPERMARKET QUEUE IS REALLY LONG AND THE CHECKOUT PERSON IS VERY SLOW. DO YOU:

a) Realise that being impatient will not speed your journey to the front of the queue?
b) Glare at the people in front of you and comment loudly on their lack of organisation?

A FAMILY MEMBER CRITICISES SOMETHING YOU HAVE DONE. DO YOU:

a) Consider the points that have been raised to see if they are valid?
b) Take it as an intentional personal attack?

WHAT DO YOU THINK OF THE PHRASE 'LIFE IS FULL OF LITTLE ANNOYANCES'?

a) It's true, but most of the time they can be overcome?
b) It's true, and they make my life ten times harder?

IN A MEETING AT WORK, ONE OF YOUR COLLEAGUES FORCEFULLY DISAGREES WITH YOU. DO YOU:

a) Agree to differ – after all everyone has their own opinions?
b) Shout down your colleague, then leave the meeting?

A FRIEND BEHAVES BADLY AT YOUR PARTY. DO YOU:

a) Ignore it and avoid him?
b) Tell him that his behaviour is unacceptable and ask him to leave?

YOU CONTROL YOUR ANGER DURING THE DAY. DO YOU FIND THAT THIS:

a) Stops you from overreacting.
b) Makes you so angry that you randomly explode over something that is quite minor?

HOW ANGRY ARE YOU?

If you answered mostly a's, you have learned to curb your anger, annoyance and aggression because you can differentiate between what is serious and important and what needs to be viewed with a more tolerant perspective. This, however, does not mean you aren't assertive when assertion is needed; rather, you know how to judge when such expressions are required. This will ensure that you keep your blood pressure at a healthy, even level.

If you answered mostly b's, you are set off by life's small irritations quite randomly and unjustifiably. This indicates that you have a high level of hostility – and a low level of self-confidence, not to mention a blood pressure reading that goes up and down like a yo-yo. You must work on coming to terms with your feelings and gain self-control. You will like yourself more and other people will find you much more approachable.

The Angry Man

Hostility towards other people and the world in general is one of the greatest personality-related risk factors of heart disease. Anger raises blood pressure and cholesterol levels. And, by making relationships with others difficult, it deprives people who become ill of the social support that they need to get well.

Mark is 45 and a successful businessman, with several restaurants; he is married with two teenage children. He is proud of his achievements and knows they are due to his competitive nature. However his temper plays a role too. About a month ago Mark suffered severe chest pains, and was taken to hospital. He was told that he had had a mild heart attack. He returned to work after the attack as though nothing had happened but soon found that his rages brought back his chest pain. He returned to his doctor who prescribed some medication to relieve the pain, but she also told him that to heal his heart he would have to make important changes in his life, including learning to control anger.

WHAT SHOULD MARK DO?

Mark needs to come to terms with both his heart attack and also the reasons that led to it, and the sooner he does this the better for the health of his heart. He needs to learn to control his anger and stress levels. Diffusing potentially angry situations before they erupt is essential for preventing strain on his heart. Mark needs to learn how to deal with work problems in a calmer manner by instigating more efficient procedures, placing more trust in his staff and improving his own management skills. He also needs to communicate with his family more effectively and without anger. He should attend a course in anger management at the coronary care unit of the local hospital.

Action Plan

HEALTH
Go to anger control classes, and practise relaxation exercises. Exercise more to burn off stress and feelings of hostility.

WORK
Set up more efficient procedures. Learn better management skills. Hire an assistant manager to relieve pressure. Delegate more to junior staff.

FAMILY
Ask family to support attempts to control anger and be more forgiving during lapses. Spend more relaxation time with them.

WORK
Work can be a source of stress and coping mechanisms are important to avoid difficult situations and confrontations.

HOW THINGS TURNED OUT FOR MARK

Mark acknowledged his anger problem and began to use the behaviour modification techniques and relaxation exercises he learned at the coronary care unit. Despite some setbacks, which he refused to let get in the way of his recovery, his relationship with his family and staff improved. Although he suffered occasional chest pains, Mark was lucky and did not have another heart attack and he felt in control of his life.

HEALTH
People with an angry and competitive personality can cause serious damage to their health.

FAMILY
Family members often don't know how to deal with an angry person in the family – they either accommodate the person or fight back, and then things just get worse.

ANGER-OFFLOADING EXERCISE

Anger is one of the most persistent and destructive of the negative emotions. The following routine is often taught in autogenic training classes (see page 42) to deal with anger. Practise it any time you feel angry.

Concentrate on the object of your anger

Raise arms in front of you

1 *Choose a quiet place, where you will not be disturbed or overheard. Stand up with your elbows bent, arms raised in front of you up to shoulder level. Concentrate on something or someone who is the target of your anger and frustration.*

Grunt loudly

Straighten arms

Lift leg

2 *Bring your arms down quickly; straighten your elbows and grunt as loudly as you can. At the same time, bend one knee and lift off the floor, as if you were snapping a stick across your thigh.*

Shout out your anger if necessary

3 *Continue the exercise until you feel you have had enough. The more vivid your imagination, the more effective this exercise will be, so do not hold back your feelings!*

avoid feeling it, if possible. People who are not easily roused to anger are healthier and less likely to suffer heart disease than other people with similar lifestyles who get angry easily. People who are angry almost all the time are most at risk of heart disease. And while it may prove difficult, they are the ones who, for the sake of their health, most need to learn to control their anger.

Defusing hostility

If you are one of those people who is always angry, you need to learn to short-circuit your anger as soon as it starts. Specialists advise spending 20 minutes every day learning how to behave in a less hostile way. Just as your angry personality was not formed overnight, you cannot expect change to come easily. You will need to work on curbing your anger over a long-term period. But the effort will be worth it. Changing your behaviour could save your life.

Keep a diary

The first step is to record how often you become angry every day, what situations trigger your rage and how you feel afterwards. Once you know what makes you angry, the next step is to learn to control your feelings. To do this, you need to recognise that you are often angry and admit that your anger is almost always inappropriate. The questionnaire on page 153 will help you to identify situations in which you get angry. Record these in your diary and write down alternative ways of dealing with them. This will serve as a useful reminder for what kinds of situations to watch out for and how to handle them.

You will need to decide whether your anger is really justified. Chronically hostile people almost always believe that they are right to feel angry, so that changing this belief is an important first step.

Change your anger

After realising that you are angry, you need to change your mood. There are several strategies that can help. First of all, you can reason with yourself. For example, you can tell yourself that there is no need to feel angry because the waiter brought the wrong order. Everyone makes mistakes and this one can be easily rectified. Putting things in perspective is important for reasoning away anger. Most anger-generating situations are really not worth getting worked up about and usually pass quickly anyway.

DIFFUSING ANGER

Anger needs to be diffused as soon as possible. Try some of these methods as soon as you feel angry thoughts beginning:

▶ *Count to 10 silently before you speak or act.*

▶ *Think about something pleasant like a party you are going to or a holiday.*

▶ *Leave the situation if possible: walk outside for a few minutes.*

▶ *Take your anger out on a cushion: beat it with your fists.*

▶ *Go somewhere private and yell out your anger.*

▶ *Write a letter to the object of your anger, then burn it.*

Stop your thoughts

If you can't reason anger away, you can try to stop it. Simply ordering yourself to stop thinking in an angry or hostile way can be suprisingly effective. You can either silently tell yourself to stop, or you can, if you are alone, shout 'Stop!'. Another method that can be used to stop angry thoughts is to think about something else. This works because you can't think about two things at once. Decide in advance what positive thoughts or situations you will turn to when something makes you angry – some people think about a delicious dinner, a funny film or making love. Then, when you feel angry, instead of dwelling on the event that has annoyed you, you should turn your thoughts to the pleasant distraction you have prepared for yourself.

Learning to meditate (see page 36) is another method that will help you feel less hostile. By meditating, you will short-circuit your body's reactions to your anger. Instead of instantly switching into overdrive, with a pounding heart, increased adrenaline and raised blood pressure, you can learn to shift into low gear. You will need to learn a meditation technique and practise it every day in order to use this method of blocking angry feelings. Then, when you feel angry, meditate for a few moments until you feel a lot calmer and more in control. Not only will it take your mind off your anger, but it will switch off the physical reactions that are so damaging to your heart.

A CHANGE FOR THE BETTER

Hostile people are usually very suspicious of others. They cherish a world view in which other people are out to get them and are against them. These beliefs are self-perpetuating. If you act as if the world is against you, then it will be.

Studies have shown that hostile people have poorer social relationships than other people; other studies prove that people who have no close relationships are less likely to survive heart disease. By learning to have better relationships, heart patients will improve their network of social support.

In a book called *Anger Kills*, published in the USA, Doctors Redford and Virginia Williams propose a number of strategies to make the angry person more caring and trusting. They recommend learning to listen to others and to become more empathetic,

tolerant and forgiving. To improve personal relationships, they advise keeping a pet, becoming involved in your community by doing voluntary work, and improving friendships by finding a confidante.

Angry people also tend to be cynical about the motives of other people. By adopting a more positive attitude, this cynicism can be overcome. Learning to laugh at yourself can often stop you from getting angry at others. The Williamses also suggest looking beyond ordinary daily situations or viewing them from a balanced perspective, and believe that becoming more religious or spiritual will help you develop a more positive mental attitude.

THE LAST DAY

One strategy is to pretend that today is your last day. If you have survived a heart attack or have to live with heart disease, you have probably used this technique without realising it. If today were your last day on earth, would you want to waste it yelling at the dry cleaner for failing to have your clothes ready on time, or swearing at the driver who cut across your lane, or complaining about your neighbours? Wouldn't you rather spend it telling your loved ones how much they mean to you or simply enjoying every moment of the day?

ASSERTING YOURSELF

Sometimes you will find that your anger is justified. Perhaps your boss is criticising your work, imposing impossible deadlines and generally making your life miserable. Instead of suffering in silence or blowing up, you can make your boss aware of how you feel by asserting yourself.

Assertion means telling someone else, in a reasonable and calm way, how his or her behaviour makes you feel and then discussing how to resolve the issue. Unlike anger, it allows you to express a grievance without your getting out of control. Other people are more likely to respond positively to assertive behaviour than to aggressive behaviour, meaning that you can get what you want without raising either your voice or your blood pressure.

INDEX

ACKNOWLEDGMENTS

Carroll & Brown Limited
would like to thank
Ellen Dupont
Sue Mimms
Garet Newell
Dr Mike Roth

British Heart Foundation

Tunturi Fitness Equipment supplied by
Bolton Stirland International Ltd.

Photograph sources

8 British Library, London/Bridgeman
   Art Library, London
9 (Top) Zefa; (Bottom) Rex Features
10 Gordon White/photo courtesy of
   Harefield Hospital patients
11 Robert Harding Picture Library/
   Westlight International
12 Robert Harding Picture Library/
   Sharpshooters
17 Professors P.M. Motta and
   S. Correr/Science Photo Library
18 Royal College of Physicians,
   London/Bridgeman Art Library,
   London
21 Zefa
24 Zefa
32 Palazzo Corner Ca'Grande,
   Venice/Bridgeman Art Library,
   London
35 Zefa
39 Zefa
41 CNRI/Science Photo Library
42 (Top) Mary Evans Picture Library;
   (Bottom) supplied by BAFATT
46 Tony Stone Images
84 Image Bank/Don King

93 Zefa
94 (Top) Science Photo Library;
    (Centre) Science Photo Library;
    (Bottom) Zefa
98 BSIP Ducloux/Science
    Photo Library
99 Mary Evans Picture Library
101 Wellcome Institute Library,
    London; (Right) Sally and
    Richard Greenhill
104 Tony Stone Images
108 BSIP/Science Photo Library
110 Harry Smith Horticultural
    Photographic Collection
115 Tony Stone Images
117 CNRI/Science Photo Library
118 Harry Smith Horticultural
    Photographic Collection
120 News International/Rainbird
122 Mary Evans Picture Library
124 Stanford Eye Clinic/Science
    Photo Library
126 (Top) Secchi-Lecaque/Roussel-
    Uclaf/CNRI/Science Photo
    Library; (Bottom) Professor P.M.
    Motta/G. Macchiarelli/University
    'La Sapienza', Rome/Science
    Photo Library
128 (Top) Hattie Young/Science
    Photo Library; (Bottom) Gca-
    CNRI/Science Photo Library
129 Chris Bjornberg/Science
    Photo Library
130 Zefa
137 Zefa
140 Zefa
144 Lionel Delevingne Photography
147 Zefa
150 Mary Evans Picture Library

Medical illustrators
Joanna Cameron
Richard Tibbitts

Illustrators
John Geary
Christine Pilsworth
Paul Williams
Angela Wood

Graphs
Nick Roland

Photographic assistants
Nick Allen
Sid Sideris

Hair and make-up
Rachel Attfield

Picture researcher
Sandra Schneider

Food preparation
Maddalena Bastianelli
Eric Treuille

Research
Laura Price

Index
Sharon Freed